GENERATING SOCIALISM

Recollections of Life in the Labour Party

DANIEL WEINBREN

Foreword by Tony Benn

SUTTON PUBLISHING

First published in 1997 by
Sutton Publishing Limited · Phoenix Mill
Thrupp · Stroud · Gloucestershire · GL5 2BU

British Library Cataloguing in Publication Data
A catalogue record for this book is available from the British Library

ISBN 0 7509 1193 X

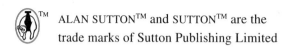

ALAN SUTTON™ and SUTTON™ are the
trade marks of Sutton Publishing Limited

Typeset in 10/14 pt Times.
Typesetting and origination by
Sutton Publishing Limited.
Printed in Britain by
WBC Limited, Bridgend.

Contents

Foreword

This book is a must for anyone who really wants to understand Socialism in Britain, the Labour Party, its roots, its members, its activities and its debates over the last century. And it does all this by collecting the memories of those who worked in it at the grass roots level, with only a passing reference to the leaders who tend to monopolise the media coverage of politics and whose memoirs mainly deal with their own careers. It is the best introduction to what we are about that I have read, and it completely disposes of the idea that New Labour, with its spin doctors, gimmicks and soundbites, could ever supplant or destroy the real Labour Party. For it is a story of commitment to a cause and of a major educational programme which actually created a public opinion that, in its turn, created the Welfare state, the Health Service and the other advances that this generation has enjoyed. It also tells of people who faced and overcame far more difficult problems than those which confront us now, and reminds us that history is made by the people and not by leaders. We hear of the campaigns for trade union rights, better wages and conditions, for peace, against fascism, racism and repression, and for good houses, good schools and full employment. For me, one of the most interesting passages describes the continuing debates that have always gone on in the party between people of very different opinions and how these arguments have shaped our thinking. The role of the Communist Party is quite properly given appropriate recognition as a school for socialists and a power to be reckoned with in the affiliated trade unions, and we learn about some of the ideological arguments between them and the Trotskyists which still go on and how discipline has so often, and so foolishly, been used to settle those arguments. But the overwhelming impression given in these recollections is of the good will and comradeship that has characterised our cooperation together from the very beginning and of the immense amount of work that was – and still is – undertaken by local parties.

Oral history, now made much easier by the invention of the tape recorder, has, for the first time, allowed us to hear from the rank and file about their experiences, and they are deeply moving and encouraging. We can see it still in the backing given to the miners in the eighties and nineties and today for the Liverpool dockers, the Hillingdon hospital strikers and all those who are engaged in struggle. Parliament and local councils have a part to play but their successes depend almost entirely on the activities of those who do the doorstep work and organise the rallies, canvass, raise the funds and circulate the broadsheets and leaflets. It is fashionable now to dismiss the activists as being out of date and irrelevant, and socialism as being a thing of the past, to be replaced by a new life that must be lived within the capitalist system trying to ameliorate its harsher features by consensus with those who detest Labour and all it stands for. But history does not work like that and it is strange that at a time when the public are clearly deserting the capitalist philosophy of the eighties, some Labour voices should be heard promising a certain continuity of those very policies. Even were such a compromise to be sensible, which it is not, the thinking that lies behind it leaves out of account all those who want to see a genuine change in an international system that causes such unfairness and widens the gap between rich and poor so blatantly.

Those who read the memories contained in this book will find it impossible to believe that the Labour and trade union movement and its rank and file members are ready to fade away to make room for the pollsters and the advertising agents whose only constituents seem to be the media proprietors, editors and correspondents. This century has seen socialist ideas of many kinds tried in many countries, and we know that communism failed because it forgot democracy, while social democracy failed because it forgot socialism, but deep down we also know that market forces which elevate profit above people can only lead to tragedy and disaster. In every generation, at every stage in the human story there have always been two flames burning: the flame of anger against injustice and the flame of hope that a better world could be built, and this book shows how powerful those flames have been in moving good men and women in their own lives to help society to move from barbarism towards social justice. I hope that the oral history project continues to flourish for it gives us a view of history and how it can be changed that our school text-books and the daily diet of press, radio and television deny us so systematically. The job this generation has to do is a formidable one but if fascism could be defeated and apartheid overthrown it is not beyond our reach.

Global capitalism is strong, but international solidarity can provide us with a force strong enough to tame it, and reading this book should remind us that there are millions more activists at work in the world and if we knew more about them and their hopes we should never be tempted to give up. As Tom Paine wrote 'We have it in our power to begin the world over again. The birth day of a new world is at hand.'

Tony Benn
Chesterfield
January 1997

Acknowledgements

The Labour Oral History Project was established in 1993. Its aims are to enlarge, enrich and restructure the history of the labour movement through the creation, assessment and preservation of its oral records. Thanks are due to Simon Fowler, Kay Parkinson, Andy Byrom and to all those who made grants, sponsored a tape or gave donations to the project, particularly the Eva Reckitt Trust, the British Library and Labour Heritage. I am also grateful to the staff of the Imperial War Museum, the Science Museum, the British Library Newspaper Library and the National Sound Archive. Some participants received training in the techniques of oral history, others simply set out, with their Labour Oral History Project Interviewer's Pack, to record older activists. It is thanks to those who recorded themselves and to the following that such a diversity of members have been recorded: Louise Brodie, Ron Burgess, John Casson, Betty Costello, Roy Gore, Chris Gregg, Sheila Haines, Elizabeth Hall, Carol O'Mahony, Chris Hubbold, Barbara Humphries, Anne Lubin, Shabana Mansuri, Margaret Morey and Martin Plaut.

Activists recalled their motivations, hopes, struggles, successes, practical activities and memories of key local and national figures. I am most grateful to the informants who gave their time freely and provided me with many weeks of fascinating listening. A number also loaned pictures and other autobiographical material. Together these recollections can be employed in order to reshape the history of the Labour Party, and to clarify our understanding of the nature of parliamentary democracy. As Tony Benn wrote, when offering his support for the Project:

> Unless the memories of our pioneers who worked so hard are collected in this way, we shall be deprived of the knowledge we need to understand how the labour movement became so strong, and how the socialist tradition was sustained in very difficult times.

The Oral History Society's international 'Red Tapes' conference in 1994 provided a valuable forum for discussion of a number of the issues raised by interviewing left-wing activists. I am grateful for the support offered by political and academic figures. Michael Foot MP wrote: 'I read of your project with much interest and do wish you the best of success. I am sure there is much to be learned from this form of history.' Professor Paul Thompson of the National Life Story Collection called the Project: 'a tremendously important piece of work both historically and politically'. I am obliged to Middlesex University, where I was encouraged to run a module in Oral History. Some of the work of students on that course is included here. Rob Perks, the Curator of Oral History at the National Sound Archive, has been very supportive of the Project. Philip Dunn and Stephen Bird of the National Museum of Labour History have been very helpful. Swindon Arts Media assisted Anne Lubin. Rebecca Ferguson transcribed and proofread material, found images, made useful suggestions and allowed me to find the time to complete this book. Her intelligence, generosity and interest sustained me.

Daniel Weinbren
London

1

Speaking Out For Labour

Here are the voices of a selection of Labour Party members recorded by interviewers from the Labour Oral History Project. Included are Labour Party activists born in every year between 1905 and 1928 and members from many different places and backgrounds. Between them they can recall every General Election since 1918.[1] They told us, often with verve and enthusiasm, about why they became involved and stayed involved in the struggle to create a more just society. The richness of their insights make these memories a distinctive source for those interested in the development of the Labour Party and the spread of socialist ideas. The nature of the party as a social and familial group, as well as a political machine, is revealed.

The Labour Party exists not only to ensure that there are as many Labour MPs as possible, but also to secure election to all representative bodies and to build fellowship in a practical fashion. These aims, encouraging the acceptance and understanding of constitutional structures and finding ways of cooperating in order to improve conditions, are central to the Party's ethos. Activists' reflections on organising social and political public events, on training and socialising political representatives from councillors to Prime Ministers and on building alliances and maintaining civic networks also indicate the nature of active citizenship within a democracy. Finding out how the political minority has been sustained through listening to them allows us to gain a better grasp of the nature of British society.

The familiar story of Keir Hardie's political career illustrates the interweaving of these elements within an activist's lifetime of commitment. In 1856, an illegitimate baby was born in a one-room cottage in Legbrannock, Lanarkshire. The child had spent just one day at school before, at the age of eight, he started to work for his living. He was frequently moved around Scotland as his drunken stepfather sought employment. He started work in the mines aged ten, where he taught himself shorthand using a pin to scratch out the figures on to stone. He learnt to write in his late teens and later described how:

> for several years as a lad I rarely saw daylight during the winter months. Down the pit by six in the morning and not leaving it again until half-past five meant not seeing the sun, and even on Sunday I had to spend four hours down below. Such an experience does not develop the sunny side of one's being.

He became involved in trade union activities as a result of which he at the age of twenty-three was sacked and blacklisted. It was difficult to find alternative work in an area dominated by coal mining, and he became a union agent and journalist for a Liberal newspaper. In 1888 he stood in a Parliamentary by-election against a Liberal, calling himself a National Labour candidate. He was unsuccessful and, realising the importance of a party machine, helped to found the Scottish Labour Party a month later. He became the party secretary. That the son of a Scottish laird, R.B. Cunninghame Graham, became President is of interest for, although the Labour Party relies on working-class support, it has never sought to exclude those from other backgrounds. In 1892 Hardie stood for Parliament once again. He won, and travelled to the Commons in a wagonette pushed by his constituents, clad not in a frock coat and silk top hat as other MPs were, but in a cloth cap and tweed suit and accompanied by a band playing revolutionary song tunes.

Hardie and his fellow campaigners were struggling against poverty, and pushing for wealth redistribution, but they also believed in the importance of autodidactism and in the power of song – a combination which has sustained the Labour Party ever since. His concerns were echoed in many of the interviews[2]:

I saw the most appalling poverty. Little children running around in mid-winter with nothing on but a little vest. No underpants, no shoes, no socks. Their skin a bluey-grey, and no doubt they were covered in lice. Eating bits of cabbage stalk out of the gutter of dirty, slimy water – and this wasn't the exception, this was what we were fighting to end in the Labour Party.

Patricia Meitlis, Liverpool

We used to go to dances, we used to have local rambles quite a lot, debates on different things. I also joined the Workers' Educational Association, to study economics through them . . . I did quite a long course with the Workers Educational Association on economics and political structures.

Tom Riley, Tottenham

We used to sing *Jerusalem* at the start of the meeting and *The Red Flag* at the end of the meeting.

Jean Goldie, Sunderland

Again and again in the interviews Labour activists' ability to combine social, political and economic concerns was made apparent. In this book the strands of Labour life are separated and analysed individually. Always present, though, are two themes which stress the importance of the Labour Party to socialists and others. Firstly, Labour is where people learn organisational and debating skills in order to go out and explain to people what socialism is; and secondly, it is where activists can retreat after confrontations with people about socialism.

Promoting democratic socialism

Activists' most important contribution to the working of democracy is their promotion of debate and introduction of ideas within their communities. They initiate campaigns, channel information and legitimate policies. It was activists who organised a campaign to ensure that housing regulations were enforced in Kingston in the 1930s. Stanley Bell, one of the campaigners, reported that some local private tenants were able to claim up to two years back rent, and the rats were cleared out of their homes. The Labour Party activists responsible for these victories were treated 'like heroes' and a tenants' rally attracted 2,000 people.

> Another campaign which helped our cause was the formation of the Norbiton Tenants Association. There was a lot of old property in poor condition let out by private landlords to tenants. The demand was so much that, when one become vacant there was a queue for it, so the landlords just increased the rent. Unfortunately for the landlords, we found out about the Rent Control Acts, which enabled us to get two years back rent of the increase for the tenants. Imagine the wrath of the landlord, but the almost hero worship of the tenants. In addition to this the property was in such a poor state, with rats running in and out of the halls, we could also apply to the sanitary inspector for certificates for 'want of repair', which enabled us to deduct that proportion of the rent covering repairs. The sanitary inspector's office was inundated with demands, and how they all hated us. Except the tenants. I remember one packed rally in St Peter's Church Hall when we persuaded the Countess of Huntingdon, an activist for tenants and probably a Communist, to come and address us. The Tories packed in as many of their lot as possible and they couldn't believe that we had a countess on our side – and we made the most of it by addressing the meeting as 'Your Grace, Ladies and Gentlemen', when they expected 'Comrades and Friends'.
>
> [In the 1945 local elections Labour gained 16 seats and Stanley Bell became a councillor.] As a group we set to work, took most of the chairmanships of committees, built houses and flats not only in Kingston but, because of shortage of land, outside as well by compulsory purchase order. We improved the health services and allied services. There wasn't a piece of playground equipment for the children until we got in. We soon altered that. Recreation grounds that were out of bounds for games, especially Sundays, were soon altered and the whole complexion of the borough changed. Unfortunately, they united their forces and we lost control after about two years, but we changed the scene in that period. It was exhausting but most rewarding.
>
> **Stanley Bell, Kingston-upon-Thames**

Activists have worked not only to aid the election of Labour to local or national government, but also to aid socialism elsewhere. Hugh Chaplin recalled the war in Spain in the late 1930s:

3

We joined a thing called the Spanish Medical Aid Committee, and its job was sending every kind of medical help to Spain. And there was a very active local branch in this neighbourhood, organised by a lady called Dr Porter Hollman, who was the secretary of the local branch, and we were very active in that. We used to go round collecting money for medical aid and, at one point, we ran for a short period, a few weeks, a shop in the Euston Road. We took an empty shop and we called it the 'Spanish Medical Aid Shop'. We had it all decorated in Spanish colours and the local people used to run a lorry which used to go every week to Spain taking medical equipment and bringing back Spanish produce, which we sold for the funds in London. My wife was manager of this shop in the Euston Road. It didn't last very long, but it was a rather interesting event.

Hugh Chaplin, Holborn

Stanley Bell was trained in the procedures of civic activity within the Labour Party. Many interviewees recalled how, through engagement in left-wing politics, they gained confidence and learnt to realise their ambitions and stretch themselves. Tom Carbery was in the Co-operative Movement, May Banks in the Independent Labour Party and Doris Ashby in the Labour Party:

In the 1930s, British activists raised aid for Spain worth over £2 million

NMPFT/Science & Society Picture Library

Young left-wingers were trained in all political activities, including open-air speaking

NMPFT/Science & Society Picture Library

On three Fridays out of four you generally had a business meeting, and there would be debate and motions discussed and that is where we learned to be secretaries; where we learned to be chairmen, that was where we learned to apply the *ABC of Chairmanship* by Citrine, and I still can't find a better organisation than the Co-op and the trade unions to produce good chairmen.[3] The average chairman of a Co-op Women's Guild from the Sixties, Seventies, or Eighties would take the vast majority of people who purport to be chairmen, would take them to the cleaners in their knowledge of basic chairmanship.

Tom Carbery, Glasgow

Although we were in the Borough of Ealing, we came under the Harrow constituency, and the Labour candidate was Helen Bentwich. It was a lost cause, because the Tory candidate, Isidore Salmon, who was a member of the Lyon family or the firm of Lyons, and Harrow being the sort of area it was, we didn't stand a chance to get an MP in.[4] But Perivale certainly had Labour councillors and, in particular, we had a woman councillor, Mrs Olive Davies, a forceful, keen woman who was very keen to train other women. She was particularly interested in the Women's Co-operative Guild, and tried to train the other women in positions of authority in the branch.

Doris Ashby, Perivale

I became ward secretary, membership collector and secretary of the very lively women's section. The section had weekly meetings with visiting speakers, debates etc. For many years we took part in the annual speakers' forum, which involved a chairman and speaker. We won the silver cup, presented by Mrs Cathon JP, on many occasions. Many of our members were encouraged to attend further education classes and subsequently gained degrees.

May Banks, Salford

'My other family'

For many the Labour Party is a home from home. It is where they can enjoy debates, social activities and shared expectations. A number of individual members emphasised the importance of comradeship. Ian McGarry said 'You make real, close, long-standing friends'. An orphan whose husband and sons had died, Vera Thompson became a Party activist because she preferred this to 'sitting at home feeling sorry for myself'. Dorothy Tarry said of the Labour Party that 'it allows me to meet with like-minded people'. Jewish refugee Lucie Hauser mentioned 'I like the companionship of the party . . . I've made a great many friends and, certainly since my husband died and both my daughters married, this companionship has come to mean a lot to me.'[5] Jean Goldie made the link explicit when she said: 'The Labour Party's my home, my other family'. Within it are opportunities for socialist family activity, marraige and avoidance of the right-wing media.

We were both into the Labour Party, you see. That was more or less my private life . . . How do you think I met my first husband? In the Labour Party . . . In 1969 I remarried, Percy Tipple, who was a member of the Labour Party I had known for years.

Josie Tipple, Winsford

There was a Socialist Film Guild. We used to go to that. They showed films on a Sunday night in a place on Elm Row, which is still a cinema place. And we saw *Potemkin* and all those modern Russian films. I went with my parents to that.

Margaret Lawson, Edinburgh

The emphasis on discussion has not been at the expense of working to win elections. Social activities attract people to the Party and the two elements are difficult to separate.[6] A survey of Labour ward secretaries carried out in 1958 found that 42 per cent responded to 'what would say are the satisfactions that you get out of political activity?' by saying that they liked to help people.[7] One said, 'I feel a better person since joining the Labour Party because I am working for something I believe will bear fruit eventually.' Three others said: 'I enjoy political discussions', 'Comradeship is the greatest thing in the labour movement', and 'I meet people I wouldn't ordinarily meet. I enjoy discussions.' Others mentioned a sense of self-expression. One considered 'politics is the core of my being . . . I must articulate my opinions and feelings through a political party.' Another felt 'practically my whole life is politics. I am chairman of a theatre group and even that is political.' A third added; 'I feel that I am contributing in a small way to the determination of policies and actions'.

Historian Ross McKibbin suggested that Labour Party members are often enthusiastic joiners: 'the same kind of people who founded pigeon breeding societies also founded the Labour Party'.[8] Over half the ward secretaries surveyed in 1958 belonged to another organisation and almost all of them did if unions and other political bodies were included. A survey made in 1969 found that party members were often in a trade union and were 'more likely to belong to churches than non-members and much more likely to participate in the activities of voluntary associations'.[9] Such activity can indirectly promote the party. A 1960 survey of over 1,000 inhabitants of Wanstead and Woodford concluded: 'a close community, the extended family, informal and formal collective organisation and socialism are all of a piece'.[10] Others have drawn attention to the links between Labour's success and close communities.[11]

The Labour Party was not the only group on the left to offer a blend of political and social activities. Rafa Kenton, who moved to Lambeth from the North East in 1938 to take up a new job, found that transferring to the Young Communist League 'enabled me to have friends immediately and not to suffer the lonely fate of other young people coming to London to work in the civil service, of miserable bed-sits and only the girls at work to go out with'.[12] Jim Mortimer left Portsmouth for London and found a circle of friends within the Young Communist League. Raphael Samuel considered that, 'for my mother's generation, communism, though not intended as such, was a way of being English, a bridge by which the children of the ghetto entered the national culture'.[13] For somebody alone in a new town or country, who was unable to appeal to a family left behind in a poorer area or country, the left offered the possibility of entry to a social network; a place within a community seeking to improve the overall status of a least a segment of the working class.

In telling their tales, a number of interviewees shaped their accounts in order to emphasise the moments which highlight the nature of local political networks and their perception of socialism as a seamless part of their lives, their families and their communities.[14] May Banks argued that, even though her mother was not a suffragette, she was influenced by the campaign for the extension of the franchise. May combined her memories with what she learnt later, placing herself and her mother within a politicised, and feminist, context. She went on to stress the ways in which left-wing politics had pervaded her family.[15]

Whenever I hear the strains of Schubert's Funeral March, my mind goes back 80 years. I was walking up Elizabeth Street on my way to Buckingham Palace Road Library, when I heard that sound. My library books slipping from my grasp, I ran towards the sound and there, at the corner of Buckingham Palace Road, I saw a lengthy procession. I saw a large grey, preceded by a procession of ladies in all-white dresses, with purple, green and white sashes over their shoulders. I learnt afterwards these were all women who had been in prison for the suffrage cause. On the dray was a coffin draped in an enormous green, purple and white plaid. In front of it were many women, and some men, then an empty carriage full of beautiful flowers. I've learnt since that this carriage should have been occupied by Mrs Pankhurst. She had been sent to prison on that very day. The procession over, I changed my books and went home, full of it. In the next day's paper I read that it was the funeral procession for Miss Emily Davison, the suffragette who pulled the King's horse down at the 1913 Derby and hadn't been killed. She was badly injured and died a few days later . . . My mother, who had always opposed the suffragettes' fight, never once missed her vote until she died at the age of 90. . . .

My husband became very involved in the politics of the Labour Party, being chairman of the Trades Council and constituency party, with Margaret Beckett, then Margaret Jackson, as his secretary. Our daughter was very active in the Young Socialists, and I became ward secretary, membership collector and secretary of the very lively women's section. . . .

My husband worked for the party until a few weeks before his death in 1981. My daughter still works but I am able to do no more than address envelopes. I have never regretted that I joined the labour movement. The happiest days of my life have been spent in its company. It is the most caring of the three political parties.

May Banks, Salford

Anne Matthews recalled how, when she left her post at the Labour Research Department and moved to a new town after her marriage to Stephen Swingler in 1936, she found the Labour Party a good means of meeting people. They helped to organise the first May Day march and meeting in North Staffordshire for years, and he became the Parliamentary candidate for Stafford in 1938.

We joined the local Labour Party, that's what we decided to do. [My husband, an adult education lecturer] couldn't ever go to meetings because he always had classes in the evening, so I used to have to go to the Labour Party. Had to go? Well, it was a bit like that at first as I was the only woman and I was also young and I wasn't even from north Staffordshire. Quite awkward really in some ways, but I was determined to go, and I joined. We met in a room in a pub up Hesketh Street up the hill, and within the second meeting I was made secretary. They were on to a very good thing. I found it difficult to say no, and I could take minutes and goodness knows what, so there I was. It was a very, very small Labour Party but we revived it in many ways. Made new members and it was part of the constituency which later [from 1945] Harold Davies represented because it was in Leek. It was a good, solid Labour part of Leek. It was very important to him. We organised a meeting in the Kidsgrove Town Hall. [Labour Party leader Clement] Attlee came, '37 probably. We were trying to get that area made into a Distressed Area, because if it were made into a Distressed Area we would get a bit of money to do a few things. So we went round with a petition, getting people to sign it. Most people didn't know what we were talking about but, anyway, we got a big petition and we sent it in.[16] We got Clem Attlee to come and speak at a very well-attended meeting at the Town Hall, and that was a way of stirring things up a bit. Sometimes 'foreigners', as it were, come in and revitalise and that's what was happening in North Staffordshire. The new WEA [Workers' Education Association] people who were coming in were revitalising. It wasn't that it was moribund but it needed a bit of a kick. A lot of outsiders were coming in, liking to live there because the people were extraordinarily friendly and easy to get to know and revitalising various organisations. A tremendously exciting time. It wasn't at all a comfortable time. We were working very hard and we also had some fun. We used to love to go to the local pubs and drink beer with all our friends and have occasional parties and things like that. It was very exciting.[17]

Anne Swingler, Kidsgrove

A Leeds soldier stationed in Norfolk during the war recalled how, through his interest in the 1945 election, he helped to create a political and social network for himself:

There was nothing in Hunstanton. I thought, 'I'll have to do something here.' I went to the local Co-op and asked to see the manager. I asked him: 'Are you a member of the Labour Party?'
'It so happens I am. Why?'
'Where is the Labour Party?'
'We haven't got a Labour Party.'
'How about forming one?'
'It's a good idea. Look,' he says, 'go down the railway station.' The railway station clerk was the station master, signals, porter, clerk, luggage man – he was the whole lot. And he was delighted. I said 'Do you know anybody?' 'Yes,' he says, 'I know a bus driver and his wife who are Labour.' And there was also the War Agricultural Officer, the man who looked after the farms. I went to see this lad and I've been friends with him ever since. 'What are we going to do?' he says. 'We're going to form a Labour Party.' We called a meeting. We had about a dozen people. None of them were public speakers. I was the only one who could stand up in public . . . I'd go travelling round the villages making public speeches. Our candidate was a Major Wise. The headquarters were in King's Lynn – but we won the blessed seat. We won it![18]

Debate attracts new members, it encourages those already in the Party to continue to raise money and win over voters and it ensures that people do not become disillusioned or have their socialism nullified by the traditions of the Town Hall or Westminster. Debate is also central because there is no one definition of socialism to which all members adhere, it is constantly being refreshed, reinvented and applied to new circumstances. Both Scott Garnet and John Crawford recalled how enthusiastic they were about discussion within the Labour Party in the 1930s.

In 1935 I went along to Long Eaton Labour Party [South Nottingham] and they only had dull business meetings once a month, but later on I struck up with the Beeston Labour Party, which had far more meetings. Moreover, the enthusiasts in Beeston used to meet before the main Labour Party meeting to thrash over articles and clear their ideas and to brace themselves and prepare themselves for political intrigues, and I sided up with the left-wingers in the Labour Party who had a sort of running issue with the right-wingers.

It was in the Beeston Labour Party that I served my political apprenticeship . . . I ran errands for the Labour Party secretary. Because I was a cyclist I was the ideal person. I could cover the ground very quickly. And then I became literature secretary, possibly because I was a cyclist, but of all the jobs that I've done for the Labour Party, and I mean of course unpaid work, I think this job of literature secretary is the one that I did best. In the years 1937, '38, '39 I found it quite hard to get political pamphlets, but as World War II broke out the *People's Bookshop* in Nottingham opened, and then it was possible to get a whole store of political pamphlets of all kinds, and I bought mainly Labour Party pamphlets, obviously, but also some Communist, some ILP, some Liberal. I can't remember buying a Conservative pamphlet, but I wouldn't swear that I never did. I certainly bought quite a number of HMSO pamphlets, and if anybody of a progressive frame of mind had written a pamphlet or small cheap book I took it along and sold it to party members, Labour Party or not. I thought they ought to know what ideas were going around.

I learned in the Beeston party to argue my corner, to put my point of view, and it was there that I had my early training in speaking. I had, earlier than this, tried public speaking in Long Eaton. The Long Eaton Library, which I used quite a lot had, in my opinion, been taken over by the right. When all the progressive councillors were absent some right-wing councillors on the rural district council that ran Long Eaton decided to take out of the library all books on politics, which meant they would have taken out seven, eight or nine books of a socialist kind to one Conservative, and it would have made any sort of political reading extremely difficult. Now, this was due to councillors not turning up for an important meeting in the town of Long Eaton. The Labour Party got a chair and the

Communist Party got a chair and I managed to borrow the chair that the Communist had used and I spoke, and what a feeble effort it was! I felt furious. Ideas were bubbling up in my mind, but turning them into words, and words that could be heard in an open market place, was very difficult. So, as I say, I needed badly to learn to turn feelings and emotions and ideas into speech, and this I did arguing my corner in the Beeston Labour Party.

Scott Garnet, Nottingham

I got involved in what I'd call 'ginger group' activities, the Labour Party wasn't moving quickly enough for me. I became a member of the Left Book Club, which was quite leftward leaning, which suited my political stance at the time, indeed suits it today for that matter.[19] We had a little meeting room in the attic of the Co-op Insurance Society offices, Nan [later his wife] used to come to these meetings, which I thought were very good. We used to have a speaker each week, friends of mine. I can remember one who was killed in the war, chap called John Gallacher, who would perhaps talk about Soviet Communism, somebody else would talk about the need for a National Health Service, before there was one of course, we'd talk about education, all kinds of things. We were very earnest, that's the only way you can put it. We did try for a very short time a theory that we could go into pubs, have a drink, and then at some stage stand up and start trying to explain to the bar what we were about, but we only lasted a couple of evenings doing that. We were soon emptied out by the chap who was running the pub.

John Crawford, Chester

Labour MP Hugh Jenkins drew attention to the importance of Labour's tradition of a socialism drawn from many sources including John Wesley, Robert Owen and Karl Marx:

That is why the Labour Party has a collection of beliefs rather than a single dogma. We still have those beliefs. We must never lose them. We must never degenerate into a mere electoral machine.[20]

Interviewees also emphasised the value that they placed on Labour as the place where discussion of the issues of the day could take place and from which they could go on to further education:

I think the Labour Party then was openly a party which held an enormous number of different opinions. There was an acceptance of the fact that we're not all machines, and that it's quite right that people think for themselves. I think subsequently that got a little bit stilted, you got to follow party policy.

Ron Whitworth, Hornchurch

We used to have speakers out. Not partisan speakers. Speakers that were giving us all sides of the story. And we would have speakers out speaking about the shipbuilding industry and the decline of it. People that worked in the industry. We really had excellent speakers. And I think that really is the purpose of the Labour Party, instead of all these minutes and all this bumf that comes out from Transport House and has to be read all the time.

Helen Cameron, Glasgow

In those days we had political education officers who used to run monthly events. I remember one of the events which was running in Ealing North was when various members of the party on a panel, right across the board: a schoolteacher, a journalist, solicitor – I think we even had a doctor – spoke about why they were members of the Labour Party and what had made them come into the Labour Party. We used to have weekend schools at Beatrice Webb House [a Co-operative building in Surrey]. At one of these weekends we had as a speaker Kenneth Kaunda, who later went on to become President of his country [Zambia]. He was here, I assume, at LSE or at London University doing a degree at the time and politically active.

Marianne Elliott, Perivale

When the NCLC [the left-wing, trade union-sponsored National Council of Labour Colleges] went out of existence it left a vacuum, and the vacuum is still there. The Labour Party spends a lot of time on explaining how to run elections, and that seems to be the sum total. They've never taken political education seriously. There have been efforts to do it in localities, of course, but that is not the same as having a centrally-directed activity to explain the various facts of socialist understanding and particularly, of course, the role of Marx. Because Marx, his views were greatly influential in the Labour Party and still are today, to a great extent, but they are not brought forth out of the enclaves of sectarian activity and that needs to be dealt with, and only the Labour Party can deal with that, with trade union finance, in my view.

Syd Bidwell, Southall

Debate can lead to considered positions being placed before Labour Party leaders. Bea Serota stressed that the Party is not simply a one-way street with orders passed down the line, that activists can have an effect not just locally but nationally:

There is a structure which goes right through the Labour Party. National Conference is the ultimate body, with the national executive operating throughout the year, and all the normal paraphernalia of resolution-building process through the constituency parties and trade unions. There is also a series of committees and commissions which are sitting now. It evolves partly from the grass roots and partly the National Executive machinery, I would say. Presumably moving

Campaigns ran more smoothly when canvassers knew local people well

NMPFT/Science & Society Picture Library

towards the period when we will be in government, but conference is the ultimate body. Not that government always follows conference decisions. We're seeing this process this current year [1995]. We're told that a number of policy documents and range of services will be coming forward for consideration by conference. That is the Labour Party in action, which is quite different from the Conservative Party method. That certainly doesn't come from the grass roots.

Bea Serota, Hampstead

Labour Party activists' efforts, on behalf of their communities, bolster democracy. Their watch over the professional politicians helps to ensure that socialism remains on the political agenda. In order to gain a better picture of our democracy, attention needs to be paid to far more than the written rules of the Labour Party, to understand its social mores it is necessary to listen to the activists. The left has provided a haven from the capitalist world, a social web, a means of expression of the political culture of the British working class. It has also provided opportunities to oppose capitalism through education, debate, organising for elections and direct action on local, national and international levels.

II

Becoming Involved

The Labour Representation Committee was founded in February 1900 and changed its name to the Labour Party in 1906. Its initial aims were to represent its principal founders and funders, the trade unions, in parliament. In addition to the trade unions, a number of socialist societies were affiliates, but there were few individual members as only three local Labour Parties permitted individual membership before 1918. The socialist affiliates included two organisations to which a number of interviewees refer: the Fabian Society, a forum for intellectuals founded in 1884, and the Independent Labour Party (ILP), formed in 1893.

In the autumn of 1900 there was a General Election and two of the Labour Representation Committee's 15 candidates, one a Liberal and the other the independent labour candidate, Keir Hardie, were elected to Parliament. The following year a controversial court case increased support for Labour. Strikers involved in a rail dispute were judged to have broken their contracts, damaged company property and disrupted normal trading. Their union was fined £23,000. As a result, unions flocked to support the Labour Representation Committee, which was committed to a reversal of this decision.

At the next General Election, in 1906, the Labour Party stood 50 candidates and won 29 of the 670 seats. That year the Party lobbied successfully for the passing of the Trades Disputes Act which restored the unions' right to strike, free of legal retribution, and went on to win a number of seats at by-elections. In 1908 the coal miners' trade union voted to affiliate to Labour and their 12 MPs swelled Labour's ranks to 45. However, in 1909 the Liberals introduced a controversial budget, and the rejection of this by the Conservative-dominated House of Lords, together with the issue of Home Rule for Ireland became central to party politics. Labour, being mostly concerned with trade union issues, was sidelined. The number of unemployed fell and Labour MPs found themselves arguing over their views on the Liberal reforms instead of initiating policies.

Some ILP members questioned the value of focusing on returning Labour MPs, instead of seeking to persuade more people of the merits of socialism. They broke away to help form a new party, leaving those committed to parliamentary socialism more firmly in the control of Labour. By the outbreak of the First World War there were 37 Labour MPs, the Party controlled 179 locally elected bodies around the country and there were over 250 Labour councillors. However, the party was still not very well organised for elections. Most of the two million trade unionists who were affiliated did not concern themselves with the party and it had to rely on supportive campaigning bodies, including the National Union of Women's Suffrage Societies, and 'the enthusiasm of local political activists'.[1] Among these were some of the parents of the interviewees. Although few people now have clear memories of the period before the First World War, a number of informants refer to the activities of their parents during this period and carry an understanding of the early development of the Labour Party. When considering the main influences on their decision to become involved in politics, many people mentioned politically active older relatives, friends and colleagues. This accords with the results of a survey of 100 people who were active in left-wing politics between the wars. Most had activist fathers or attributed their sense of social justice to a parent.[2]

Family ties

Given the restrictions on membership and the limited franchise prior to 1918 there was little chance that those born before the First World War Armistice would grow up within an atmosphere of support for Labour. Sam Waters said: 'All my relations were strong Tories, even Masons' and Scott Garnet and Doris Partridge both came from Conservative backgrounds. Nevertheless, a number of those born early in the century mention a left-wing parent. Olive Parsons was born in 1892 and her family holidayed with Ramsay MacDonald (who became Labour Prime Minister in 1924). Syd Bidwell's father was in the ILP. He 'used to go on about the philosophy of socialism, and Marxist literature was on the bookshelves at home and we thought, 'Well, wish the old man would shut up about it'. Despite this original lack of interest, Syd went on to become a Labour MP. Fred Combes' parents were not left-wing but he did share with his sister and brother a life-long interest in Labour Party politics which kept them together: "We had our own banner [in the Labour League of Youth], my younger sister made it, and I carried it on demonstrations to Hyde Park". Almost 50 years later he chose his sister to be his mayoress when he was mayor. Harold Edwards' mother was a keen co-operator, the mothers of Isa Paton, Aileen Plant and Owen Heather were all suffragettes and John Crawford's father was an active trade unionist.

During the 1920s and 1930s, local Labour Parties were created all over the country, and it was to these new Labour Parties that many interviewees and their parents were attracted. In April 1935, the Labour Party League of Youth's journal *New Nation* published 'Why I Joined the League', in which L.V. Thomson wrote: 'I have been brought up in a Socialist family, on the writings of Blatchford, Wells, Shaw and others. If heredity and environment count for anything, I cannot be anything but a socialist.'[3] Many of the recruits to Labour in the interwar years had previously supported the Liberals.

My left-wing inclination? I think I must have been born with it.

John Horner, Hampshire

'It's a natural thing for a working man to be, is Labour.' That's what my father used to say.

Lew Smith, Tottenham

[My grandfather] used to have a conference on a Sunday with his family. He had a son, and his wife, and my mother and my father and, of course, his wife. And me as a kid just sitting listening. And they had to read, they only had the one *Reynolds' News*. But he would have certain articles in it and he would read them and then they discussed what was your opinion and what did you think of that, and do you think that we should pursue this line or that line? And then they would have a sort of quiz situation, spelling bee they called it, and that ended up the evening. And we didn't have any electricity or anything like that in these days, it was the old oil lamp in the middle of the table and that, basically, was where it all started.

Alex Kitson, Edinburgh

My father was a very strong trade unionist, in fact he organised the firm in which he worked, and I can remember his putting up in our front window bills in the election . . . My dad was a convinced socialist, and he brought us up on socialist principles. And those teachings, a lot of them I still live by.

Tom Riley, Battersea

My father wasn't a member of the Labour Party. He always was very active. My mother had been a member for some time. He always helped, but he was rather more left wing, although not a member of any particular party.

Doris Ashby, Perivale

Very strong family environment, but one which was always surrounded by politics and the trades unions. Never was there a day went by but what those subjects were mentioned in the house, because they were of importance in those days. And they are today.

Les Horne, Yorkshire

Both my parents were in the Labour Party in Edinburgh. My father had been in the Communist Party in the early twenties but, by the time I was noticing things, they were both in the ILP and then, when the ILP disaffiliated from the Labour Party [in 1932], they both joined the Labour Party . . . My father accused my mother of being right-wing, of being right, and he was more left. And I couldn't work out how somebody, a person, could be right and another could be left . . . And then they would have recourse, in a joking way, to family history, because my mother was a Jacobite, came from a Jacobite family, and my mother would say, 'Well, you fought on the wrong side at Culloden' . . . History, with some people in Scotland, still lives.

Margaret Lawson, Edinburgh

I'd come home from school and Dad'd start talking to me . . . it would be, he called it municipal housing and, I tell you something, this was the old socialist view of the day. If you was a socialist you had no right to be thinking of buying a house. 'Buying a house? Want to be an owner? No. Damn good municipal housing. That's what you want. That's what you've got to strive for, my girl' . . . Dad said, 'Don't sit there criticising your country and the Labour Party. Get up off your arse, get out there, and do something about it.' And, so you know what, I was 16, I sat down and thought, he's got something there . . . So I said to him, 'How old do you have to be to join the Labour Party?' and he said, 'Collector'll be round Sunday, we'll ask him.'

Vi Willis, Ilford

My father was in the ILP of course, which he regarded as a socialist ginger force in the Labour Party itself. I recall he'd go out canvassing at election times, but he didn't play his role as an activist in the local political scene itself because his hands were very full, he'd quite a young family, five children. Mass poverty was in the thirties, which greatly influenced me, and I fell into tune with my father's observations.

Syd Bidwell, Southall

A guy called Fred Barker knocked on the front door. My father suggested that I went and talked to him, and within three weeks I was the ward secretary and was one of those running round collecting subs as well. And the subs then were on the penny-a-week stamps and we went round and stamped people's cards.

Harold Tomlins, Chester

How I came to actually join Labour was my elder brother was already a member of the Labour Party before. When I left the [children's] home at fifteen, their last piece of advice to me was not to join the same organisation as my brother, so the first thing I did when I left there was to say to him, 'Take me to one of the Labour League of Youth meetings', which he did, and I was about fifteen and a half, and I joined the Labour Party then.

Olive Rainbird, Tottenham

My mother-in-law said to me 'They're looking for a secretary for the Labour Party, they're going to come and see you' . . . I had a visit from the then treasurer and chairman of Davenport Ward Labour Party and it wasn't to ask me to be a member or something, or to rejoin, it was to ask me to be secretary. It was an astonishing situation . . . I said I'd be a collector and they were satisfied with that. I later did become secretary. In those days collectors were the most important people in the branch.

Jim Tucker, Stockport

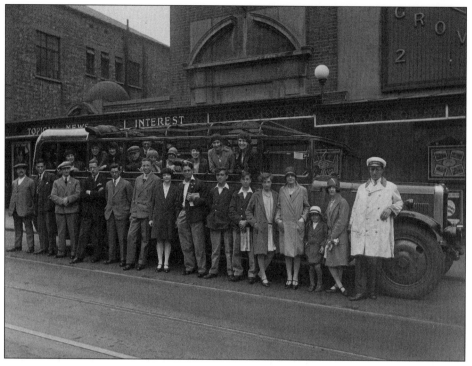

Olive Rainbird and her brother join other Tottenham socialists setting out on a day trip

Olive Rainbird's private collection

My father was a stonemason, that in a way was my introduction to the Labour Movement. I've always been it because my father was a keen trade unionist and secretary of his branch of what was then called the AUBTW, the Amalgamated Union of Building Trade Workers. So my introduction to the Labour Movement was really from birth . . . My second brother was always interested and later became a member of the national executive of NUPE, his interest was in the trade union side, much as my father's had been, rather than the purely political. My third brother, who worked in the aircraft industry, was chairman of the shop stewards committee where he worked. My youngest brother was very interested in politics but he was an armchair politician and never did anything except criticise me for being far too right-wing.

John Crawford, Chester

I'd grown up always in a socialist household. I was passionately interested . . . My father went to that [Pankhurst] Hall, his elder brother, who shared the hat-blocking firms, he was ten years older, he also was there. They were very active there. One aspect of their activity was a dramatic society. My mother was passionately keen on dramatics and apparently she had a friend who went to Pankhurst Hall and they wanted some more young women in the society. She said, 'I know a young woman simply dying to join a dramatic society'. My mother went down to start with for the dramatic side but, of course, she soon became converted. She was a very easy convert, because at that time she was being prepared for confirmation and one of the things that was being taught to her was about the churching of women. Women during childbirth were considered unclean, and when they finished the birth they had to go back to the church and have a ceremony to be declared clean again. She thought that was a most dreadful insult to womanhood. That stuck in her mind ready to be thinking. Also, of course, at that period there was the ideas of Darwin evolution, starting to permeate society. She was very interested in that. Her thoughts about evolution rather than God just creating the world, and also her disgust at their feeling about women. So when she went down to Pankhurst Hall she soon imbibed everything. That is how my father and mother met . . . They were passionate walkers, passionate cyclists. They of course joined in the Clarion cyclists, spreading the socialist doctrine out in the countryside by cycling out to rural areas. Naturally, when they came to Stockport they joined the Labour Church.

Aileen Plant, Stockport

[Mother] was a suffragette, a member of the suffragette movement . . . I remember the pride with which my mother greeted the fact that the first woman had been elected to parliament [in 1918] . . . In the immediate postwar years my sister was in a pushchair and my mother went round speaking in the back courts, if you know what I mean by back courts. You know, in tenements as we have in Glasgow, there was a common back court where there was a wash house, very often run down. And my mother went round these in the afternoons, very often with her pram. She was really very good. In fact, she was asked to stand as a councillor in the Kingston ward . . . but she felt that having four children she couldn't do that, and Jane Roberts got the nomination and went on and was councillor for many, many years, finishing up as the first Glasgow Lord Provost. She didn't like to be called Lady Provost . . . Part of the reason, my mother did admit to me later was, of her turning down the offer of a nomination, that my father was beginning to have ambitions towards council work but, of course, being in full-time employment it was a different story in those days. And he was just enough, she felt, of a chauvinist to resent her being a councillor when he's not.

Isa Paton, Glasgow

Both my mother and her mother were quite active suffragettes. The Preston group or branch of the suffragettes was moderately strong. On one occasion, when Winston Churchill came, he was then a minister in the Liberal government, came to speak in Preston, they were successful in disrupting his meeting.

Owen Heather, Preston

Owen Heather's father was a Labour supporter but, as an Inspector of Taxes, was barred from party political activity. His mother was a suffragette and his maternal grandfather worked for the election of Keir Hardie. However, politics were not discussed at home. It was not until he was aged twelve and a fee-paying pupil at the prestigious Manchester Grammar School, that Owen read the murder stories of Douglas Cole and then his work on economics and politics. In addition to his interview he wrote some biographical notes in which he explained:

My introduction to socialism came from G.D.H. Cole. I had read a number of his detective stories and progressed to his very lucid explanations of socialism. I was hooked! I joined the Labour Party at the age of fifteen and was taken under the wing of William Luby, an elderly engineer, very much of the manual working class, a fine fellow. Within a few months he had secured my election as secretary of the Withington ward party.

Owen Heather, Withington

My mother joined the Labour Party about '35, '36, I don't know exactly when . . . She was a collector. I remember the long sheets for collection. I think it was six shillings a year then to be a member of the Labour Party. People used to pay quarterly or half yearly.

Marianne Elliott, Perivale

Perivale Labour Party was very lively. I can remember that my mother was a collector for the Labour Party and there was only one house where she didn't collect subs from. She used to go round every month and, I can't remember how much it was, but it was something very small, something like tuppence or thrupence. But she called at every house with the exception of this one.

Doris Ashby, Perivale

Breaking away

Analysis of recent voting behaviour has shown that once people have made a choice they are generally unwavering, and that the most accurate way to estimate how a person will vote is to discover their parents' preferences. When both parents support the same party, 90 per cent of people will support that party at their first election. This figure drops to 80 per cent in later years. A survey of young Labour Party members made in the 1960s concluded that:

The further left a Young Socialist the more likely he [sic] is to have actively radical if not revolutionary parents, parents whose own politics were shaped in 1917, 1926 or 1931 . . . Of those who are active the great majority are merely continuing a family habit of enjoyment in public affairs. Often the critical politicising experiences that brought the family into politics lie three generations away, the Dock Strike [1889], the Revolution of 1905, the Great War.[4]

Such consistency was impossible during Labour's early years, until the extension of the franchise gave many families the chance to vote for the first time. However, even when this is taken into account, the interviews and survey evidence demonstrate a significant realignment of political attitudes as the Labour Party grew. Isa Paton spoke of the shift in personal terms, explaining that her father was initially a Conservative. A survey carried out in the 1960s found that, of those people old enough to vote in 1918, 38 per cent said that their fathers were Liberals. However, only 18 per cent said that their own earliest preference was for the Liberals. Of those who voted for the first time between 1922 and 1935, 13 per cent voted Liberal, although 25 per cent of their fathers had voted that way. These figures indicate a striking shift, suggesting that 25–30 per cent were changing their votes each decade and 50–60 per cent between generations.[5]

In a survey of people born between the 1870s and early 1900s, only 43 per cent of the working-class men interviewed reported having the same political loyalties as their fathers. None of those with Labour fathers became either Conservative or Liberal, but ten of those from Liberal homes became Labour supporters, as did seven from Tory homes and six from neutral or no-answer homes. The younger the respondents the more likely they were to switch to Labour, and those with Labour-supporting fathers were youngest of all.[6] Labour's supporters either came from Labour homes or had switched allegiance, particularly from the Liberal Party. John Uzzell's remark indicates his awareness of this shift: 'My parents were very much in the mould of having left the Liberal tendency, the old Liberal Party, on the formation of the Labour Party.' Among the Ministers in the 1945–50 Labour government there were three similar examples. Stafford Cripps, whose father was first a Conservative MP, became a Liberal peer and then joined Labour; John Strachey, whose father was the former editor of the Conservative periodical the *Spectator*; and George Strauss, the son of a Conservative MP who joined Labour shortly before his death. Harold Edwards remembers speaking at Liberal Party meetings before there was individual membership of the Labour Party. Those who had the vote before 1918 may have changed their voting behaviour as a result of the war or political instability, but perhaps Labour gained most from generational replacement, people growing up and choosing Labour. A survey of young political activists conducted in the 1960s concluded:

The principle of family succession is what emerges most clearly among young activists. Four out of five come from families with a record of political activity. Seven in every ten support the same party as their most politically active parent. The main patterns of innovation appear to be for children of . . . once active Liberals to become Young Socialists.[7]

In later decades the generational persistence which was parodied by W.S. Gilbert when he noted that every child born alive was either 'a little Liberal or else a little

21

Conservative' reasserted itself. By the 1960s the Labour lead over the Conservatives was greater among those born in the 1920s, the children of the first significant Labour generation, than it was among any other age group.[8] The pioneers, their children born during the interwar period, and many of their grandchildren, formed the core of Labour's support. The memories of these people, who grew up within the households of the early Labour voters who had bucked the trend of British politics, supports other evidence which suggests that parental influence was important for left-wing activists.[9]

As Labour became more established, many of those who did not follow their parents into Labour still adopted left-wing politics. Helen Lilly, the daughter of a travelling showman, recalled:

> My Dad's family were all active in Labour Party politics, and one of his uncles was on the Jarrow March, which he was quite proud of. My dad was always active in politics, even though travelling showmen were quite conservative . . . My mother . . . her family were all strong Labour. My grandmother was very strong chapel with Labour connections through Primitive Methodism . . . By this time I was thinking about politics, thinking about joining the Young Socialists. I was fifteen . . . By then the '64 election was coming up, so we were all knocking on doors wanting to chuck the Conservative out. [Labour MP] George Brown came up [to Newcastle] I went and listened to him and booed him and heckled him. Heckled Labour, heckled the Conservative . . . I joined the Communist Party when I was eighteen.[10]

Jimmy Allison was appointed Glasgow Organiser in 1971. He 'disagreed with Militant's views', but his daughter was elected to the Labour Party Young Socialists' Scottish Committee as a Militant supporter in 1972.[11] Labour's appeal was due in part to its ideology, but also to the fact that it quickly became established as a central element of working-class political culture.

Some parents were uninterested in politics or were worried about the implications of commitment to socialism. Instances of discrimination against left-wing activists are rife. Keir Hardie was sacked for his trade union activities. Mr Ruffard, born in 1897, the son of an agricultural labourer, recalled the difficulties of political activism.

> Seven of us had the nerve to start a Labour Party here in Culverton [Somerset], out on the road, under a window. We asked later if we could go to a pub room, but once the landlord knew what it was for, he said 'You can come this once, but I don't want 'ee afterwards'. So we had to hold all our meetings in one of the old cottages . . . I lost my job over it once or twice. When Labour started standing down here, they had a rough old time. Some people are afraid, even today.[12]

Once people had joined, life was not always straightforward or even pleasant. Ralph Morley 'received a blow in the face' and had his hat destroyed at an early Chichester

Labour Party meeting, and W.F. Toynbee's leg was broken when a platform was overturned in Cookham, near Windsor. A woman who put up Labour posters in the window was told to remove them by her husband, who feared that he would 'never get another job'.[13] Martha Feeney and Margaret Lloyd remember how their families suffered because of their fathers' views, and Syd Bidwell and Doris Partridge recall that their mothers were unenthusiastic about left-wing politics.

My father was an agitator, and that was his role in life, to agitate. Unfortunately, he wasn't a good provider because of that. He was a great dole man. He was on the dole a lot. And it was unfortunate for my mother because she didn't marry a Communist. She didn't marry a political man. So she was left, and she wasn't well. And my father was following the Communist diktat all the time. Going into jobs and trying to start the Trade Union movement, and sort of bringing Communism in and trying to get people into the Party and all that kind of thing, which wasn't always helpful for the family.

Martha Feeney, Glasgow

When I was born my father was the Labour Agent for St Helens. You'd have called him a Communist these days. When he worked in the pit he was boycotted from every pit. That's why he got the office job . . . He used to write to the paper, my mother said I used to be afraid of opening the paper. On a weekend we used to get two papers: *The Reporter* and the St Helens newspaper, and my father's name was across, he'd been writing about what happened in the pits. And they were so badly done to and he knew it because he was working among them then, I suppose.

Margaret Lloyd, St Helens

My mother's attitude to politics? It wasn't for the likes of her, and my father used to denounce that as a 'Kids and Curtains' mentality. I'll always remember that, 'cos there weren't so many women in the Labour movement at that time, but if there were, of course, they were well to the fore in the Co-op Women's Guild, which brought many women out of their shell. Later on I was able to help in that process when I was the organiser of the National Council of Labour Colleges . . . When I look at the pressure for women's rights and women's participation in everything in tune with menfolk, I'm thinking of the deep-seated prejudices, not only amongst men, not having women too prominent in party affairs, but also the attitude of the women themselves; and it was pretty well known that if they had to make choices they would vote for a man, if they did come to meetings they would be inclined to think, well, a woman's place is in the home. Certainly my mother had that view.

Syd Bidwell, Southall

In those days, it wasn't respectable to be a socialist and the adjective always used was dirty socialist. I can't tell you why. But dirty socialist, that was the phrase, and many a person's been offended by that.

Isa Paton, Glasgow

My parents were Tory. It was considered in my town, which was a Labour-controlled town, that the Labour people were very common and very rough. My mother said, 'She goes in the mayor's car to collect her fish and chips.'

Doris Partridge, Barrow-in-Furness

My father's family had been very strong Conservatives. My father's father was a bank manager. My father was converted to socialism because of what he saw going on all around him and the conditions that people were living under and he saw socialism as a way of improving people's lives and, as happens with most people who are converted, they are very strong about it. He and my mother joined the ILP in 1914, before war broke out.

Isa Paton, Glasgow

John Crawford and Mervyn Jones both recalled rural fears of intimidation in the 1950s.

I became what was then called propaganda secretary. Ideally suited job for me, because I'd been doing this for years before the war, when most of the others hadn't. It was very interesting. I enjoyed it. I especially enjoyed going to the Duke of Westminster's villages to sell, I remember, on one occasion a pamphlet we'd produced which was an excellent pamphlet, called *Green and Pleasant Land*. We were supposed to sell these for sixpence and we did very well. Even in the Duke's villages. People would take them and say 'Between you and I, don't tell anybody'. We've even gone to some houses and they've given us more than the sixpence, they given us half a crown, five shillings, and said, 'That's for the funds, keep it under your hat'. It was like a secret society going round some of those villages and I imagine, to be honest, it is still the same today.

John Crawford, Chester

There were people who didn't dare say they were in the Labour Party. They felt they would get the sack, they were tenants, they'd be turned out of their houses. In fact this was an unreal fear. But it dated back to the old days of the tied cottage and the old days in which a farmer or a landowner could, if he thought somebody had the wrong ideas, he'd say 'Right, you're evicted.' At the time I'm speaking of, this was no longer legally possible but this kind of folk memory went on, and I remember John Beadle [agent] telling me once that he went into a village and eight separate people and each of these people said to him, 'Yes, I'm Labour in my opinion but of course it's useless 'cos I'm the only one in the village.' As a matter of fact there were eight of them or so. John Beadle introduced them to each other and started a Labour Party branch in the village.

Mervyn Jones, Chichester

Josie Tipple accepted the risks attached to Party membership:

I found that politics interfered with promotion; partly politics and partly being a woman. I went for eleven headships in twelve months and didn't get any of them. I ended as a deputy. The Labour Party is worth it.

Josie Tipple, Winsford

Comrades at work

Important though the family was as a base for isolated left-wingers, the principal funder of the Labour Party was the trade union movement, and a number of people mentioned the importance of school and work-based contacts. Those interviewees who did not follow their parents' preferences may have been influenced to vote Labour by changes in neighbourhood, school, workplace and leisure time pursuits.[14] Many of those who were educated between the wars were bound together by their experiences of elementary schooling. They learnt a similar religious doctrine, saw the same films, had access to the same national newspapers, could follow teams in the same national Football League and engage in similar adolescent leisure pursuits. Many went on to similar semi-skilled jobs. In the past there had been greater divisions between religious denominations, and the possibility of improvement, through a scholarship or an apprenticeship or even a regular job, had appeared greater. These young voters tended to support the general and industrial unions and the party which offered, in its very name, to take up their concerns. Important occupational, status and regional differences were maintained but there was a considerably more economically, socially and politically united working class than there had been previously.

I delivered some leaflets, I remember, when I was about ten, for a friend of my father's, a teacher at the school, who was standing as a council candidate in West Norwood. And that was for the [1937 local] election just before the '39 war.

Maureen Dewar, Tottenham

I had distinctly left-wing views. We had a very interesting teacher of history at Bromley Grammar School. Although he did not directly proselytise for the Labour Party, he taught his history with a very distinct attitude towards the idea that the whole of English history had been a struggle for ordinary people to get freedom of speech, freedom for their political views and to improve the conditions of life and that made a considerable impression on me, and although I did not join any labour movement at that time I had a very considerable sympathy for the attitude of the labour movement, and was indeed very favourably disposed towards them.

Edward Britton, Guildford

It was the Sunday School Superintendent that was a member of the Labour Party. There had been Labour candidates, of course, in Northwich constituency. I joined on my birthday when I was 21, in 1939 when nobody could say I couldn't. Of course the war came then, so I didn't get my first vote until 1945. Percy Clerk was the man's name, who recruited me and he and a man called Fred Hewitt, who is still alive and in his 90s, used to put a bit of money in the Post Office Savings Bank every week so that there would be something with which to start again after the war.

Josie Tipple, Acton Bridge

I joined the Labour Party League of Youth in 1933 . . . I was a railway worker and went to work on the vans at Paddington. I was what they call a van guard on the horse-drawn vehicles around the Paddington district. Of course, being greatly influenced by the older workers that I was involved with at an early stage. When I think of young people these days, what they're missing, particularly if they're young, is associating with older workers who will have some influence in their lives, and some care about them as well.

Syd Bidwell, Southall

I'd been doing vacation courses at the Royal Aircraft Establishment in 1935–6 and soon decided that was the place I wanted to work. I should be a civil servant if I went there. Funnily enough that was the place which introduced me to politics, a civil service establishment . . . Extraordinarily enough, the civil servants there were very left wing. We had a Left Book Club, that wasn't started quite as early as 1935 or '36, but the RAE was described in journals at the time as a 'red' establishment, (several of the aeronautical press people were right-wing and they thought it was appalling). They were university-educated people and I was invited to go to a discussion group straight away.

Alan Yates, Farnborough

It was towards the end of the war when I met a fellow who made perhaps politically the strongest impression on me. He was on his way. He was in trouble. He was invariably in trouble. He was a guy who refused to carry out orders that he thought were wrong or ill-conceived for whatever reason. Sometimes I thought he was right. Sometimes I thought 'Well, you're making a rod for your own back.' A fellow named Green . . . I talked to him a couple of times and realised what sort of man he was and he was the sort of man I wasn't. I had become conditioned, if you like, to doing what people expected me to do. He made me think if I can be me, think for myself, that was the start. He was a Communist.

John Morris Clarke, Liverpool

I joined the Labour Party because one of the lads at work, he would put up at a local election as a Labour councillor and I promised to help him out canvassing and all that sort of thing, and then I got collared for membership.

John Tuffey, Wandsworth

Being in the trade union movement obviously attracted Labour Party people. I joined the Labour Party in 1945, so I sought out the local branch and worked with them.

Mike Turner, Yeovil

Joining difficulties
There were times when recruitment was rather haphazard. Helen Cameron and Isa Paton joined before the Second World War and Frank Booth, Bea Serota, Alan Yates and Irene Wagner joined in the 1940s.

I tell you, I'd a heck of a job joining the Labour Party. It was very difficult to get somebody to tell you where you contacted your local Labour Party . . . And eventually, through a colleague of my father's we managed to join the Labour Party . . . When we moved in 1946 we again had this dreadful business of finding out where the Labour Party met, when they met and there was a fellow called Joe Gerard was secretary of the City Labour Party, as it was then (all these things have been done away with now) and we wrote to him, but he never ever made any contact with us. But, eventually, another colleague of my father's managed to give us the address and where the meetings were held, and we were very active in the Labour Party.

Helen Cameron, Glasgow

In the Thirties when I tried to join it was the same thing [as it is now], I never yet got a reply to my application to join the Labour Party, or I might have been in before the war.

Isa Paton, Glasgow

There was a by-election [late 1945] and I went there one evening and I said 'Could I help?' and that's how I started. Finished up as secretary of the ward and on the council for 17 years . . . They asked me 'Would I go on the count?' I said 'I'd very much like to do, but I'm not a member of the Labour Party.' She said 'Oh, that doesn't matter, but in any case we'd better put that right hadn't we?' I joined up then and I've been a member ever since.

Frank Booth, Stockport

It took both of us three or four months to join, because we found from Transport House who the secretary was. We wrote, then nothing happened, because the organisation was still very chaotic.

Irene Wagner, Holborn

We moved to Hampstead to live in some flats by Chalk Farm Station at the very beginning of 1939. This was very important for us as we'd only been in the flat a few days when somebody knocked at the door and pushed a piece of paper through the letter box. We went to see what it was and it was something from the Labour Party. 'Join the Labour Party' . . . We flung open the door and rushed into the corridor and said 'Did you put this through our door?' and they shrank back. And we said 'We want to join,' and they were taken aback. We all joined the Labour Party from that moment . . . We'd just gone through Munich, which scared us all stiff and made us very political. We knew that war was a possibility.

Alan Yates, Hampstead

I don't recall much going on when I first arrived [in 1942]. I think the political temperature began to rise in Hampstead in about 1944. But in the earlier years I had been to Fabian Society summer schools . . . The Hampstead Labour Party didn't come on to my horizon until I think '43 or '44, when one of the then prime movers in the Marylebone Fabian Society, somebody called Bill Fiske who later became leader of the LCC and the GLC and, in fact, became a member of the House of Lords eventually, started something called the Young Voters group, with a view to getting young people involved in the work of the Labour Party for the forthcoming General Election. That was a very active organisation and a whole lot of us, some from the Fabian Society, some from the LSE [London School of Economics] who were living locally and young people generally, I think, all probably under the age of twenty-five, I suppose, then became very active in the Young Voters Group and joined the Labour Party, which was then being reconstituted because it had been disaffiliated. I went to my first ward meeting, I'll never forget it, in Parliament Hill in Harry Smith's house. I walked in, and the first thing I saw was a picture of the King and Queen on the mantelpiece and this was so remote from my conception of what the Labour Party was, the King and Queen and the Union Jack in the centre of the mantelpiece and I thought, 'My God, what have I come to?' The wards were being re-formed and eventually we had a Town Ward and that's where I was made secretary. I became a member of the GC and I eventually became chairman of the party.

What I sensed coming into the party after the period of disaffiliation was a great deal of the bitterness still remained. The people who'd been expelled and the people who'd stayed on – there was a sense of tension. But I wasn't part of that. It made the existing members of the party very suspicious. Perhaps because we were so young. They seemed to be very suspicious of newcomers, which is quite natural in some ways, but they would always talk about the ones who'd been expelled and there was a great feeling of resentment about those who were in the Communist Party. I remember that very clearly, deep resentment there of the people who'd gone to the Communist Party, or who had stayed in the Communist Party during the Hitler/Stalin pact. That went very deep into people's minds . . . I remember Mrs Cayford looking round the GMC, as we called it then General Management Committee, saying 'I can see a lot of strangers here today.' Whereas we all thought we would be very welcome. Mrs Cayford was the queen of Hampstead. She was undoubtedly. She had been on the council, stayed in the party, stayed on the council right through the war, and was indeed a remarkable woman. One must be fair about it. But by our standards she was terribly reactionary and right-wing and resentful of the new look.

Bea Serota, Hampstead

Left-wing politics is often associated with rebellion against the established order. For some left-wingers, becoming a socialist meant renouncing kinship and class ties. A number saw this as a move towards a morally superior position, and some expressed the view that socialism is a practical form of Christianity. Becoming a left-wing activist could mean the creation of a new supportive structure based on a sense of a workplace or on international comradeship. However, most of those who have remained within the Labour Party for most of their lives grew up in households in which their activities were accepted and who took a left-wing newspaper which bolstered Labour. In a survey of thirty-five Labour Party ward secretaries (twenty-six men, nine women) in Manchester in 1958, 58 per cent claimed that a relative was interested in politics. 77 per cent belonged to a union, and three had fathers who were full-time officials, one was a Labour Party organiser, another a union official and a third a secretary of a local co-operative society.[15] The survey concluded that 'it is almost as difficult to disavow inherited politics as it is to disavow inherited religion'.[16] Among those who did take the initiative was the woman who had helped as a child with street meetings and who added that, as 'my sister was a founder member of the ILP . . . it was natural that I should join.' Another said that 'it was rather a matter of drifting in . . . my father was a trade unionist all his life, my grandfather was secretary of the ward and secretary of his trade union . . . my uncle took over the secretaryship from grandfather . . . uncle was also a councillor.' Others said: 'I was born into it . . . it was and is a way of life, my family was active', and, 'I grew up in the labour movement.' The latter went on to say that he and his wife joined the party partly to make friends. Another pointed out that joining the party was a means of affirming, or creating, a sense of family, saying 'I wanted to fill a gap in my life. I just suffered the loss of my sister.'[17] To campaign for Labour was an expression of loyalty to a community and if there was revolt it was against those responsible for poverty and degradation. For many, being active for Labour meant more than an extension of household relations, it also led to new experiences and contacts.

III

Youth, Faith and Cooperation

Founded in 1893, there were about 10,000 Independent Labour Party (ILP) members by 1895, and many more people had heard of the ideas of its central figure, Robert Blatchford, editor of the *Clarion*. A million copies of his socialist tract *Merrie England* (1895) were sold for a penny each. In 1894 he founded the Clarion Scouts, who cycled around the countryside, slapping stickers promoting socialism on almost any available surface. He also encouraged the formation of a Glee Club, a Camera Club, a Field Club and Clarion Club Houses. The Clarion Cycling Clubs alone had 7,000 members within a few years. Linking socialism, sport and social activity was clearly very appealing, and the ILP influence was widespread until at least the 1920s. Jim Tucker recalled the nature of the ILP: 'The ethos of where we were. The ILP was part of the framework . . . My interest and inclination had always been socialist. I hadn't studied it, it was more emotional than academic.' Fred Neuner remembered the left-wing Austrian Social Democrats in a similar light:

> My parents and my grandparents were all Social Democrats, so I had a good upbringing. Not so much from my parents, because I hardly was with them, they were always travelling, but my grandparents, my grandfather was an old party member, and I got into the movement because I had friends. They went camping, and that was lovely to me, so I went with them from the early days.

Labour Churches, first opened in the 1890s and mostly defunct by the end of the First World War, were closely intertwined – in terms of membership, speakers and even the form which meetings took – with the ILP. Indeed, the inaugural meeting of the ILP was held in the former chapel which the Bradford Labour Church used for services. By 1898 at least seventeen Labour Churches were running Socialist Sunday Schools, and even after the Labour Churches declined in the early part of this century, the Sunday Schools continued, often run by the ILP. Even though, as Helen Cameron noted, 'most of the people that were in the Socialist Sunday School never joined the Labour Party', they provided an alternative perspective to that which Jean White learnt at school: 'At school there was always a big blank in the history they taught you. They seemed to teach you up to the time of King Harold who got an arrow in his eye, and there was nothing until the time you were living in.'

Socialist Sunday Schools

In May 1893 Keir Hardie MP, the owner-editor of *Labour Leader*, proposed the formation of groups of youthful 'Crusaders', and in the next two years 1,000 children enrolled. Hardie urged his Glaswegian colleagues to establish classes, and a number of local activists took up the idea. Margaret McMillan, later a leading advocate of child welfare, started work on a primer and, in February 1896, the Glasgow Socialist Sunday School was inaugurated. A former member of the Glasgow Christian Socialist League, Archie McArthur, took over the editing of the 'Crusader' column in *Labour Leader* and, by 1900, there were seven Socialist Sunday Schools in Glasgow and one each in Paisley and Edinburgh. The number had risen to ten in Glasgow and fourteen in Scotland as a whole by 1910. Jessie Stevens attended a Socialist Sunday School in Glasgow:

> We were taught the Ten Socialist Commandments. I can remember a few of them: 'Honour all men, bow down to none'; 'Love learning, which is the food of the mind, and be grateful to your teachers as to your parents.' They all emphasised the value of man for himself, not his rank or position.

She joined the ILP aged sixteen, sold *Labour Woman* and recalled that, 'We worked, we went on marches, we knocked on doors, we spoke on street corners'.[1]

The Socialist Sunday School Hymn book of 1911 included a socialist ten commandments:

1. Love your school fellows who will be your fellow-workmen in life.
2. Love learning, which is the food of the mind. Be as grateful to your teachers as to your parents.
3. Make every day holy by good and useful deeds and kindly actions.
4. Honour the good. Be courteous to all. Bow down to none.
5. Do not hate or speak evil of anyone. Do not be revengeful, but stand up for your rights and resist oppression.
6. Do not be cowardly. Be a friend to the weak and love Justice.
7. Remember that all the good things of the earth are produced by labour. Whoever enjoys them without working for them is stealing the bread of the workers.
8. Observe and think in order to discover the Truth. Do not believe what is contrary to reason and never deceive yourself or others.
9. Do not think that those who love their own country must hate and despise other nations, or wish for war, which is a remnant of barbarism.
10. Look forward to the day when all men and women will be free citizens of one Fatherland and live together as brothers and sisters in peace and righteousness.[2]

In 1911 a founder member of the Glasgow Socialist Sunday School organised a 'Proletarian' Sunday School, which did not prove very attractive. When the war broke out in 1914, the Schools' ruling body adopted the resolution that 'The only flag we recognise is the Red Flag and our only War is against Capitalism'. In May 1917 Glasgow's Red Sunday School launched its own ten commandments:

1. Thou shalt inscribe upon your banner: 'Workers of all lands unite. You have nothing to lose but your chains: you have a world to win'.
2. Thou shalt not be a patriot, for a patriot is an international blackleg. Your duty to yourself and your class demands that you be a citizen of the world.
3. Thou shalt not usurp the right of any man or woman, nor shall you claim for yourself any natural advantage over your fellows; for every man and woman has an equal right to an equal share in the product of their collective labour.
4. Thou shalt not take part in any bourgeois war, for all modern wars are the result of the clash of economic interests, and your duty as an internationalist is to wage class war against all such wars.
5. Thou shalt teach Revolution, for revolution means the abolition of the present Political State, and the end of Capitalism, and the raising in their place of an Industrial Republic.
6. Thou shalt demand on behalf of your class, the complete surrender of the capitalist class and all the means of production, distribution and exchange, with all the land and all that it contains, and by so doing you shall abolish class rule.
7. Thou shalt wage the class war, by pointing out that the history of all recorded societies is a history of the Class Struggle, and that the emancipation of the working class from wage slavery must be brought about by themselves.
8. Thou shalt take part at all times in the political and economic struggles of the working class. Thou shalt renounce craft unionism, and work for the organisation of the working class into one vast industrial union, to take and hold the means of life.
9. Thou shalt perform a mission in society by achieving an ideal of a fuller and higher life for all, in the abolition of classes, and by the regulation of industry by the Industrial Republic, which shall end the Political State.
10. Thou shalt remember that the economic structure of Society determines the legal and political superstructure and the Social, Ethical, Religious and intellectual life-process in general. It is not men's consciousness which determines their life; on the contrary it is the social life which determines their consciousness.[3]

After the war the great thing in the ILP was propaganda. Propaganda meetings, propaganda meetings, it seemed to me to be about every Sunday and, from about the age of eight, my mother would take me on a Sunday night to the propaganda meetings, which were held in cinemas in Glasgow. The East End was very popular, Jimmy Maxton's seat, Campbell Stephen, people like that, and that was the entertainment on a Sunday evening, to go to the propaganda meetings with my mother. But during the day we attended the Socialist Sunday School. Oh, it was wonderful. We went there as a family at 12 o'clock on a Sunday and we met in a rather dingy shop in a rundown part of this area Kingston, and we sat on wooden benches and with a slightly raised platform at the end, and at a table there sat the chairman, who happened to be my father's cousin and if there was a speaker, we got speakers in those days, and they told us just about municipalisation and just local history. And on the wall behind it there was a big picture which probably one of the members had drawn, and it was the curve of the world, and above the bright sunshine, and the rays of the sun came on to the world, and they formed paths. And on these paths the children of all the countries in the world were walking towards this – walking, joining nearer each other, closer to each other to this wonderful sun. And I find that what I want for the Labour Party. I still want that for the Labour Party. And I'm not for devolution and all those things . . . The [Socialist Sunday School principle] I like to think about often is 'observe and think in order to discover the truth. Do not believe what's contrary to reason. Never deceive yourself or others.'[4]

Isa Paton, Glasgow

In 1900, Archie McArthur moved to London and reinvigorated the Socialist Sunday Schools there. By 1907 there were twenty schools and by 1912 a formal council of schools had been established. In addition to the unaffiliated schools there were fifteen affiliated schools in Glasgow and eighteen in London. Schools ran orchestras, choral singing, folk dancing, rambles, libraries and other activities designed to improve children mentally and physically. The movement continued between the wars but declined in popularity. By 1964 there were only seventeen Schools remaining, nine of them in Glasgow.

There were social evenings that they would organise, they would organise a dance occasionally, Christmas party, a Socialist Sunday School in Heston and Isleworth. That was run at the Labour Party headquarters in Heath Road. Two of my own children went there. They had an annual school sports day on Parliament Hill Fields with other Socialist Sunday Schools in London. Fulham, particularly, had quite a strong Sunday School. There was something like a Ten Commandments, which were very good. Teaching moral principles and concern for other people. Teaching internationalism, that all people have equal rights. Brotherly feeling towards other people, these were the sort of things.

Jim Mortimer, London

All these [Socialist] Sunday schools had adults who were dedicated. They ran them. They'd have one in Govan and one in Kingston and one in all the working-class areas. The one that lasted longest was the one in Pollock. My husband, after the war, used to go out on a Sunday and lecture to the children . . . They had choirs, and things like that, and there would be what we called Kinderschools, competitions with other areas. But that wasn't to any great extent. The Co-op Party did that much better, because they had money . . . Most of the people that were in the Socialist Sunday School never joined the Labour Party. They all became either in the Communist Party or they dropped out altogether. At that time in Scotland, before the war . . . although there was a lot of unemployment and a lot of poverty, it really wasn't the done thing not to be going to church. And my father wouldn't let us be in the Guides or the Brownies or the Scouts, or any of those things, because he thought they were militaristic organisations. You didn't go about shouting, 'I go to the Socialist Sunday School', because they really thought fundamentally that you were spitting at photos of Jesus or something – and you wouldn't have dared let the teachers know that we went to the Socialist Sunday School.

Helen Cameron, Glasgow

We moved from London to Manchester and, in 1922, my future husband and I were taking a walk one Sunday evening down Camberley Road in Salford, when we came across a crowd in a croft and went to investigate. A middle-aged man was addressing his listeners and telling them Salvation Army lies to throw a penny on the drum, the drum being a small piece of land around his feet. He was speaking on behalf of the Independent Labour Party and, after a few attendances of similar meetings, we became members of the West Salford ILP. West Salford ILP had its own premises, Milton Hall, and sponsored its own MP in collaboration with the Labour Party. We were busy. We had a proper kind of meeting on Monday evening, choir practice on Tuesday, events committee on Wednesday, dramatic society on Thursday, League of Youth on Friday, social and dancing on Saturday, and Sunday afternoons we had a Socialist Sunday School. I was soon recruited into service, and eventually became secretary. Our baby daughter, Jill, was named in the Socialist Sunday School. It was a beautiful service. On Sunday afternoons we filled the hall with our members; sometimes having a concert, sometimes a speaker or a debate and, once a month, a full business. As a result of one of these meetings, my husband and I went to a conference in Leicester when I heard the young Jennie Lee, still in her teens, tear a strip off Oswald Mosley, who at that time was still a member of the ILP. At the three ILP buildings in Salford: Milton Hall, Hurst Hall and Hyndman Hall, we had many happy meetings with well-known speakers including Ramsay MacDonald and Manny Shinwell. They were great days, never to be repeated. In 1932 we joined the Labour Party and left the ILP, and have worked for the Labour Party ever since.

May Banks, Salford

Faith in socialism

Apart from the nonconformist-based Socialist Sunday Schools, religion led many to the Labour Party; from Josie Tipple's Baptist father who took her to hear striking miners singing Welsh hymns, to Aileen Plant's mother, who was horrified at the discriminatory practice of churching women. Alice Taylor was born in 1892 and left school aged thirteen. She described her relationship to the labour movement:

> To me it was a faith. It was something which informed your whole life. We were Methodists, and I believed that the inequality of people was an affront to man and God. I can truthfully say I learned my socialism in Sunday School . . . The Labour Party was our social life as well. There was nowhere else for young people to go.

After a lengthy description of her life and times she concluded:

> I think we may be going through a bad patch, but goodness will come of it. People will come back to the fold, you see I'm speaking like a good Methodist. Some people do describe the Labour Party as a church. There has to be a moral sense there, care and compassion.[5]

George Hodgkinson was born in 1893 in Beeston, Nottingham, and became secretary-agent of the Coventry Borough Labour Party. He attended Bible study classes where:

> I picked up the rudiments of my socialism. Christ had socialism in him . . . My political life was governed by a sense of decency and morality. I've always seen in life a moral purpose, even in a system that was crude and savage.[6]

In 1918 Labour contested parliamentary seats in Cardiff for the first time. They did not succeed then but, in 1919, Labour's first four councillors were returned to the city council. There had been Labour candidates before, in 1908 in Splott for example, but the most successful working-class candidates had not stood on a platform of independent labour. By 1921 the party had an office and a full-time secretary. Splott and Adamstown soon became Labour strongholds, and in 1929 Labour won all three constituency seats. A report in *Picture Post* in 1939 referred to the virtual absence of night life in Cardiff, but on the left there were a range of social activities including co-op dances and a meeting place, the Ruskin, or Cosy Café underneath the Trades and Labour Hall. The Trades and Labour council ran whist drives and outings and held lectures and an annual Fancy Dress Ball. Hugh Dalton, Labour's candidate in Cardiff East in 1923, found the constituency 'disheartening. Amazing meetings, with an atmosphere of religious revival and people weeping readily at references to war and poverty, but this was only an unhealthy facade. No organisation.'[7] Bill Herbert made a similar connection with faith in the city:

I'm a socialist. Always have been. You don't need to be a member of the Labour Party – of which I've been a member for many years – but you don't have to be a member of a party to be a socialist. I look upon socialism like religion. It isn't just something you read, it's something you practise . . . What you must do with religion, you mustn't just be a member of a church, you must practise it. Socialism is exactly the same. Whether you're a member of a party or whether you're not, socialism is something to be practised. Practise it outside by helping other people. It's as simple as that.

Bill Herbert, Cardiff

Chapel was very – not left – but very Labour oriented and pro-trade union. We had all kinds of preachers and lots of them they didn't mix their words, they were Labour and they believed in the trade unions.

Maurita Matthewson, Bargoed

Do you know what Jesus Christ was to my dad? The first socialist to get around to people.

Vi Willis, Ilford

I used to go with my mother to Women's Guild meetings and also we got tied up with the suffragette movement. Not the suffragettes who brought a lot of ignominy to the whole thing. They were thoughtful women who had an idea, they had a policy, and from them I became an ardent equal opportunities advocate. Even in those days, when it was almost unheard of. In the trade union I pressed always for equal opportunity and equal pay for equal work . . . It had a tremendous effect on my thinking. It complemented my religious beliefs that in Christ there is neither male nor female, bond nor free, and it complemented that.

Harold Edwards, Warrington

I'd always been against prejudice, no matter where I was. I hate prejudice. I hate things like that. I certainly hate racism and the thing that goes on up here, which is Rangers and Celtic, Catholics versus Protestants. We're moving away from it very gradually, but it's slower than it should be.

Jimmy Allison, Paisley

I think we must have absorbed a tremendous amount of our nonconformist upbringing in our attitude. I don't think that there are enormous differences between a religious outlook – a Christian outlook – and a Labour Party outlook – a Socialist outlook. I'm sure that my children haven't got an outlook that is very different from the socialist outlook that I've always had.

Alan Yates, Leyton

In 1871 there were 10,000 Russian and Russian-Poles resident in Britain. They were mostly Jewish and the majority settled in London, Leeds and Manchester. The government-sponsored pogroms in western Russia speeded the flow from 1881 and, by 1914, over 150,000 had arrived in Britain. Three Jewish interviewees mentioned international concerns in their interviews when they spoke of their influences, and another placed Labour within the European social democratic tradition.

That great wave of immigration which started in, I suppose, the late 1880s from central and eastern Europe; consisted of people who were, after all, escaping both from poverty and from discrimination, and it was natural for them to be politically minded and of the left. [My parents] were never members of the Labour Party, as far as I can remember, but they used to go to Labour Party meetings.

Bea Serota, Hackney

My father was a great reader who taught himself English soon after he came to this country . . .The house was intellectual with a small i. Money was never discussed but always political, social, musical ideas were the subject of argument and discussion . . . My father refused to go to synagogues but he was a very fervent believer in the Jewish religion, as was my mother, who lit candles on Friday night . . . I was bar mitzvahed. At the age of fifteen or sixteen I found myself less interested in religion and more interested in questions which really ought not to occupy such a large part of the mind of a young fifteen-, sixteen-, seventeen-year old, that is the hunger and the unemployment, the evils of avaricious capitalism and the beginnings of Hitlerism in Germany when I was seventeen. All overwhelmed me and I had very little time for either religious belief or for many of the normal pursuits of a sixteen- to seventeen-year-old . . . I joined the Labour Party in 1944.

Joe Kahn, Hackney

I was in politics right from the start. I was interested in people who were hard up, and I wanted to know why. I'd think to myself, 'Why are we poor and all this, when we were such a rich country?' That's how it all started. And we controlled the biggest empire the world had ever seen, and that kind of business, and I wanted to know why it was.

Lew Smith, Hackney

We were always wondering about the emblem of the Labour Party, the flame with the pen and the spade. But in 1916 they suggested the rose as an emblem. And it's taken all this time for the European Socialist Party to take up the rose at first, the folded hand with the stylised rose, before the Labour Party thought about that.

Irene Wagner, Holborn

Youth organisations

The Labour Party's own youth organisations owed something to the church and the Socialist Sunday Schools. An important initial contribution was also made by women. In 1918 the Women's Labour League, which had been established in 1906, was formally disbanded. Members could become individual members of the Labour Party and join the Women's Sections. These had representation on the General Committees, usually on the Executive Committees of the Constituency Labour Parties to which they were affiliated, and on District and County Labour Parties. One of the first items which was discussed at a conference of Women's Sections of Greater London, held in 1919, was an issue outside the political mainstream: the possibility of Juvenile Sections.[8]

Some Labour groups joined Kibbo Kift Kindred ['Proof of Great Strength'], a radical youth movement founded in London in the 1920s, but many withdrew following a split in 1924. Others joined the Woodcraft Folk, which was also established at this time but was not formally attached to the Labour Party. Some Women's Sections had Junior Sections, but these were mainly for organised play. As *Labour Woman* emphasised in 1925: 'It is undesirable to bring children of tender years too closely in contact with political movements, and instruction in political doctrines should be avoided'.[9] Wood Green Labour Party recruited forty children and arranged sports events for them. Southwark South East offered free entertainment, including sweets. In 1920 the Young Labour League was created by Arthur Peacock in Clapham. It produced a newspaper, *Young Labour*, and members helped out in Harry Gosling's by-election. Labour Parties around the country began to establish youth groups or to work with ones run by a variety of organisations; including Women's Sections, the co-operative societies, the ILP and the Socialist Sunday School movement.

The Labour Party acted to co-ordinate and control these changes and the Young Labour League merged with official Youth Sections. By May 1925, there were 185 Young People's Sections. The Labour Party decided to establish a London Young People's Advisory Committee, but the first chair was expelled for his membership of the Communist Party. Spurred on by the establishment of potential rivals, in the form of the ILP Guild of Youth in 1924 and the Young Communist League, and also by the effectiveness of social-democratic youth groups in Germany and Sweden; the Labour Party established the League of Youth for party members under the age of twenty-five in 1926. According to the Labour Party there were 229 branches by the following year, but many of these probably only existed on paper. The League was granted relatively little autonomy, and was strictly reorganised under central control in 1929.

Figures for individual membership of the League of Youth are not reliable because not all branches communicated with the Head Office, which sometimes inflated figures for propaganda purposes. Membership turnover in the League of Youth, where the upper age limit fluctuated between twenty-one and twenty-five, meant that figures were rapidly outdated and, anyway, it was easy to lapse. To join, a person completed a card and made a payment to the Labour Party. Sometimes parents would join on behalf of their offspring and names were rarely removed from the lists thus compiled. Active membership indicates more about the impact of a branch than analysis based on the size of any branch. There were perhaps 200 branches by 1932, but only 2,000 members took regular copies of the League paper *New Nation*. In 1936 the Conference was not convened because of Communist infiltration, the publication of *New Nation* was suspended, and the upper age limit reduced to twenty-one. The League, however, recovered and there were probably around 12,000 activists in the League that summer.

London was one of the most active areas with sixty branches by 1933 when a national 'Call to Youth' was orchestrated. East Fulham alone recruited eighty-one youths aged from ten upwards. During 'Socialist Week' that year the Fulham League made over 1,000 flags and provided speakers and canvassers for seven days of intensive propaganda. There were eighteen outdoor meetings, at which no speaker was over thirty-five years of age, and thousands of leaflets were distributed. There were also poster parades, which involved a dozen members delivering leaflets while one gave a speech.

As well as owning its own hut, the South Tottenham branch was a generous financial contributor to the Hostel Building Fund. A house in Hoddesdon, Hertfordshire, was taken over, furnished and decorated by League members and opened as a hostel in July 1933 with two pavilions for dancing, a camping field, tennis courts, kitchen gardens,

The Hoddesdon hostel was a popular meeting place for many young activists

NMPFT/Science & Society Picture Library

Access to the countryside was a political issue in the 1930s. The *Daily Herald* sponsored this ramble
NMPFT/Science & Society Picture Library

lawns, flowers and a sports field in the 10-acre grounds. There was accommodation for 400 people and a library, educational classes and lectures. Most of those who used the facilities came from North London and East Middlesex, but they were available to all League members. Thirteen thousand people camped there in the summer of 1934, and It was sometimes used by the University Labour Federation.

Many in the League stressed the importance of its social activities. In 1930 the League invited fourteen- to seventeen-year-old youths to write an essay entitled 'Why I am a League member'. The first prize was awarded to Nora Crowther of Hebden Bridge, who detailed the activities of the branch: lectures, discussions, sports and rambles, and concluded that such activities 'combine to unite us into a happy band of young people, all eager to learn, fitting ourselves for the time when we shall be old enough to join the Labour Party'. The Labour Party issued guidelines as to suitable League activities, which included rambles, sports, visits, socials and play reading as well as 'Mock Parliaments', debates, speakers, canvassing and study groups. On Coronation Day (12 May 1937) 150 League members took part in a ramble. There was also considerable activity at Hoddesdon according to one reporter for Mass Observation.[10] A week after the Coronation, 200 League members went on a coach trip followed by a supper and dance. In response to a fascist rally in Trafalgar Square 2,000 took part in a march, and this was followed by a poster parade a fortnight later.

My brother was elected chairman and I was responsible for the Labour League of Youth. I thought this was some sporting or cultural activity and had great difficulty in recruiting a few members, mainly sons and daughters of other members, and knowing what to do with them. They were even less political than myself. I can see us playing Bung-a-Barrow – a form of leapfrog. However, on reflection I can see this was the beginning of a new life in many ways. Because of the difficulties with the League of Youth it was suggested I went and met our neighbours, the Surbiton Branch, who were a little more intellectual. The leader was a Dora Berry from Sheffield. With her strong Labour background she was an active member of the Surbiton Labour Party and a keen supporter of the League of Youth. In the end we decided to amalgamate our branches and in the end Dora and I got married.

Stanley Bell, Kingston-upon-Thames

I did have a boyfriend, who I eventually married, who was in the Labour Party, and I met him as soon as I joined the League of Youth.

Olive Rainbird, Tottenham

Olive Rainbird (third from left), with her husband and son (in hats), joins a socialist expedition

Olive Rainbird's private collection

As a youngster, all my social activity was tied up with the League of Youth. Whatever they were doing, I did it . . . We were a very friendly crowd, and what we did cost very, very little money. 'Cos, fortunately, the Labour Party then had a sports club, 25 acres, down on Tottenham Marshes, and in the summer time all the spare time we used to be down there, which used to cost nothing. We used to ride our bikes over there and play cricket, rounders, you name it – anything.

Tom Riley, Tottenham

We used to run these social evenings and rambles . . . there'd be anything from ten to twenty of us and we all got a cup of tea out of one little teapot and a primus stove. We had a great deal of fun in those days as well as serious politicking . . . We used to have, over the other side of the marshes [Tottenham Marshes], a hut on a piece of ground there which used to be called the Five Acres, and we had cricket and football. All fun, we didn't have a cricket team that went and played anywhere. We had the equipment and we used to play cricket over there; sometimes stay weekends.

Olive Rainbird, Tottenham

'I had an egg I'd fried, the first time I'd fried anything, and they nailed it to the wall of the hut.' Olive Rainbird
Olive Rainbird's private collection

The official paper of the League of Youth was *New Nation. Advance* was more left-wing

I first went to the Labour League of Youth at about the age of sixteen. I think that was the minimum age, and that's when I would have gone. Mainly political discussion, but bit of table-tennis, dominoes, it was a sort of social club, some political education.

John Crawford, Chester

Following the General Election of 1935 I formally joined the Labour Party. I spent all my days and hours helping in that election. I played a major part in forming a Redcar branch of the Labour Party League of Youth. I was its first chair. We got a nice contingent of young people, largely based on canvassing the sons and daughters of existing party members . . . My activities in the Labour Party League of Youth were such that I got to know Ted Willis very well . . . He helped to produce an unofficial Labour Party League of Youth newspaper called *Advance*. The Redcar branch of the Labour Party League of Youth used to take copies of *Advance* and we would send in contributions to *Advance* about our activities, such was our inspiration. I remember the subtitle of the paper *Advance* was 'the future is ours to decide', which was a useful thing to say.[11]

Jim Tucker, Redcar

I joined [the Co-operative Society's Comrades Circle] when I was about fifteen and they used to have quarterly meetings in various towns in Fife and the East of

Scotland, and you went on Saturday and listened to a speaker. They also had dances on a Saturday night, which was supposed to encourage people into the Comrades Circle and make for an interest in the social side. And we'd have rambles on a Saturday.

Helen Cameron, Glasgow

The Young Labour League had a drama section, a choral section, a football section, a rambling section. We rambled all over the vale that was within walking distance of Barry, sometimes covering 20 miles.

Douglas Hawkins, Barry

At Monday meetings it was really political style of thing, as far as it could be; but in between you'd ramble, or dance. We used to always go rambling . . . Would we go to Rufford? Would we go on this ramble, this Sunday, this farmer was closing a footpath? So she would meet us there and we'd climb this gate. Would we climb this gate, and walk up this path (he must have put a gate on), and sing *Rule Britannia*? Well, I'd never sung that in my life, and I'd no intention of doing. I couldn't climb a gate. I think they put me over. But we did walk this path. It's a good idea probably, you're keeping footpaths open. But I thought, 'I'm not singing *Rule Britannia*.'

Betty Crook, Chorley

I remember a group of us setting off [to trespass on Kinder Scout, a popular destination for walkers and the site of a well-publicised mass trespass]. Unfortunately, they were spotted by gamekeepers. I was the only one who wasn't spotted, but that was only because I was wearing a green jacket and green trousers and blended in too well with the scenery, but when the others were rounded up I had to go back. There was no point in a mass trespass on your own.

Owen Heather, Withington

Owen Heather's diary entry for 1 May 1938 makes clear the resourcefulness of League members:

The Divisional Labour Party had decided not to have a tableau in the May Day Procession. The Withington League of Youth decided to do so and had a first-class tableau for two shillings. This was how it was done. The motor lorry we had belonged to Dolly [Rock]'s father so he only charged ten shillings; then we persuaded the Divisional LP to pay. A large poster was done on a sheet that Jack Willock secured from work. The smaller posters were made of shelf paper from home and wood left over from last year's tableau. Our only outlay was material for a red flag. Our tableau featured the summer camp that the League of Youth Federation was going to run that summer. We had posters advertising it on the sides of the lorry. On the lorry we had a small tent and eight of us dressed suitably, some for hiking and cycling, some for tennis and one in a bathing wrap. In addition, we had a superb red flag measuring 6 feet by 5 feet. When we arrived at Platt Fields I detached this, and we walked round the meetings with it, the flag, flapping in the breeze. I rather annoyed a speaker from the Socialist Party of Great Britain by flapping it in his face. We were the only League branch with a tableau. The Federation were going to have one but it flopped at the last minute because the young engineers who were going to man it failed to turn up. The May Day procession in Manchester was one of the largest ever. It was about two miles long and must have included at least 7,000 people.

There was a big argument within the Labour League of Youth about wearing political uniforms. And, sadly to say, my friend, who was secretary, was strongly in favour, while I strongly opposed it. And happily the thing was dropped. It was round about the time when the fascists were going about in uniforms. [This was outlawed under the 1936 Public Order Act.] Why they should want to do it, I don't know.

Fred Combes, Islington

We had this (ILP) Guild of Youth Conference at Rivington, and we had a marquee, and a lot of tents, and they came from all over . . . We'd no cars or anything, so you'd meet 'em, different ones of Guild of Youth would meet somebody on station and then somebody would take them up to Rivington, then another would meet the next lot. There wasn't cars, it was more or less train and bus to Rivington.

Betty Crook, Chorley

Of course, the thing is, we hadn't television in those days, and people made their own amusements. Similarly, they had meetings in the school, and we had a monthly social and, apart from television, a lot of people didn't even have radio, so they went out for their entertainment and interest.

Doris Ashby, Perivale

We started holding fairly regular film shows. Showing films in support of the Spanish Republicans, showing a number of Russian films, and a number of what one might call anti-imperialist films.

Owen Heather, Withington

In 1934 the Kingston Labour Party was so tiny that when nineteen-year-old Stanley Bell went to his first meeting he was immediately given responsibility for the League of Youth. Soon afterwards the Party was disbanded for trying to form links with the Communists. What turned things around for Labour was help from the well-organised Surbiton League of Youth which went out on to the streets. Eric Voysey, who was active in the Kingston League of Youth in the late 1930s, recalled that street meetings were 'a fundamental feature'.[12]

ARE YOU satisfied with things as they are—Rising Prices, Prospects of another Slump, of War, of Fascism ? . . . or

DO YOU find yourself without interests and friends in life ?

THEN JOIN THE

WITHINGTON LEAGUE OF YOUTH

(open to all young people between 16 and 25)

Headquarters :

WITHINGTON LABOUR HALL, LANSDOWNE STREET
OFF MAULDETH ROAD (Near Wilmslow Road).

● FRIDAY MEETINGS ●

FEBRUARY 4th——Visit to film " Spanish Earth."

FEBRUARY 11th—Rev. Ettienne Watts (of All Saints), on " Christianity and The People."

FEBRUARY 18th China—Grim Realities," by a long resident of China.

FEBRUARY 25th—Joint Meeting with Left Book Club on "Hollywood Exposed"

MARCH 4th———" Spain," by a comrade who has recently been fighting in the International Brigade in Spain.

MARCH 11th———" Communism," by one of the local leaders of the Communist Party.

● DANCES ●

held Fortnightly on Tuesdays, from 8-0 to 11-0 p.m. (Tues., Feb. 1st, Tues., Feb. 15th, etc.). Admission 6d. only. Band—Al Jones and His Swing Aces.

SPECIAL NOVELTY DANCE ON SHROVE TUESDAY.

VISITS to B.B.C., Breweries, Newspaper offices, etc.

DRAMATIC SECTION, producing plays and sketches.

JOIN NOW ! Write for a Syllabus from the League of Youth Secretary— H. O. HEATHER, 10, Danesmoor Road, Withington.

The League of Youth combined political activism with films, dances and excursions

Owen Heather's private collection

I was well away with the Red Falcons, Rote Falken. That was the sort of youth organisation of the Social Democratic Party [in Germany]. They were really quite way ahead. They used to go on walks and rambles and that sort of thing. Friendships were created and I think a lot of girls actually did go to bed with the boys.

Irene Wagner, Dresden

This was an idea of bringing in those who were too young to play an active part in politics. I'd heard of the Co-operative Party having Woodcraft Folk and I thought, well, we'll try something of our own and call it the Red Falcons. I think the name came from a similar organisation in Germany. Just for boys – it was thought to be easier. There was a fair amount of hanging around and talking. A number of games were played, we had table tennis and some card games, a certain amount of leafleting was done.

Owen Heather, Withington

Owen Heather also mentioned the Red Falcons in his diary. This is how he recorded the events of 27 December 1937:

Went down to the club in the afternoon to get ready for the 'Red Falcons' party this evening. Two of their mothers turned up and got the food ready. There were about twenty-four at the party, including only five girls. It turned out that they had brought a lot too much food. They were rather unruly, and it was difficult to get them to play games properly. Land, Sea and Air went down with them, also Spinning the Trencher but not Musical Chairs or Murder. They had a passion for kissing games – I'm afraid the girls got rather overworked, but they didn't seem to mind it. I joined in, of course; their kisses were a trifle damp. We concluded at 11.30 p.m.

The Red Falcons held a meeting on 16 January 1938 and then another on 23 January, after which the diary entry read:

Evening: the Red Falcons. I have decided that a much more military structure is required; everything is lax. I realise that a military structure is not as good as Communist comradeship, but it is certainly better than we have at present. After I have gained more experience then I might institute comradeship. I have also decided to start with propaganda on them – speakers etc. They proposed a cycling run to start at 10 p.m. next Saturday night to Wincle, camp out and come back on the Sunday. Seems a wild scheme but I am ready for anything if they are.

February 13th 1938: Young Luby came down with slides and gave Red Falcons a lantern lecture. It went remarkably well, they keeping very quiet.

Owen Heather's recognition of the need for fair administration of the rules, even if this was time-consuming, was shared by others. Although such tasks could be dauntingly complex and appear to be a long way from socialism there were useful skills to be learnt.

To begin with [the national membership scheme] was absolutely horrendous, because nobody knew what was what. The information was six months late. It was wrong. God knows where they got this from. But now, I must say, the information comes once every fortnight. It is accurate. And provided you provide them with the information, and it takes a hell of a lot of time for the Membership Secretary, then the scheme works well.

Irene Wagner, Holborn

The majority of people who came were working-class people. We had a lot of trade unionists, they far outnumbered the others . . . We had a particular item of business and a very well-known and quite well-revered man in Chester labour movement, a chap called Alderman Ted Ashton, got up. I said 'Alderman Ashton, you can't speak on this business.' 'What?' he said. 'I can't speak on this business? It's got to do with the railways,' he said. I said, 'Yes, I know.' He said, 'I'm the branch secretary of the NUR. What do you mean, I can't speak on it?' I said, 'Because you are the delegate from Broughton Ward Labour Party, you are not a delegate from the NUR here.' 'Oh, bloody ridiculous.' He came to me later and said: 'You were quite right.' It was quite a test because he was a forceful character and I had to get him in order, otherwise I'd have lost it.

John Crawford, Chester

[The British Federation of Young Co-operators] had two meetings each week. A Tuesday night and a Friday night. On the Tuesday night it was entirely social. You played table tennis, you had a quiz, you had a beetle drive, things like that. It was all pleasurable and, at the same time, revenue raising . . . We would have a dance once a month, and again that was revenue raising. And then, on an informal basis, and I stress the informality of this, a lot of the crowd, on a Friday . . . would arrange to go Youth Hostelling or go camping on the ensuing weekend . . . Almost every other weekend I would be out of town camping or at a youth hostel.

Tom Carbery, Glasgow

In the Co-op movement, we were trained from a very early age. We had the Children's Circle, which took in children from eight years old. And we learned

Many left-wingers enjoyed camping trips like this one at the Clarion Hostel, Hoddesdon in 1938
NMPFT/Science & Society Picture Library

chairmanship and how to take minutes, how to give votes of thanks to speakers that we had. So we were educated from a very early age in this sort of thing.

Josie Tipple, Acton Bridge

The links between the political and the social were made within the Communist Party as well. Mancunian Communist Joe Garman, who was born in Hightown in 1916, said 'Literally, you could say if you playing table tennis you were playing it with an anti-fascist feeling about it . . . The theatre was part of the struggle against fascism.' There were lectures and rambles. 'It was a wonderful thing for Jewish children to do and rambling became as important a factor in Jewish progressive life as anything.'[13]

There was 100 members [of the Young Communist League] in Kensington. We had a football team, a netball team and even a drum and fife band.

Dot Welsh, Paddington

After the war some of the activities of the youth sections continued.

We used to do overnight trips to Durham. It was funny, we used to take – our League of Youth used to take – sandwiches and a flask, and we would set off about maybe nine o'clock at night on a Friday night, and we would walk to Durham. At halfway through there was somewhere arranged where we would get two or three hours sleep, some farm or something where there was a barn. Somebody would arrange this. It was all very proper, all great fun. We'd arrive in Durham the next morning, we'd go to the skating rink and go and have a lunch somewhere and then get the bus back home . . . I've made lifelong friends. 'Cos I think, when you're young, you do tend to make friends and keep up with them as you get older, so people who were friends and close to me in my youth still remain. People who were in the League of Youth in Sunderland I still keep in touch with.

Jean Goldie, Sunderland

I joined the Labour Party when I was sixteen and was in the YS [Young Socialists] . . . We had a Perivale branch first of all and then we had a constituency branch. We used to have camping and drank a lot of cider.

Marianne Elliott, Perivale

Jean Goldie stressed the emphasis placed upon encouraging young people to become involved:

[The local party] involved the Young Socialists or the League of Youth in everything. They were determined that the League of Youth should be trained up. There was a very positive attitude about young people at that time . . . The strange thing is that nearly all the people who were in that first Young Socialists, they all became – I used to say I'm the only one that hasn't become either famous or done something big with my life. And I think it was because you got so much support from the parent party, and I think it's really served them well.

Jean Goldie, Sunderland

The Co-operative movement

Although co-operatives existed before the establishment of a shop in Rochdale in 1844, the modern movement dates from that year. The Co-operative movement runs retail outlets, farms, factories, educational activities and social events. Inspired by Robert Owen, the aim has been to create communities and institutions which provide members with greater security through mutual support. There has always been a strong political element to the Co-op. George Holyoake, the great publicist for the movement, stood for Parliament in 1857. Others contested seats and, by the last decade of the nineteenth century, many perceived a need for greater political involvement.

In 1892, a Joint Parliamentary Committee was established, with representatives from the significant co-operatives. In 1917, delegates from over 500 co-operative societies met and established a new department of the Co-operative Union, the Central Co-operative Parliamentary Representation Committee. This later became the Co-operative Party, of which interviewee Harold Edwards was one of the earliest members. Retail co-operative societies established local branches, which were open to members of the Co-operative Party and the Labour Party. In 1918 the new party stood its first candidate, who lost a by-election, but at the General Election one MP was returned. There was no written agreement with the Labour Party and some co-operative candidates stood against Labour until 1927, when it was agreed that Co-operative branches could affiliate to Constituency Labour Parties. However, just as the TUC is not affiliated to the Labour Party, so the Co-operative Union is not affiliated to the Labour Party nationally. The number of Co-operative MPs rose slowly and it was only in 1945 that it reached double figures when twenty-three Co-operative Party MPs were elected.

In those days there was an age limit for joining the party. I was too young, but I was essentially a party member, although I was not a member, right from being old enough. I think it was at the age of twenty-one that I actually joined, but I had the association building from before that. From the days of 1917, as a matter of fact. It was the Co-op Party influence that pushed me straight away into the Labour Party. I was going to the Liberal Party meetings and I was speaking sometimes there. I remember that they wanted me to be one of the Young Liberal Association. For some reason they seemed to think I might be able to speak. However, I was so disillusioned that I very soon broke away from that kind of thing and then, for a time, my association with the party was inspired by Co-op activity and my Co-op movement and Co-op Party meetings were the place that I did most of the discussion.

Harold Edwards, Warrington

The Co-operative movement at that time, they had wonderful facilities, they had the Children's Guild, which I attended, they had the Woodcraft People, they had the Comrades Circle for the teenagers, Women's Guild, Men's Guild, they had their convalescent homes, they had their camera club, they had their elocution club, they had nursing club which, we're talking of pre-war, pre-National Health and there you could, from this organisation, Co-operative organisation, nursing organisation, you could hire such things as bed pans, crutches and so on. You take all that for granted now, but people didn't know where to get these things if an emergency, a medical emergency, arose in their home. The Co-operative did all these things and the Labour Movement had a very strong side of – we on Sundays went rambling out into the country, as far as the tram would take you for tuppence and then you walked the rest and the men would carry an urn and you would picnic where there was a supply of water and so on. And you had your music festivals. The Labour Party, the Socialist Movement in Glasgow at that time could run a festival every year, a festival of music in St Andrews Hall. And they did that. There was that. There was the little ones, and then there was the older children and there were choirs and Hugh S. Robertson, while his wasn't a socialist choir, he was a well-known socialist, or a slant towards that, and the William Morris choir was run by a socialist, Willie Robertson, who became my boss in later years. And his sister-in-law May Carruthers took the junior choir, and there were socialist choristers, and Tom Kerr, who was a Labour councillor for many many years in the Govan area, he had a choir. It was all these aspirations to a little bit of culture. And you'd your cycling clubs, the Clarion cycling clubs, and the camera clubs. There was a reaching out for something more than just a new carpet.

Isa Paton, Glasgow

My family were and are Catholics, and they were very wary of the extreme left-wing Communist influence in the Labour movement, and so there was some apprehension in the house when I said I was going to the Co-op Comrades Circle. On the other hand, it was the Co-op: we were members of the local Co-op Society, my father and mother knew that the Co-op ran in harness with the Labour Party and Trade Union movement and therefore they did not object . . . By sixteen I was the Glasgow District Secretary for what was, at that time, the British Federation of Co-operative Youth.

Tom Carbery, Glasgow

My mother was a member of the Co-op. Her share number I can still remember now, 6683. As a child I went to the Children's Co-op Guild. It did play quite a big part in my life, the Co-op . . . These two women used to tell us all the history of the Co-operative movement, about Robert Owen and about the industrial revolution, which I found very interesting, and the Tolpuddle Martyrs . . . You used to pay a penny to go to this guild and then there was a woman who used to play the piano and teach us to do ballroom dancing. That was when I first did early steps in ballroom dancing.

Jean White, Wallasey

In 1942/3, the government introduced a provision that all young people, from the age of sixteen, had to be in an acceptable youth organisation. And the Scouts, and the Boys Brigade and the Girl Guides and things like that they were all deemed suitable. The things like the Air Training Corps and Army Cadet Forces, and so on, they were clearly deemed suitable. The Co-ops found themselves in trouble because neither the Woodcraft Folk nor the BFYC [British Federation of Young Co-operators] was deemed to be suitable. Now this was because they were deemed to be too political. So the Co-ops, rather than see people drift away to the bodies that were acceptable, set up Co-operative Youth Clubs. But all they did was play table tennis and have dances and things of that nature. I don't know how the hell that was supposed to help the war effort.

When I came back from the Forces in 1947 I joined both the Labour Party and the Co-operative Party. The Labour Party was by far the more exciting of the two. That's not to say it was a thrill a minute, but it was certainly a livelier organisation than the local branch of the Co-operative Party.

Tom Carbery, Glasgow

There were Co-ops all over the country. In 1914 there were 3 million Co-operators

Please CUT THIS OUT and POST IT NOW to Vic Butler, LCS, Ltd., Rainbow House. Palmerston Road Wood Green. N 22

Application Form for Membership of the Co-operative Party.

I, ... of

Address ....

....

declare myself a Co-operator, assert my belief in the Co-operative Commonwealth, and agree to work for its establishment through the objects and programme of the National and Local Co-operative Party

I will do all in my power to promote the political policy of the Co-operative Party as declared rom time to time and approved by the Co-operative Congress.

Many Labour Party members also joined the Co-operative Party

I feel the Co-op has been very badly treated by the Labour movement. I don't think their contribution has been quite recognised as it might be. They're always at the tail end of everything, the Co-op. If there's speakers it's unions, and then the Labour Party and then the Co-op at the tail end.

Isa Paton, Glasgow

Both [my husband] George and I were members of the Co-op Party for quite some time and it's really rather cynical, but we joined the Co-op Party because our ward, which is the Bloomsbury ward, always had a lot of people who were interested in politics and the Labour Party, and therefore we always filled our quota of GC [constituency party General Committee] members. So by joining the Co-op Party we could provide extra members of the GC, so my ward having let's say five members on the GC, we then had George and me, plus three others from the Co-op Party on the GC as well.

Irene Wagner, Holborn

That was the shop we always used. My mother was extremely grieved if she had to go anywhere else to buy anything. The Chester Society wasn't a political society. Its board of directors at one time was under Conservative control, later it was split fairly evenly and later still, when I was a member of the Board of Directors, we had quite a strong Labour majority and we tried on two occasions to accept affiliation to the Co-op Party and each time we failed, so we were never a political society.

John Crawford, Chester

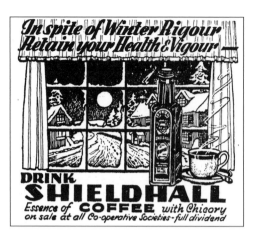

The Co-op advertised its products and services regularly in the socialist press

The Co-op was a great part of our lives. We did all our shopping – we bought everything there in those days, everything we ate, we were clothed there; milk, bread, everything and the divi [dend] was very good, it was about one and six in the pound.

Maurita Matthewson, Bargoed

My wife and I have been members of the Co-operative movement since our marriage in 1938. We still support the Co-operative movement. We buy our groceries at the Co-operative and so on. We must never forget the tremendous contribution that they have made to the living standards of people. In fact, during the years of experiencing poverty, the Co-ops never, ever demanded people to pay. They helped them to pay their bills whenever they possibly could.

Albert Huish, Cardiff

There was a very large Co-op in Camden Town. I used to go and do all my shopping there. But the Co-op was so dreary, the underwear was unspeakably horrible and the hats were unbelievably dreadful. But the materials were very good.

Irene Wagner, Holborn

You came into the world, you got something out of the Co-operative, and they took you out. They had an undertaking department as well.

Alex Kitson, Edinburgh

That Alex Kitson's words echo Labour's state socialist ideal of cradle-to-grave welfare is unsurprising for when, in 1945, the first majority Labour government was returned to the Commons, many of those in positions of authority sought to implement policies based on the pre-war comradeship of the labour and co-operative movements. Labour's postwar Chancellor of the Exchequer Hugh Dalton used the language of the campsite when writing in 1940:

It is not far to the Land of Heart's Desire, not more than a day's march if we could see the way, if the clouds would lift, if we had the will to make the journey. From man as he is to man as he might easily be, it is not so far; from this society to another without war or want, not far.

Seventeen years later Dalton used similar imagery to a number of other interviewees when he wrote about the 1945 government:

We all knew that within us, and because of us, and around us, something had changed.
'England Arise, the long, long night is over;
'Faint in the East behold the dawn appear.'

Edward Carpenter's socialist hymn at last found fulfilment. After the long storm of war, after the short storm of election, we saw the sunrise. As we had sung in the shadows, so now in the light,

'England is risen and the day is here.'

The successful running of Socialist Sunday Schools, League of Youth branches, film shows, whist drives, dances, drama groups, public meetings, May Day parades and discussions required from activists considerable organisational, presentational and leadership skills. It was from within the ranks of dedicated activists that the leadership came and it was with the activists that they shared a vision of the socialist commonwealth. When Herbert Morrison spoke of the spirit of modern socialism as being a 'sober sense of social responsibility', when the *Daily Herald* argued that the leaders of the Labour Party needed citizens with 'an active and informed interest in political affairs' and when Attlee referred to 'an active spirit of service to the community' they were looking to Labour's supporters and to the experience of politics in the 1930s. After the 1945 election, a moral argument was made in order to encourage further recruitment. According to party literature the government required 'active personal support' if it was to realise its goals, and Labour voters could do this by joining the Party and becoming active. Discussion groups were encouraged to form and examine a series of specially produced pamphlets. A journal, *Labour Forum*, was established to aid the process, and the National Executive Committee considered the possibility of establishing left-wing book shops. Owen Heather's belief that he would see 'The Funeral of Capitalism' and his analysis that 'We were very optimistic in those days' were reflected both within the wider movement and within the Parliamentary Labour Party. Clement Attlee said that the party had to work 'to convert to its faith many millions of workers who still cling to Capitalism'.[14] In order to change society, activists had to take responsibility to shop at the Co-op, to join the union, to talk to workmates and friends about Labour. Such zeal led to enduring friendships which, to many, demonstrated Labour's route, its goal and the only basis on which it could succeed: fellowship.

IV

The Culture of the Left

To find out about events around them, or to communicate socialist ideas, many people turned to the alternatives to the Conservative-dominated press. Frustration at the mainstream media led to attempts at new forms of communication: ranging from flyposting, singing and leafleting, to talking to friends and workmates. Activists helped to spread the ideas of socialism through public meetings and spectacles such as May Day parades as well as through fund-raising events. They also helped to maintain communities and support for Labour.

The press
Labour has never had much access to the mainstream press.[1] A Sheffield newspaper editor told a Labour Alderman between the wars that the paper ignored Labour speeches because: 'We aren't in the business of giving you free publicity'.[2] Patrick J. Dollan, leader of the Labour group on the Glasgow City Council, argued in 1922 that 'unless municipal Labour can maintain a local press it will not hold ruling power for more than a term'.[3]

Although there are left-wing films, the cinema newsreels were often biased against the left.

> [Neville] Chamberlain [Prime Minister] came back [from a meeting with Hitler in September 1938] bearing his little piece of paper [which he erroneously claimed meant that Britain would avoid war]. I saw this on the newsreel when I went to see a film. I went with great indignation to the cinema manager and asked him how he dared show such a piece of blatant political propaganda. He was very polite, but I don't think he was greatly impressed.
>
> **Scott Garnet, Nottingham**

A left-wing press did emerge, and many people referred to it. From 1850 the National Co-operative Press published the Sunday newspaper *Reynolds' News*, which had sales of over 400,000 in 1937 and peaked at 712,000 in 1951.[4] Robert Blatchford's popular *Clarion*, which was published from the 1890s, was often mentioned as an important influence. In her survey of 100 inter-war activists, Pamela Graves discovered that:

> Just over a third had a background in non-conformist religion, mostly Methodist or Primitive Methodist, and about the same number had a shared socialist culture that included Socialist Sunday Schools, the Labour Church, the *Daily Herald* or *Reynolds' News*.[5]

57

The national Sunday newspaper *Reynolds' News* always made its political stance clear

National Museum of Labour History

Just before the First World War the left-wing *New Statesman and Nation* started publication, Robert Tressell's novel, *The Ragged Trousered Philanthropists* was published posthumously, and the Labour newspaper the *Daily Herald* was founded by striking Fleet Street printers. It was the official Labour paper from 1923 until 1960. In 1964 the TUC sold its shares and the paper became the *Sun*.

> My parents read the *Daily Herald* and *Reynolds' News*, which were the two socialist papers of the day, and later I myself took the *Clarion*, the *Leader* and the *New Statesman*. It was a reading family. My father was very bookish. I used to go to the library to change his books.
>
> **John Crawford, Chester**

> We used to have the *Co-op News*, which cost three ha'pence per week, and surreptitiously on Sundays we got hold of *Reynolds' News* . . . I had read *The Ragged Trousered Philanthropists*, I had avidly followed the *Daily Herald* and

the *Women's News*, and the League of Youth *Clarion*. But I was not allowed to join the Labour League of Youth.

John Uzzell, Swindon

When the *Daily Herald* come, they'd read a Liberal Paper till then. The *Daily News* I think it's just called and then, as soon as the *Daily Herald* come on the show, it was the *Daily Herald* and we had it and, of course, Sunday for a while – now, what was the Sunday paper for a good while? It was another Liberal paper for a long time. We got the *Reporter*, then there was the local papers. Oh, and an evening paper, the *Liverpool Echo*. We'd plenty of papers always about, and then it was *The Guardian*. We got the *Manchester Guardian* for a long time.

Margaret Lloyd, St Helens

My mother used to deliver *Daily Worker. Daily Worker*, 1d.[6]

Olive Rainbird, Tottenham

One consequence of limited press access is that Labour has often concentrated its efforts on local activity, for which personal contacts can be important. In these circumstances people have sought publicity through the production of local newspapers, flyposting and lobbying Parliament. During the General Strike George Hodgkinson, the Secretary of the Labour Party in Coventry, organised propaganda:

When [the TUC] began to publish the *British Worker*, we sent a runner by motor bike up to London every day to get copies, and we also invented a strike bulletin of our own, a foolscap sheet printed on both sides, punched out by a stencil on a

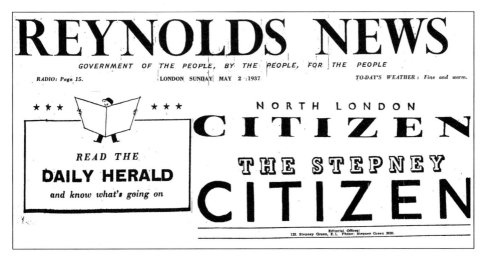

The left has always tried to maintain alternatives to the mainstream press

typewriter and ready every morning at six. Every morning, too, the newsagents were waiting outside. We had made a bargain with them. They did not sell the [government's] *British Gazette* and, in return, they were the sole distributors of our newsheet. They sold it at a penny a copy and our Gestetner made £47 and paid for itself.[7]

Douglas Hawkes established and helped to edit a local Labour Party newspaper, the *Challenge*. There was a print run of 400 copies a month and it sold for 2*d*. The commercial rival's prophecy that it would only last for six months proved to be accurate. His venture was probably more successful than Dot Welsh's avian propagandist, but other local party papers enjoyed greater longevity.

The first [whitewashing] I remember doing was 'Down with the Rich Man's Budget – Chamberlain Must Go'. I tell you, there was a couple of girls that I recruited into the Young Communist League, and one of their mums was looking after a parrot for somebody and us three used to stand in front of this parrot saying, 'Chamberlain must go. Chamberlain must go', trying to get the parrot to say 'Chamberlain must go.' It never did. Or it might have done years later, I don't know, but it never said 'Chamberlain must go' then.

Dot Welsh, Paddington

In North Kensington they had a paper called *The Citizen*, which my mother used to take around. And she became very friendly with a dentist, and used to place piles of her leaflets in his waiting room, which he used to find very amusing.

Doris Ashby, Perivale

I remember folding up *Citizens* and I remember delivering with my mother. My mother delivered in Perivale until about two years before she died. When she was in her eighties she still delivered in Perivale, and I remember very well delivering in Perivale at elections. Sitting on the floor folding up *Citizens*.

Marianne Elliott, Perivale

There was the *Hayes News*, which tried a Southall circulation. When I was a councillor, I used to write a column on Southall events for the Southall edition of this paper, but it was not under the control of the Labour Party, as such. But it used to be circulated by newsboys calling from house to house and selling it on Friday evenings, as distinct from delivering it through newsagents, in fact some newsagents wouldn't touch it. But the boys used to make some money out of it. I think they used to get 6*d*. Actually, the cost of the paper was tuppence ha'penny at the time, so it was quite a profitable activity for *Hayes News*-round youngsters. We did try a Southall edition, which was circulated through Labour clubs.

Syd Bidwell, Southall

The *Citizen* produced many local editions, all sharing the same basic editorial content

We used to do fly posting . . . my job was usually being cave and watching out for the police, which I forgot sometimes and let them get caught. And then they would be fined 10*s* and we would have a collection amongst the members to pay the fine.

Olive Rainbird, Tottenham

My Dad, who died in 1931 when he was only thirty-six years of age, always had the weekend papers, both socialist. One *Reynolds' News* and the other the *Clarion*. Robert Blatchford for the *Clarion* is supposed to have turned more people to socialism than anyone else. Well, in Chorley we had Elijah Sandham. He was elected to the town council as a Tory in 1908 but saw the error of his ways, so he resigned his seat and stood again as a socialist and was elected. He was a wonderful speaker and could recite poems beautifully. He had another newspaper, the *Northern Voice*, and we would go out with Elijah. He would speak at street corners and we would knock on doors and try to get readers for the paper. Money was scarce then, but we usually managed to sell one or two. We had a building on Elijah Sandham's land, and over the platform we had a banner, 'Socialism – the hope of the world'. I believed it then, and I think I still do.[8]

Betty Crook, Chorley

Performing

Some activists turned to singing and acting as a means of promoting their ideas. Ewan MacColl recalled the nature of the street theatre in which he was engaged during the series of 'more looms' strikes, which involved thousands of people in Lancashire in 1931 and 1932:

> On every street corner of a town, putting on a show lasting about four minutes, collecting contributions and then moving on to the next street. You took a barrow with you, or a hand-cart, and collected food, and bundles of clothing, and money, and it all went into the strikers' relief fund.[9]

Tom Thomas wrote the script for and produced *The Ragged Trousered Philanthropists* in London in 1927 and the play soon reached Stockport, Cheshire, where it was performed by a Labour dramatic society. May Banks of Salford also remembers the period:

> In 1926 we gave performances in towns all over south-east Lancs, raising funds for the miners' soup kitchen. We played excerpts from *The Ragged Trousered Philanthropists*, Sheridan's *School for Scandal* and Shaw's *Major Barbara*, a splendid play satirising the influence of the arms maker Andrew Undershaft.

In the early days of socialism in Britain people used song to encourage comradeship. The Aberdeen Socialists would picnic in the countryside and then return to the station and 'sing till our train came in'. Socialists evicted from Lichfield Cathedral 'revenged ourselves by gathering outside singing *England Arise*'. Fred Jowett of Bradford recalled how, in the 1890s,

> Sometimes in summer time the joint forces of Leeds and Bradford socialism tramped together to spread the gospel by printed and spoken word in neighbouring villages. And at eventide, on the way home, as we walked in country lanes or on river bank, we sang:
> 'What is this, the sound and rumour? What is this that all men hear?'
> 'Like the wind in hollow valleys when the storm is drawing near,
> 'Like the rolling on of ocean in the eventide of fear?
> 'Tis the people marching on . . .'
> And we believed we were![10]

Song continued to be part of the repertoire of the left. In 1926 *Melody Maker* reported that seven Nottingham miners had been fined £3 each for 'forming a jazz band' and making life difficult for a blackleg.[11] Edwin Greening recalled how, during the General Strike,

> In that beautiful summer of severe austerity, in 1926, we swam in the now clear waters of the river Cynon; watched the numerous jazz and character bands as they practised and then strutted and marched in the carnival competitions in all

the Aberdare districts; we went to the Go-As-You-Please competitions in the miners' institutes and theatres where the local talent: Esmee Preston and Ida Jones's dancing troupes, entertained the locked-out miners and their families.[12]

Megan Morgan also recalled that 'for all the bitterness, it was a happy time' when 'the jazz bands would walk from the Rhondda, half starved as they were, parade the streets and then walk home again'.[13]

One of the other things about the Labour Party in those days was that it was a very caring party, and they had jumble sales and fêtes, summer fêtes and Christmas fêtes, and socials on Saturday evenings – I think it was probably once a month, but it seemed like once a week. Everybody, the whole family, went and we all had a lot of fun. Different kinds of dance. Most of them were the fox-trot and dances like that but, at the end of the evening, we would all get in lines and do a very mad dance. I'm not sure what it was called. We all held each other's

Worldwide, music and socialism have always been linked, as they were by these Spanish Republicans
NMPFT/Science & Society Picture Library

Socialist songs were so popular that complete song-books were produced

NMPFT/Science & Society Picture Library

shoulders and went stamping forward and swinging our legs to the left and to the right and we would end up singing one of the songs that's connected with the Labour Party, like *Jerusalem.* Building-you-together-in-a-group sort of songs.

Patricia Meitlis, Southampton

[We used to sing] 'England arise, the long, long night is over. In the East behold the sun appear.' Our chairman said, 'Well, there's not much point us singing *England Arise*', so we sang *Scotland Arise*.

Isa Paton, Glasgow

We used to get together on Saturday evenings and sing all the Bolshie songs. I could sing the *Internationale* in three languages at one time.

Magda Clarke, London

Sang the *Internationale, The Red Flag* and then, later on, 'Harry [Pollitt] was a Bolshie, he was one of Lenin's lads' and then 'Wage the class war slickly, get it going quickly, hang the rich on the lampposts high, but don't hang me'. [One version of this continues: 'Stick to Marx, my hearty, Damn the Labour Party, Keep the hell fires burning bright for the bourgeoisie.']

Maurita Matthewson, Bargoed

So we're coming now into the summer of '39 and we're having lots of meetings and selling *Why You Should Be a Socialist* for tuppence door to door. Can you imagine it? In villages we did it. Amazing. John Strachey's *Why You Should Be a Socialist*, and there was another one which had to do with foreign policy and the war which we were selling too and putting on plays, Clifford Odets' plays in the town hall.[14]

Anne Swingler, Newcastle-under-Lyme

One of the things I got involved in at that time was Unity Theatre.[15] I was never an actor but we enjoyed those political pantomimes. I immediately offered my services and they said, 'If you're an engineer you can come and do the lights', so I did three nights a week doing the lights. It was chaotic. We were all part-timers and unpaid. I remember fading up the dawn at the beginning of the play. Dawn had gradually to illuminate the stage for the first ten minutes and I gradually pushed all the dimmers up and dawn wouldn't break so I thought 'Gosh, the chap last night must have done something', so I touched all sorts of switches and suddenly dawn broke. The language from the producer in my ear was something terrible. It was a wonderful period. We had Paul Robeson playing there. I met Alfie Bass and Bill Owen. Those two I took to the underground stations once the war began, to entertain people sleeping on the platforms. I just plugged in a spotlight on London Transport's electricity, introduced them and they did a variety turn and then we just jumped in a train and went to the next platform and did it all over again. Unity Theatre was very active in those days. That was a good introduction to the left-wing movement.

Alan Yates, Hampstead

A number of people commented that campaigning in these ways was enjoyable, and formal meetings often less so. They linked the decline in attendance to the limited repertoire of current party activities:

The Labour Party is very hard working, it sticks to its course, but very often it doesn't know how to enjoy itself. People get tired. Even important members of Labour groups get tired, and they need some mental refreshment from time to time, and solid discussion of serious points of view doesn't give that.

John Crawford, Chester

I don't think branch meetings have changed during the time I've been in the Labour Party. I'd like to think they had. You've got a fixed agenda when they take in the correspondence and the minutes of the previous meeting, and then half an hour is spent discussing whether the secretary got the proceedings correct or not, and that's what's driving people away from the Labour Party. At one time we used to have branch meetings of forty to forty-five, but that's steadily gone downhill, and in the two branches which I'm a member of at the present moment [as a county councillor his division covered two branches] we're lucky if we can get eight there . . . One of the problems of the Labour Party is that the greater the majority the less people want to come to the particular branch meeting.

Harold Tomlins, Chester

Many left-wing activists are used to performing. Some of those with a lifetime of left-wing commitment communicate in a pedagogic fashion, or emphasise the importance of the collective rather than the individual. One interviewer recalled recording a Communist who 'speaks on tape exactly as he speaks at a public meeting . . . he is making political statements. This has to be taken into account in evaluating the answers.'[16] Communist Jack Dash (1907–1989) said:

I always wanted to go into the theatre like my mother [an actress]. I suppose being a public orator is something like theatre because, whether you're aware of it or not . . . if you're a good orator, it's acting. I don't mean you're false, but your whole presentation when you want to warm people up, it's like when you're delivering lines.[17]

Some interviewees made it obvious that they were influenced by current events and their contemporary consciousness. My interview with Margaret Lawson was interrupted so that we could watch a live broadcast of Tony Blair giving a speech at the Labour Party conference. At the time when Betty Crook was being interviewed there was a major debate about the Labour Party's constitution which may have led her to give it greater historical emphasis: 'You talk now about this Clause Four and doing away with it, but that were the chief one in those days, weren't it? That were the chief plank o' your politics.'

Fund-raising

A number of activists emphasised how, through being integrated into their social activities, the otherwise mundane task of fund-raising became enjoyable and an aid to recruitment. It has been suggested that its commitment to electoral politics has led Labour to become too focused on raising money and that this has distracted it from other goals.[18] In 1938 an activist of twenty-five years' standing argued that the declining membership of the party was not due to its policies but to its 'unbusinesslike' local administration.[19] However, activists sometimes linked raising money with raising morale, their own or that of other people. Leslie Hilliard recalled the dockers on short time and in receipt of meal tickets, relief tickets and 'perhaps a couple of quid' who, in the 1930s, still 'paid their 1*d* a week when bread was 2*d* a loaf'. He went on:

> I was ashamed sometimes that we should collect money from an unemployed docker who was sitting in a home where all the furniture had had to be sold to qualify for relief, where they were sitting on soap boxes, with a candle, and where they would insist on paying their penny rather than buying a loaf of bread because they were making an investment for the future. I was convinced we would win.

Vic Lock said 'In the Labour Party you meet all kinds of people. You call at their houses to collect their subs and have a chat . . . I've got great satisfaction out of my Labour party work.' Harry Blanks reported: 'I've raised hundreds of pounds for the Labour Party in my time, perhaps thousands' and mentioned dances, sales of Christmas cards and collecting subscriptions. Mervyn Jones noted that Labour was 'astonishingly well organised' in Chichester, where he was the candidate in 1955, with three employees: an agent, a secretary and a fund-raiser who organised a tote. In 1991, 9 per cent of Labour's income came from subscriptions and, if donations are added in, then a total of 26 per cent came from individuals. This amounted to around £2 million, which is more than the affiliation fee of any one trade union.

> For local elections it was local collections, because the subscription in those days was a nonsense. When we first started up here after the war, it was six shillings a year. In these early days it was a farthing a week, called for once every four weeks, then it became a ha'penny, called for every two weeks, then a penny, called for every week. That was in 1928. The sub was then 4*s* 4*d* a year. They were able to run quite a lot of things, raffles, sale of work and that kind of thing. When we came to Parliamentary elections we did it by collections at meetings. We relied a lot on the adoption meeting, selection meetings and things of that kind. Trade unions used to put money in and we used to have collecting sheets, and that is a good way of raising money.

John Crawford, Chester

> Used to go out every Sunday morning with his little book, collecting, and it used to be 1*d* a week . . . You couldn't say, 'I'll leave it till the end of the month,' 'cos they couldn't afford 4*d*.

Sid & Vi Willis, Ilford

> I started going round collecting subscriptions. At that time subscriptions were in the shape of a stamp – a book of stamps. And I think every stamp would cost 6*d*.

John Tuffey, Tooting

Membership money. We did that. I collected for years 'Sixpence a month,' and stood up for a lot of abuse. I've stood at many doors for my sixpence and they've told me, 'We're better socialists than you are'. We went around collecting all over the area, we collected money. Once a month. Sixpence a month. Six shillings a year. And that's it. Most of them never came to the meetings.

Helen Cameron, Glasgow

The days of mass membership have gone, primarily because the subscription rate is too high and when I'm talking about we went round and canvassed and got hundreds of members it was coppers, and I remember going home with my pockets full of coppers from the subscriptions. The question of recruiting members in 1945 is easy, we made hundreds of them. Now, ideally, if you take a ward and it consists of say fifty roads, you can split that up into areas and, if you're luckier still, you take every road of those fifty and you can have a street captain. Now that street captain knows that road and knows the people. So when you come to polling day he goes along and knocks on the doors and says 'You know you're Labour and it's voting and you'll be along there, won't you?' and that, of course, is the ideal basis of Labour Party organisation which, regretfully, I don't ever see coming back again.

Stanley Bell, Kingston-upon-Thames

I became the social secretary and we ran the weekly whist drive, which seemed to raise a few bob for the constituency . . . We were fortunate enough to be running these whist drives once a week and that kept the branches going, but the constituency had its own fund-raising activities. They ran a football competition which provided a lot of income, but most fund-raising activities in the Labour Party taper off after eighteen months or so and you've got to think of something new.

Harold Tomlins, Chester

The women of the group, as always, were great ones for running fund-raising things. We used to hold whist drives in our house for funds. And the women made tablet and sold it, and some made jewellery and sold it. We were just repeating what my parents did, because my parents used to run whist drives in their house for the ILP at that time, that was in the Twenties.

Helen Cameron, Glasgow

I recall that when I was a schoolboy one of [mother's] recreations was whist drives. She would go to the ILP rooms in Consett. She was as much interested in winning. I wouldn't have called her at that stage a political activist but it was part of the ethos of where we were. The ILP was part of the framework.

Jim Tucker, Consett

We used to run a bingo school on top of the Co-op greengrocer down the high street here. Then, when the Co-op sold that off, we carried on in Durrington Hall.

John Tuffey, Tooting

They ran a Tote, and that's how the income of the party came in really, with some objections from older non-conformist elements of the party who thought running a Tote was gambling, it was immoral and a socialist movement shouldn't do it. However we did, and brought in lots of money from the Tote so we had a headquarters, we had a staff of three and we had 2,500 members and it really was quite a flourishing Labour Party.

Mervyn Jones, Chichester

We were always organising socials to make money – Burns suppers, they're great for Burns suppers in the Scottish Labour parties, and socials, things like that.

Margaret Lawson, Edinburgh

There was a large amount of people in the Labour Party. So much so that they had their own executive committee, which used to meet in somebody's house, and I can remember my mother organising refreshments for a fête which they held in Perivale School, and I would think that nearly everybody in Perivale came there that day. It raised a tremendous amount of money for the party.

Doris Ashby, Perivale

We had a very active ward, all sorts of things, football coupons, dances at the Adelphi, dances at the Town Hall. There was a lot more activity in those days than they appear to have now.

Frank Booth, Stockport

Maureen Dewar and Tom Carbery pointed out that raising money could lead to disputes, which might undermine the central purpose of the party and its efforts to encourage discussion. Alan Yates recalled the time when Menon was invited to speak for only twenty minutes because an administrative matter was considered of greater importance.[20]

I joined the Labour Party down there in Farnborough. I immediately became speaker finder and I got Krishnan Menon to come and address us in the Cove Labour Party. I met him at the station, he came down from London to speak, and we didn't have a car but I took two bicycles and said, 'Can you ride a bicycle? It is only a mile to the Labour Hall.' He looked a bit dismayed. Typical of the Labour Party, it was about half past nine before he was called upon to speak, although he'd been there since eight o'clock, because there was a big debate going on about the price we should charge for the Labour Hall to the Women's

Institute for their whist drives. Krishnan Menon was finally asked and we said 'Well, Mr Menon, you're going to speak on the problem of India, we can give you twenty minutes'. I'm afraid this is characteristic of many Labour Party meetings I've been to. It's very sad.

Alan Yates, Farnborough

The Party raises money by party subs, by running social events, prize draws, scratch cards, socials, anything. It's still the same old thing. To raise money you've got to have fund-raisers doing things. We seem to have given up on jumble sales and messy things like that, but we still do most of the other.

Maureen Dewar, Tottenham

The bulk of the people come from the local Labour Club. I remember well the great controversy as to whether or not there should be a Labour Club. When Labour built all these council estates on the perimeter of the city they enforced their no-licensed premises provision, they were temperance areas, reflecting the whole temperance element that lay on the Labour Party. At that time the Co-ops didn't have any off-licences, for example. So when they talked about having a Labour Club that would sell beer this was obviously a complete volte-face. There was great controversy. And there were people who said 'You will make money, but you will lose your soul'. And in no small measure so it has come to pass. So about 60–70 per cent of the people who attend the CLP, their entrée to the Labour Party was through the Labour Club. They were persuaded to take up, in an active way, the membership of the Labour Party which was a condition of being a member of the Labour Club. It was the *sine qua non*. And they were told to come in and support some of their own genre who had become active and were seeking office.

Tom Carbery, Glasgow

Public meetings

Listening to the great orators of the day sustained members and aided recruitment and publicity. People could also pick up hints on performing. In 1895 Liberal Party activists distributed 23 million leaflets, an average of four per elector. Gradually, other methods of communication have come to be considered more valuable. The first election broadcasts on the radio were made in 1931, followed by Labour's first television broadcasts in 1959. By 1964, 88 per cent of British households had televisions, rising to 97 per cent in 1985. People recalled the oratory of the past and recognised that interest in finding out about politics at meetings has declined.

In the week before the election the queue at the Bingo Hall, you could give them a shout. We decided in the mid-Sixties that there was no point in trying to hold meetings in halls any longer for elections.

Harry McNeill, Glasgow

[Bevan.] That was a man. He could charm anybody. He could have an audience of 2,300 people and somebody shouting from here and somebody shouting from there and he'd say, 'Just you hold on a minute, just you hold on a minute, and you just hold on a minute,' and then he'd have about three or four more barrackers and he'd say: 'Stay where you are,' and at the finish he'd go round, and he'd go back, in order, and say, 'What was it you were asking, and what was it you were asking?' It was terrific.

Walter White, Birkenhead

[Nye Bevan] spoke at some length and the whole place was packed with officer training cadets from Eaton Hall and he took them on and gave them a real roasting – that was a great night.

Harold Tomlins, Chester

During a 1956 by-election in Chester during the height of Suez . . . Nye, when he came to speak, he was barracked immensely. We knew a lot of people from an Officer Training Corps at Eaton were coming to barrack. He said to them, 'Just a minute, I've heard that some people were coming to barrack me. I don't mind barracking. The only thing I want to tell you is that you will come off worse if you insist on barracking. I would recommend to you, intelligent men, what you ought to do is to listen carefully and if you don't like what I have to say, come and see me after the meeting or write to me and I'll give you an answer.' The meeting was fine after that, except when he got on to Suez itself and there was a bit of chi-eyeing about running away and that sort of thing, which he dealt with.

John Crawford, Chester

George Lansbury came to visit the Labour Party in Bittern Park. The words 'George Lansbury' had a sort of magic ring in the same way that, in *A Passage to India*, the Indians say 'Mrs Moore, Mrs Moore'. Everybody was saying 'George Lansbury, George Lansbury' and one didn't know quite what to expect. I was chosen to present him with a pair of the most beautiful kid gloves and I'd never seen such elegant gloves. I must admit, I thought it was a bit unfair as he looked very posh and had very nice clothes on and I thought 'It's really not fair giving him these gloves' but of course I did, and gave a little speech.

Patricia Meitlis, Southampton

During the '51 election we had a Drill Hall that was packed to the rafters with people wanting to listen to Manny Shinwell, and he gave a marvellous speech.[21]

Harold Tomlins, Chester

We went down to London to visit my parents in August, and they were living in Teddington. And they were very active in Teddington Labour Party, and my mother had already bought tickets for the rally in Westminster Hall. And so we went to the rally. They all came in: Herbert Morrison, Edith Summerskill, Attlee and so on. It was very exciting.[22]

Margaret Lawson, Edinburgh

The Festival of Labour was organised by the national party at Battersea Park. I think it probably lasted three days . . . One of the marquees had handicrafts from Labour Women's Sections and paintings and one in fact was 'Achievements by Local Parties'. I think Merlyn Rees organised it . . . We had functions in Ealing during the week, the whole week. We had a meeting for women at Ealing Town Hall and the speaker was Bessie Braddock who, of course, was a tremendous draw in those days and the Co-op put on a fashion show and refreshments were served to celebrate the festival.[23]

Marianne Elliott, Perivale

May Day

The annual May Day parades provided public displays of the strength of the labour movement, the diversity and colour of its banners and its claim to the symbolic control of space. A number of people commented on the excitement generated at the spectacle of streets thronged for these celebrations.

We had a procession, it would be May Day [1921], and collected for the miners. I remember collecting.

Betty Crook, Chorley

Jimmy Maxton became an ILP MP in his native Glasgow in 1922, and rose to become party leader. Tom Johnson remembered that this popular and dramatic speaker 'had none of the heavy forbidding economic and philosophical jargon about dialectical materialism and the like then the fashion. His was the merry jest and the quip, well mixed with the stuff for pathos and tear, and sauced with apt Biblical quotation and graphic description of social wrongs.'[24]

Helen Cameron also remembered him:

We went to May Day, and we put on our best frocks and marched along, and the tiny ones were put in lorries and carts probably at that time, and we met people like Maxton, and people like that.

Helen Cameron, Glasgow

[Ellen Wilkinson] came on a march with the Finsbury Labour Party in '37. From the gasworks to Hyde Park, the Sunday May Day march. The Labour Party had a march, a big march, which everyone joined in, it went from the gasworks near St Pancras. A long march, right along the Marylebone Road, down to Hyde Park.

John Platts-Mills, Finsbury

We distributed leaflets, we organised meetings. Every year we took part in a May Day walk in Nottingham. I remember one group. Oh, I do wish that my Labour Party had had the wit to think of it. There was at the time a campaign to get rid of rats and other vermin, and we'd had a rat week to exterminate rats and on May Day people pushed a very large cart with a tremendous sign over it saying 'Rat Week – Get Rid of Chamberlain'. Oh, I did think that was clever. A rather odd thing came out of the May Day marches. A local Labour Party secretary joined in the march, of course with his wife and little boy in their pushchair, and the little boy was immensely intrigued with this march and people walking along carrying banners, and he wanted to walk along, he wanted to have his placard on a pole that he could carry. Now his parents, good *Guardian*-type progressive thinkers, didn't want to make capital out of their little boy's enthusiasm. He should be left to decide his own politics, therefore it would be unfair for him to carry a banner with a left-wing slogan on it, so they made him one especially for himself, 'Down with Donald Duck', and he walked up and down the garden path with this placard and he was immensely proud of it.

Scott Garnet, Grantham

There was a strong tradition in Manchester of a procession on May Day. The route varied, you needed somewhere large enough as the destination, large

In 1938, socialists poured into London's Hyde Park to celebrate May Day

NMPFT/Science & Society Picture Library

enough for an open-air meeting. In those days there were a considerable number of horse and carts around that you could hire fairly cheaply, so that each branch more or less would get a horse and cart and arrange for some form of construction on it. On one occasion we got into trouble with people living close by where we were assembling because we had a coffin on the lorry, labelled 'The Funeral of Capitalism'. We were very optimistic in those days.

Owen Heather, Withington

May Day marches. There was always a good contingent from Tottenham, and we used to walk from Tottenham in those days up to Hyde Park. It's a long walk. And I didn't miss a year until we were about forty-eight or forty-nine.

Olive Rainbird, Tottenham

There was a march from George Square, and they assembled on George Square, right round the square, and the side streets, and then they marched to the Green. And then there was the principal speaker. The year Hugh Gaitskell came to

May Day tableaux provided a colourful way of making a political point

NMPFT/Science & Society Picture Library

74

Glasgow, he got a very rough handling from the crowd . . . And he paid us the compliment of coming down and having a get-together on Saturday afternoon in our hall. And we put on a dinner at night in one of the local restaurants, and he and Mrs Gaitskell came to that.[25]

Isa Paton, Glasgow

I've never missed a May Day. I've always been to May Day . . . When Tony Benn came here to lead off the May Day thing, to be the main speaker, it was so sleety that we had to go into a hall.[26]

Martha Feeney, Glasgow

The older members of the trade unions used to look forward to that one-day holiday, celebrating the victories of the working-class people. I would join our union banner, as everybody else did.

Albert Huish, Cardiff

Maintaining communities

Although the press is still mainly opposed to Labour, the value of public meetings, oratory, theatre and parades as means of communication has diminished. Stronger impressions of the labour movement are gained from the television than from a show of strength on the streets. Voters can discover the party affiliation of candidates from the ballot paper and information about the parties by telephone, direct mail, web sites or e-mail.[27] Nevertheless the creation of the right political climate through publicity remains of central importance. A number of studies have shown that the local political environment can influence voting behaviour; that, for example, a middle-class voter in a pit village is more likely to vote Labour than an equivalent voter in a seaside town.[28] Harold Tomlins indicated how activists maintained Labour's position within their communities:

One of the things Labour Party people won't realise is that you've got to get associated with these fringe organisations if you want to make any progress and sell the Labour Party to its best advantage, and being a member of the local community association, chair and eventually President does the party's image no harm at all. They were surprised, I must say, the Labour Party, when I became President of the Chester Ladies Choir, and so was I, because I was taking over from some old retired lieutenant colonel who had been the most extreme right-wing Conservative in the city, but they nailed me for the job and I thought 'Well, in the interests of the party it'd be just as well to take it on'. And all that entails is you go to a couple of ladies' choir concerts and give an odd donation and everybody's happy. Am I appearing cynical?

Harold Tomlins, Chester

By talking to their family and friends about their experiences and by sharing their ideas, activists aid Labour. When memories are shared and articulated they become part of the popular historical awareness and an indispensable part of social identity. Richard Hoggart, who was born in Leeds in 1918, analysed the working-class culture in which he grew up. He stressed that the 'core of working-class attitudes . . . is a sense of the personal, the concrete, the local: it is embodied in the idea of first the family and second the neighbourhood.' There was an 'earnest minority among working-class people'. In the years 1850–1950 it was they who:

> at great sacrifice supported trade unionism when it had its way to make, they worked for Labour representation in Parliament, they were connected with the Co-operative movement and were the pillars of the local chapels . . . They worked for Hyndman's SDF [Social-Democratic Federation] in the Eighties and for the ILP [Independent Labour Party] in the Nineties. They helped to set up the Labour Representation Committee at the turn of the century . . . Many of them are today doing valuable work in political and trade union affairs.[29]

Some of the interviewees indicated the influence of such stalwarts of the party and the atmosphere they engendered:

> I started looking round [in 1967] and there was no Labour Party organisation in Woolston. I was just a member at Newton-le-Willows, and I started sussing things out and somebody told me 'Go and see Mrs Nichols in the Post Office'. She was rather elderly and rather prone to forgetfulness, but she did give me a book and she said there were names of people in there that she used to collect for the Labour Party in the 1920s and 1930s, so I went round and some of them were still there and that is how we started the Labour Party in Woolston and we joined up with Padgate, making some sort of branch.
>
> **John Morris Clarke, Newton-le-Willows**

> Prior to the 1960s our Labour Party filled any large hall at election times, but with more households and television our audiences fell and street meetings were impossible. We had close links in those days with the unions and the Co-operative Party. No Labour family would dream of shopping anywhere else but the Co-op before 1960.
>
> **May Banks, Salford**

> Winsford was a Co-op town, there were Co-op shops all the way up. You could clothe yourself, have your shoes mended, have a suit made, everything. Now there isn't a single Co-op shop, except the travel agent, left in the town. They had a lovely big store in the middle of the town, but it lost money and they closed it. We started a Co-op Party in the town, but it didn't go very well . . . Before 1950 I don't think you could buy anything in Winsford which didn't come from the Co-op.
>
> **Josie Tipple, Winsford**

Helen McElhone suggested that one of the roles of activists is to ensure that their elected representatives maintain an interest in the needs of the constituents and the community.

Up here we're more concerned for the people whom we represent and are friendly with them. Maybe we're too cosy. But I think it's probably just. We're just a different race, the Scots and the English. I think, in England, people are out for themselves. I suppose, yes, we have some people like that here but, on the whole we're out for what we can do for our people. Maybe it's because England's so cosmopolitan – the party has far too many careerists. And that doesn't mean to say that I don't believe in academics being elected as Members of Parliament and things like that. But they're too concerned about their own career rather than being concerned about people.

Helen McElhone, Glasgow

It is difficult to gauge the impact on the electorate of activists' communications, ranging from the quiet chat at work to the mass rally and parade. Certainly, voters have been mobilised both for elections and for the defence of the collective rights of the working class from Basques in Bilbao to coal miners in the Rhondda. Activists agree that the debates, rituals and rhetoric of the Labour Party gave them heart while boosting recruitment and funds.

V

The General Strike and the Depression

Immediately after the First World War, the Labour Party grew dramatically. Individual membership of the party was introduced across the country, allowing those who were not in trade unions to join. The Liberals had split, leaving members uncertain and angry. Labour, although it had had its divisions over the war, was united in its efforts to keep a watch on the government and to secure welfare reforms. Trade union membership had increased and many more people recognised, as they had not prior to the war, that it was possible for the state not only to run factories but also to fix rents and wages and be involved in everyday activities. They looked to the party which promised to voice their interests within the expanded state. There were widespread improvements in wages, educational provision, accommodation and material conditions. There was also a decline in the working-class birth rate and in the number of hours worked. These changes were beneficial to Labour. However, the party still needed people to explain and implement its ideas as set out in its new constitution and programme, *Labour and the New Social Order*. Labour became committed to advancing democratic forms of government and to increasing public ownership and control. It proposed welfare and educational measures and further taxation. The intention was to appeal not only to trade unionists but to all workers, by hand or by brain, so that Labour would become a mass party. In order to be elected, Labour needed well-organised local party machines run by activists who could legitimise socialist values, set the political agenda, mobilise electoral support, finance campaigns, and recruit, train and socialise the party leadership.[1]

The General Strike
During the First World War the coal mines had been taken under direct government control. Wages rose to the same level across the country, and the miners' union favoured the continuation of public ownership. However, the mines were returned to the private sector in 1921 and wages were cut. In protest, the miners secured the support of rail and transport workers and arranged a strike for 15 April 1921. The other two unions backed down at the last moment and the miners went on strike alone until 1 July. The unions' 'Triple Alliance' was revived in 1925 when wages were again cut, but this time the government intervened and promised to subsidise miners' wages for nine months until 1 May 1926. By May the mine owners still wanted wage cuts and locked their workforce out of the pits until they would agree to wage

reductions. The government declared a state of emergency and the Trades Union Congress called workers in key industries out on strike in support of the miners in what became known as the General Strike. In addition to the million miners, another million and a half workers were called out, and there was almost unanimous support from trade unionists. The government used troops and volunteers, many of the latter were students in the Organisation for the Maintenance of Supplies (OMS), to break the strike. Julius Jacobs was twenty when the strike broke out. He recalled the OMS in Hackney 'or, as the local trade unionists called it, the Organisation of Mugs and Scabs'. Members entered the tram depot but could not run the trams as pickets trapped them inside. The volunteers escaped over a wall,

> but they were spotted and a chase ensued along Mare Street. By Westgate Street there stood, and I think still stands, a horse-trough full of water. And here the blacklegs were caught and dumped into the trough. There were no further attempts to get the trams out.[2]

After nine days the TUC called off the action, without having secured an improvement for the miners. Many of those who returned to work were victimised and the miners came out on strike again until the end of November 1926.

Labour Party members ran soup kitchens and raised money for boots and clothing. Marge Evans sold miners' lamps on ships in the Bristol docks and adopted a miner's child for several months. There was also an adoption scheme in Chatham run by Labour activist Bertha Grieveson.[3] Many pits did not open again after the strike, and miners who had been active were often blacklisted. Edward Cain, who was active in Seaham, County Durham, was told by the manager: 'If you give up your ideas of socialism you can start'. He refused and was evicted from his miner's cottage.[4] More generally the union leadership was widely criticised, union membership fell and membership of the Communist Party, which was critical of the union leaders, rose. Peter Kerrigan was the twenty-six-year-old vice-chair of the Glasgow Trades and Labour Council and chair of the Glasgow Central Strike Committee in May 1926. Fifty years after the events he wrote of the May Day demonstration on Glasgow Green:

> Very clearly do I recall the tremendous atmosphere, the enormous feeling of solidarity flowing on that hopeful and exalted day from the huge mass of the workers assembled there . . . The other sharp picture I have is from the days after the strike, when the Glasgow Trades and Labour Council was trying to raise money for the miners, locked out in their desperate rearguard fight against the government and the coal owners. On a brilliant August day, my wife-to-be Rose and I cycled out from Glasgow . . . We carried in our panniers and haversacks all the food we could collect. The meetings were in green open fields in lovely sunshine and hundreds and hundreds of miners and their wives and children were there.[5]

There was considerable sympathy for the victimised workers and those in pit villages, and considerable bitterness towards the volunteer strike-breakers, the trade union leaders and the government:

> The government had, during the previous year, secretly financed a so-called independent movement of volunteers, public safety volunteers [the OMS]. They recruited a lot of people who were trained secretly on how to run trains and how to handle telephones and how to do various other things that ordinary people did. And they were immediately called into action. All London Transport was on strike, national transport was on strike, 100 per cent solid, and they used to bring out the buses, driven by a blackleg, with a policeman sitting beside him, and barbed wire across the front, a nice friendly atmosphere to show that the people were behind the government. And to see those trundling through the city and young students from Oxford and Cambridge pretending to run railway trains, which they couldn't do, thank God, and then seeing the army called in at the docks; the provision of essential services, and the trucks running from the docks

Buses driven by blacklegs were targets for striking workers during the General Strike

National Museum of Labour History

to Hyde Park, which was turned into a distribution centre under the military, was extremely enlightening. And you've got to remember what the miners were striking about. They had appalling wages, and they were threatened with a reduction in wages and an extension of hours. And the slogan 'Not a penny off the pay. Not a minute on the day' was the slogan of the strike. And the General Strike was not a General Strike for anything other than supporting the miners. It was secondary striking.

Jack Gaster, Marylebone

The General Strike had a tremendous effect on me because I was very involved in the sense that I felt that the miners had everything in their favour except the powers-that-be. During that I went into the mining district, preaching, and I met these people and, apart from their fight with the powers-that-be, I realised that these were people who knew what was what. It wasn't a silly sort of a grab for all; it was a determination to maintain their right to what was a right . . . There were certain odd bits and pieces of transport working, strike-breaking actually, and I walked to work and back home at night rather than use any of that transport. I was very determined about that.

Harold Edwards, Warrington

My father was on the General Strike local committee. I was very young, but I recall the workers attacking buses at the Southall bus garage, which was situated opposite the existing Ealing Hospital, and pushing a bus over – the crowd pushing a bus right over on its side, and it was being driven by a black-leg student. They couldn't do that on the railways very easily – take over railway workers' jobs – but there were of course stooges and black-legs trying to run services at that particular time. That vividly remains in my mind, but I was too young to assess it politically.

Syd Bidwell, Southall

My early political contacts occurred first of all in 1926, during the General Strike, when my eldest brother took me to Hyde Park, where the demonstrations were occurring. I have vivid memories of the rough treatment of the strikers by the police, with arms painfully twisted up behind their backs. Even at the age of eleven, I could begin to see the class struggle.

Stanley Bell, Kingston-upon-Thames

My father was a preacher in the Welsh Baptist tradition . . . he was what was known in those days as a radical liberal, of the Lloyd Georgites, and I was influenced by him. I remember when I was eight being taken to hear the Welsh miners sing when they were on strike, and that lives in my memory because my father explained about the coal owners and the conditions of the miners. That really sticks in my memory. This was in Weaverham, where I lived. They sang Welsh hymns and had a bucket and collected, and we hadn't much money but of course we did give to them.

Josie Tipple, Acton Bridge

I have vivid recollections of the miners' strike in 1926. As well as being an iron and steel area it was a coal area and, as a schoolboy, I remember seeing people known as blacklegs being escorted by the police from buses.

Jim Tucker, Consett

Some streets had no mechanised transport and many had no option but to walk or cycle. Bob Davies, a twenty-four-year-old Communist, recalled walking two miles into St Helens and said, 'what struck me most forcibly was the quietness in the streets. It was like early Sunday morning, but even more silent.'[6]

I remember the General Strike. Not, I think, politically but just because the streets were quiet and I could cycle to school without any interruption.

Alan Yates, Leyton

During the General Strike, my father stayed in the Victoria Hospital, it was on Whitegate Drive, it's not the same as Blackpool Victoria now, and mother and I walked if we couldn't get a lift from Fleetwood to Blackpool – about nine miles.

Sam Waters, Fleetwood

1926, that's when my father was mayor. The strike was just over when my father took the mayor over, and we'd been working hard. All the collections went to Grindley Labour Club. The biggest meetings you've ever known in your life. They was held at Hippodrome and theatre. Big places. They were packed. And then they would have some outside. Couldn't get in. On a Sunday, that's when they'd very often be held, because that was when the theatre'd be closed, I suppose. And we would have to put papers on every seat. We had good hymns. All the old hymns. And we had to stand on the stage and we was the choir. And my father used to say 'I think I conducted the biggest concert in the place'. It was packed, upstairs and down. And then we'd start. And we'd only piano. And it was Mrs Thackeray, her husband was alderman, and she played the piano for us and we enjoyed it. And then we had big boxes and we'd put round the collection for the strike fund, and they did get some . . . down below there was men and they were mending clogs and shoes for people around, and we was upstairs and there were big long tables together and the money was poured on it, and you'd see all that going on.

Margaret Lloyd, St Helens

Bill Carr was eighteen and a miner in Newcastle-on-Tyne when the strike broke out. He remembered:

> When the miners' lockout ended, the pit was manned by blacklegs drawn from other parts of Britain, and none of my family were accepted when they presented themselves for work. Yet the family – my grandfather, father and I – had worked in the industry for a total of 110 years, (grandfather first went down the pit at the age of eleven) . . . On November 29, it was all over. The lockout had lasted seven months, and things would never be the same again. The bitter hatred of the miners against the Tories was deep indeed, and has continued until today. This is reflected in the almost obsessional desire in every miner's family to vote Labour.[7]

Durham miners' leader (later an MP and peer) Will Blyton recalled how he had had to leave his post on the Board of Guardians when, after the General Strike, he became a recipient: 'When I was first elected to Parliament in 1945, I had a final demand for £7 2s of the poor relief; the first cheque I ever wrote, out of my first money as a MP, was to pay off the last of that debt.'[8] James Griffiths, an MP and South Wales miners' president also recalled that the miners did not receive strike pay but relied on loans from the Guardians and the Co-op. He added: 'We received money from the Labour Party and from Russia'.[9]

> The local policeman, the bobby, as we called him, was on the side of those that were on strike. And I'll tell you the reason why. Because, during the coal strike in '26, we had Irish people coming over, and they were blacklegging. And the local bobby used to go into the local pub and haul them out after hours, and lock them up for the night, and he didn't make any mistakes about locking them up, he made sure they didn't do a day's work the next day. So, you see, for once the police were on our side.
>
> **Les Horne, Yorkshire**

> When I was five years of age, 1926, I used to go to the coal tip with my dad and my uncle. We used to have a little gambol, we used to call them. Had pram wheels with a little plank on and we used to go there picking coal because we had no coal to keep warm, and I would go with them. And there was my first involvement with trade unions, because they would have meetings. I'd be there and suddenly along would come a lodge official and he'd call out and they would have a meeting there and then. They would all start talking and voting and this sort of thing. The strike was on for five months and I was going back to this tip day after day, day after day, at five years of age. I hadn't even started school. But you learned an awful lot from what was going on.
>
> **Bill Herbert, Blackwood**

My sisters (I was the youngest of the six children) they used to take me to the soup kitchens, and what a blessing those soup kitchens were. My mother used to work in them, providing or helping to provide the food for us all. They were absolutely marvellous. A very basic diet, but it was adequate, and the getting together was marvellous.

Maurita Matthewson, Bargoed

There was one terrific strike in '26, and if you told people today that there wasn't a penny came into that house during that six months – we had nothing. How we survived, God above knows.

Les Horne, Yorkshire

The miners' strike carried on after the General Strike, and one saw the miners with their begging bowls in all the streets. It was a most shocking thing. And what influenced me to some extent were all the blacklegs, who were mostly from the universities and suchlike and included one of my brothers.

Jack Gaster, Marylebone

At one time during the strike I saw a crowd of over 1,000 people assembled at Barry police station with Sergeant Spiller, the policeman from Dinas Forest, controlling the crowd whilst they listened to speakers. The collapse of the strike was seen as a sell-out and the disappointment still reverberates . . . In the General Strike the whole country was on the verge. All they needed was the leadership. But they back-tracked.

Douglas Hawkins, Barry

[My father] continued working through the General Strike of 1926 which, of course, meant that nobody would work with him afterwards. He'd blacklegged, you see.

Tessa Broome, Cheadle

Before the [First World] War, every year there was a big trades union march, demonstration, at which they used to collect money for hospitals.[10] They used to collect quite a lot, because there wasn't the National Health Service that there is now. And, during the General Strike, the medical students they blocked us. Drove the buses, drove the tubes so, of course, the reaction of the trades unions was – that's the lot. So there's no more marches after that.

Fred Combes, Islington

Once they struck, everyone got frightened after a couple of days' strike. Well, you know that by the General Strike. Everybody got very scared. 'Oh, no, we can't do this any longer, we can't fight for our rights, as you call it. The kids'll have nothing and we'll be put off.' It was a dockers' area, as well.

Sid & Vi Willis, Ilford

The 1929–31 Labour government

The Conservative government passed the Trade Disputes and Trade Union Act in 1927, which made sympathetic strikes and various forms of industrial action illegal. Some civil servants were forbidden to join unions affiliated to the TUC, and a 'contracting-in' system for the payment of the political levy to the Labour Party was established. Instead of a percentage of each affiliated union's members' dues going automatically to the Labour Party, individuals had to direct their money to Labour. Membership of and payments to the Labour Party fell, and efforts to recruit individual members became more concerted. Union leaders' support for Labour was strengthened as they sought to have the law changed. By 1928 the unions still contributed most of the money, most of the MPs and ten times as many members as those who were individual members. Membership rose steadily until 1937. At the 1929 General Election Labour received its highest-ever percentage of the total ballot. It was the first time that women aged twenty-one to thirty had been allowed to vote. Mary Stott recalled that:

> I was one of the important people because I had just got on the register in time. I wasn't a leftover from 1918. I got up very, very early, soon after the polling station opened. In fact it's possible, isn't it, that I might have been the first flapper to vote, and I put on a bright red dress because I was voting Labour and I stalked off with my head high.[11]

> The main discussions were about the sort of person we wanted as the Labour candidate, because we'd had the very charismatic Barbara Gould, who was a great influence on me. The stories about her were apocryphal. She came, I think, in 1924, but I first knew her in 1929. The young management from ICI used to follow her around and heckle her, and she used to give better than they gave her. She fired my imagination. I met her, of course, during that election. She lost the election by four votes. I was eleven then, and I cried when she lost.[12]

Josie Tipple, Northwich

Labour formed a government, but the thirty-six MPs of the affiliated ILP were heavily critical of the new Prime Minister, Ramsay MacDonald, and there were internal divisions within the Cabinet. In May 1930 Oswald Mosley, a junior Minister with responsibility for unemployment policy, resigned from the government. His calls for greater expenditure on job creation and higher tariffs were supported by many at the party conference. The splits over public works and tariffs continued and, in the summer of 1931, in the face of a prospective budget deficit due to high public expenditure, and a fall in Britain's gold and foreign currency reserves, MacDonald resigned. This precipitated the formation of a 'National' government led by MacDonald and dominated by the Conservatives, and then to a dismal performance by Labour in the General Election of October 1931 when only forty-six Labour MPs were returned. Labour did not split as disastrously as the Liberals had in 1916. The solidity of the Labour Party outside parliament, in the unions and constituencies, helped to keep it going, despite the dramatic departure of its leader. Only seven members of the parliamentary party left with MacDonald. These included the railworkers' union leader Jimmy Thomas.

> I was disgusted with Clynes, and Ramsay MacDonald and Thomas and that, and it was them that finally brought me into the party [in 1929].
>
> **Fred Combes, Islington**

Some informants remembered the shock of the end of the second Labour government:

> Then came the debacle of 1931 and I saw the Labour candidate J.W. Fawcett sitting in the Labour Club holding his head in his hands and saying, 'This is the end for Labour'. I often wondered if he lived to see the great landslide victory in 1945. Of course, after this the fortunes of the Labour Party were at a very low ebb. It hardly existed in Kingston.[13]
>
> **Stanley Bell, Kingston-upon-Thames**

> We had a beautiful picture of [Ramsay MacDonald] in our passage (we never called them halls) . . . Dad's idol. My dad's idol.

> I came home from school, sitting there waiting for him to come in, and there was such a commotion. We'd heard him come in with his key and there was such a commotion . . . There's Dad in the passage, he's got the frame round his neck . . . and he's standing like this: 'You bloody traitor, you bloody –' tearing the picture up into little pieces . . . And afterwards he came in and Mum said: 'What's all that about, about him being a traitor and all that?' So he said to me: 'You saw what I did?' 'Yeah.' So he said, 'Well, I think he's killed the Labour Party.' 'Do you, Dad?' 'Yes, I don't think we're going to get out of this.' Anyway, they called a special meeting of the ward . . . He'd become a National Government, hadn't he? So of course there's going to be, over the country there was Labour MPs – we didn't have one – so, of course, those that didn't want to be National, which was most of them. It was a terrible upheaval in the party. And it did do the party, even locally, a lot of harm.
>
> **Vi Willis, Ilford**

Local government

Excluding the wartime coalitions, Labour has been in power at Westminster for only about twenty years of this century and so the Party has usually had to rely on local activists to implement its ideas. Sometimes this has led to divisions within the Party. Labour councils paid wages and poor relief, and had responsibilities for housing, gas, education, water, electricity (until the creation of the Central Electricity Board in 1926), transport, and other municipal trading enterprises; and, between 1929 and 1934, for health provision, unemployment and poor relief.[14] When Labour won power in the town halls it had opportunities for prestige, power and patronage which were denied to it at national level.[15]

In 1919 Labour won control of London's Poplar council and the Poplar Board of Guardians. Councillors promptly raised the pay of council workers and initiated public works to aid employment. After refusing to raise a rate, twenty-nine councillors and the mayor were gaoled and 10,000 people pledged not to pay rent until their release. This was secured, and the Poplar councillors then refused to prosecute those caught removing council property to burn as fuel. They went on to make relief payments to strikers and to pay illegally high wages and relief. Ramsay MacDonald was opposed to Poplar Labour Party's policies and Beatrice Webb referred to the Poplar party as essentially a working-class benefit society.[16] The policies may have lost Labour votes elsewhere, but the ideas were popular among the poor and, as miners' MP James Griffiths recalled: 'During the years of the Depression I had been deeply impressed by the services rendered to our people by our councils. It is not too much to say that their salvage work saved our community life from complete disintegration.'[17] Riva Stanton recalled that in West Ham, where Labour councillors were also found guilty of paying out too much relief: 'We was told if Jack Jones [the local MP] gets in, he's the Labour man, he'll look after us, we'll have better RO [Relieving Officer], better this, better that.'[18] Fred Combes also made the link between his own misfortunes and social structures. He explained that, in 1922, his widowed mother, who was claiming benefits (rent, meal voucher and 'a loaf of grey bread'), was gaoled for twenty-eight days after being caught by the Relieving Officer cleaning offices and bringing home the papers from the office to sell. 'My mother's experience hit me with a bigger impact because I was only thirteen, fourteen years old . . . that moulded my political outlook.' He joined the Labour Party and later became mayor of Southwark.

In one of its publications of the late 1930s, the party noted of local councillors:

> One or two persons of energy, ability and devotion can, in this sphere, make a very real difference. Individual initiative counts for more in bringing about effective change than in the House of Commons. And that change operates on the substance of daily life for great numbers of people . . . The well-being of citizens of all ages, and especially poorer citizens, is profoundly and directly affected by the action, or the inaction, of their representative body in the place in which they live.[19]

In Stepney, electricity was supplied only to firms which employed trade unionists, and it was turned off during the General Strike. In St Helens, the council handed over responsibility for the electricity supply to the electricians' union and, in Swindon, power was cut off to some industrial firms.[20] In Hackney, the electricity profits funded a pre-election cut in rates.[21] A number of councils established their own municipal banks, and, in 1932, Walthamstow formed a company bank.[22] The Finsbury Health Centre featured in an Army Bureau of Current Affairs poster of 1943 designed to encourage people to believe that they were fighting for a better Britain.[23] Local control was an incentive for 'the impoverished and the deprived' to organise themselves for local elections for 'local politics has provided the only avenue to a recognition and public status otherwise denied by society to many manual workers'.[24]

The Means Test

There was some unemployment in the early years of the century, but the First World War produced full employment. Afterwards, although there was a brief boom in many parts of the country, there was soon a major slump. By July 1921, over two million people in Britain were in receipt of poor relief. Throughout the 1920s, there were never fewer than a million people on poor relief, and the figure had risen to three million by 1931. These official figures only include those who were insured. The total number touched by unemployment was probably about half the British workforce, as many people were out of work for a short period but then found work. Short notice periods and no redundancy payments made unemployment a major threat to many workers.

The system of relief for the unemployed of England and Wales which existed in the 1920s was based on that devised in 1834. The able-bodied poor were allocated relief only through the workhouse, and this relief had to be of a lower standard than that of the worst-off workers. The system was administered by locally elected Boards of Guardians, who appointed Relieving Officers and the Workhouse Master. The Boards were funded by the rates, and were also responsible for the relief of poverty caused by old age, low wages or ill health. Claimants applied to the Guardians for help and, if the Relieving Officer accepted their case, were given either 'out-relief', part of which could be given in kind, or accommodation in the workhouse, which was sex segregated and highly regimented. In Scotland, under the Poor Act of 1845, councils did not have to provide any relief for the unemployed and, although some did, the levels were almost always less than in England. The Insurance Act of 1911 introduced a structure whereby employers and employees paid into a fund from which unemployment payments could be drawn, but the scheme only covered some industries and never amounted to more than a supplement to the Poor Law. In addition, it was made illegal for claimants to receive benefits without being put to task work, and half of the relief was paid in kind. Wage earners were taken out of the Poor Law system by the provision of old age pensions, some health care and unemployment benefit. Vi Willis recalled one effect of the removal of an individual's own responsibility for decisions about budgeting.

Kids couldn't learn at school if their tummies were absolutely empty, and rumbling all the time. And they were cold, and they were lousy – forgive me for saying it . . . One mother had eight, nine children in one room, that all lived and slept there. An' they used to have a little bit of a paraffin stove out in the garden, and they would do a bit of cooking out there. And, do you know, those rotten old so-and-sos in the shop, 'cos paraffin was a little bit dear: 'No, it's a food ticket. Can't have any paraffin on it, 'cos it's a food ticket.' Oh, that sort of terrible thing that absolutely got on your brain and you used to think to yourself: 'Oh, if only there was a revolution.' I can't help it. Even when you was young you used to think that.

Vi Willis, Ilford

A change was made to the relief of unemployment in 1931. Unemployed workers who had used up their twenty-six weeks of insured benefit were subject to a means test to establish their eligibility for 'transitional benefit' before they fell in to pauperism. The unemployed worker had to declare all the family income, including savings in the Post Office or the Co-operative Society, old age and disability pensions or wages drawn by any other member of the household. Even free school meals and milk were taken into account by officers, who would visit and check with neighbours in order to calculate the total resources of the family. Transitional benefit could never exceed the already low insured benefit rates, themselves always less than a living wage, and yet people had to prove that they were destitute. Frank Booth remembered:

The parents were on the Means Test. They used to come round and see what you'd got in your house. Eventually we'd got rid of everything worth getting rid of. They used to come. They always let you know. This particular day I can remember seeing me mother (I was twelve) stood behind the door crying. I said 'What's up?' and she said, 'I'm waiting for the Means Test Man to come.' She was so upset that any of the neighbours should peep, and when she saw him coming up the street she opened up the door quick because they made you think in those days that it was something to be ashamed of. Not like today it's something you're entitled to, but then you were on the Means Test. It was something you should be ashamed of yourself for being on. It was the first inkling I had of something wrong . . .You had six months unemployment pay and then you had to declare all the income you had. I remember particularly that my sister worked at Tilsons and she got a two-shilling rise and the conversation for a whole week before the Means Test Man come was whether they should tell him about this two shillings, 10p now. They were frightened what would happen if they didn't tell him and he found out. Eventually he did come and they told him. It was the conversation every time my mother and father were talking, they were talking about whether to declare this 10p.

Frank Booth, Stockport

I can remember the long queues on the dole at Dorchester which stretched from what was the Labour Exchange, round the corner, right round, past my house.

And I saw all these men queuing up, every one wearing their cap, to get their pittance of dole, and I couldn't understand why this had to be. My father was usually amongst them because, as things got tighter, the farmers would cut back on labour, and then he would be on the dole, and then we would suffer.

Mike Turner, Dorchester

Teenagers left home in order not to incur the burden of supporting their parents, and there was widespread anger as workers were reduced to the level of paupers. At the Labour Party conference in 1932 there were hundreds of resolutions submitted against the Means Test. Moving one of them, Mr A.E. Eyton asked: 'Has anything known in the history of our land done so much to break up family life and unity as the Means Test? Prostitutes have been made by the hundreds as a result of unemployment and the transitional benefit inhumanity.' Veteran labour activist Ben Tillett called upon delegates to 'go out on to the street corners' to tell the people that the Means Test was 'causing the destruction of family life'. Activists united on this issue as men and women, working class and middle class, organised for change. Bea Serota recalled the atmosphere:

I don't think one could grow up in London in the Thirties and not be aware of what was going on politically. In our local greengrocer there was always a card which said, 'Relief tickets taken here,' which were being handed out to poor families – and there were boot funds. The primary school I went to, which was an all-age school then, I was in a class with girls of fourteen. There were girls running barefoot at the weekend and wearing those high boots which are now so fashionable and which we thought were so terrible at the time because they were a symbol of charity. One of my sister's boyfriends at that time went to fight in Spain, in fact he was killed, so you couldn't really grow up in London in the Thirties and not be aware of all that was happening in Europe as well as here.

Bea Serota, Hackney

The Depression

That so many were out of work between the wars meant not only poverty for them but also that many were fearful of losing their jobs. There was despair after the employers won the General Strike and the government introduced the Means Test. High unemployment weakened the hand of those seeking to improve pay and conditions. Much work was very dangerous and, in this regard, Bill Herbert's pit accident in 1934 was by no means unusual. The consciousness of many of the respondents was formed in this period, when they saw the effects of the unequal distribution of cultural and material goods and sought to uncover the causes and the route to a better society.

I saw poverty as a child. I was surrounded by poverty. I experienced poverty and that, I suppose, gave me a kind of a bitter feeling of the society that I could see about me, despite the fact that I was very, very young. My Dad unemployed. My brother and sister having to go to London to seek work. And that was the beginning of my serious thoughts about life in general.

Albert Huish, Cardiff

My class at school, and all through my primary school, there was children there, that father never worked. They'd stay off school if they had to get another pair of shoes, because they didn't have two pairs of shoes. And they were buying shoes in the cheapest shops and there was no way that those shoes were going to last. They were just probably cardboard . . . I remember one dreadful day when one of the men locally . . . murdered his wife and then committed suicide, and he was driven to this by the sheer misery of not being able to get work.

Helen Cameron, Glasgow

I used to go to work at seven and to come home about five, so during the winter you wouldn't see daylight from October because it was dark when you went down [the pit], dark when you came back . . . The roof collapsed. I went to get back, but there's a post behind my back. I couldn't get away. It hit me, hit the post, and down came the roof and I was trapped there. That was about ten o'clock on a Tuesday morning. I think it was about two o'clock on the Thursday morning that they got me out. They pulled me out and, as they pulled me out and lifted me up, so my shoulder which had been smashed and my arm, the weight fell down and bones came through the skin . . . No pit-head doctor. Nobody met us. The only people that was there was the people who brought me out and we walked home, because there were no ambulances.

Bill Herbert, Blackwood

The Depression. I can recall that as if it was yesterday. How a worker was standing on a box in the yard there at Hayes, near Clayton Road area, by the railway station. Calling on the workers to resist. They were going round the lines of benches, tapping every other worker on the shoulder to get his cards. And I've seen men actually break down in tears 'cos they had to go home and tell their families that they'd been sacked. And this was now working in towards the mass unemployment of the 1930s, when there was real poverty emanating from there, and there was no extensive welfare system, and it meant that families had to look after families, brothers had to look after brothers – and children without proper clothes and ill-fed and so on, that was the stark realities of that period of the 1930s, which had such a profound effect on what happened in later years.

Syd Bidwell, Southall

I'd got my ticket [as a merchant seaman on a tramp steamer]. I'd come home after four years or so and, of course, I was out of work, because I'd arrived back in England in the depth of this great slump when there were no ships. The whole of international trade had collapsed, there was no work, seamen were out of work. Everybody in the merchant navy, apart from a few passenger liners, but tramp steamers were finished. I was means tested. I was very bumptious, proud, overbearing, strong. I thought I was physically strong, as I was, and I thought I had a certain intellectual strength, just beginning. I was on the dole, I had no money. I'd been away from England, I'd got my ticket, couldn't get a ship, and so I had to appear before the Means Test committee. I thought a lot of myself. They thought I was worth 9*s* 6*d* a week. That was my Means Test. I remember the first thing I did was go for a walk. I remember walking down St Mary's, Walthamstow. I walked into Cambridgeshire. I walked to Ely, wanted to see Ely Cathedral. I walked through Grantchester. I looked back and thought, What an idiot of a fellow [the poet Rupert Brooke]. Here he is worrying about bleedin' Grantchester. 'Is there honey still for tea?'

John Horner, Walthamstow

I left school in 1931 in the Depression and visited this factory weekly for six months looking for a job. In the end the foreman said 'I'm sick and tired of seeing you here, so I'm going to give you a start. You get here five minutes before time, 8 a.m., and be ready to work. You go on to 5.30 p.m. One hour for lunch.' No breaks for the toilet or tea and no unions.

Stanley Bell, Kingston-upon-Thames, Surrey

[The Labour Exchange]. You went two or three times a week, not like today. They learned they mustn't do that. If the unemployed got together they'd start organising, didn't they, as unemployed. And now what they do, you don't go to them, you go to the bloody Post Office to get your money. That kind of thing. It's all different. They did that because the unemployed are the cleverest, no, not clever – they learn. Once they learn, that's what they do. What they did. No way could you let unemployed get together at Labour Exchanges. They'll organise, won't they? And they did. And that's why the unemployed were very well organised. And when they called a march it wasn't a matter of 100 people marching down the street. Thousands would come along. It was terrific. And yet there was no Labour Movement compared to today. You had no Labour MPs, or only a handful of them. And the councils were all Liberal or Tory. There was no such thing as Labour councils for many years.

Lew Smith, Hackney

The hunger marches

In 1931, when the government introduced the Means Test, there were over two million unemployed in Britain. Many of them lived in relatively compact and cohesive working-class communities. Although after 1929 there was less opportunity for local bargaining as benefits were administered by the offices of the Unemployment Assistance Board and financed by national taxation, people still gathered at Labour Exchanges and were able to work together to oppose the system of relief. There were several locally organised marches against unemployment soon after the war. In 1921 the National Unemployed Workers' Committee Movement (later the word Committee was dropped from the title) was formed from a group led by three London Communists.[25] The NUWM claimed 100,000 members at its peaks, just after its major marches of 1922–3 and 1932, when 20,000 marchers in 18 contingents converged on London.

One of its first actions was to march from London to the Labour Party conference in Brighton. This gained the unemployed some publicity, some dignity and some support from Labour Party activists. This was despite the distaste the leaders of the Labour Party and the TUC had for an organisation dedicated, according to the oath of membership, 'never to cease from active strife until capitalism is abolished'. The unemployed workers' movement challenged Guardians, gave legal advice to the unemployed and campaigned against excessive overtime and blackleg labour. The NUWM publicised the plight of the unemployed and represented them in benefits tribunals and in the Courts of Referees to which those disallowed from benefits could appeal, and its branches provided social and material support for the jobless.

On the 1922 march the Labour Parliamentary candidate for Lincoln gave his support, and in Canterbury a meal and beds were provided by the Labour Party. Around 2,000 marchers converged on London and around 50,000 took part in a demonstration when Parliament opened. Five years later, 300 Welsh miners marched to London, and there were further national marches in 1929, 1930 and 1932. In 1932 in Plymouth it was the Salvation Army which provided food and accommodation and, when the police shepherded the marchers out on the following day so that they were unable to collect money, 'the Labour Party', according to a Ministry of Health report, 'gave no support to the marchers, who were unable to collect a halfpenny'.[26]

In 1933 Ronald Kidd, who had watched the hunger marchers come to London, accused the police of employing *agents provocateurs* among them. They denied this and Kidd decided that, with another hunger march in prospect, a permanent team of observers was required. In February 1934 he, Dr Edith Summerskill, Kingsley Martin, and a number of others established the National Council for Civil Liberties (NCCL, now Liberty). John Platts-Mills' recollections of the foundation of the NCCL indicates the organisation's emphasis upon citizens' rights under the law:

When I was living with [Lewis] Clive [godson of Neville Chamberlain] we went canvassing for a Labour member, [Lewis] Silkin, way down south of London. Must have been the by-election of '32. Clive had a lot of money. His mum owned a county. Clive sloshed round money to every organisation he thought was a leftist organisation. Then we joined Civil Liberties. I was certainly one of the chaps who got Ronald Kidd to make himself into an organisation. That was liberal plus. I went to get [Elizabeth] Alan to become secretary of it after Kidd. [He was the first NCCL secretary. She was secretary until the 1950s.]

John Platts-Mills, Finsbury

93

The fifth national march occurred in 1934. Members of the Oxford University Labour Club marched with the NUWM from the Corn Exchange to the city boundary and the Labour Party in Hertford was also supportive. In 1936 the final national march was held and the Labour leadership changed its opinion of what was styled a National Protest March. It was supported by 595 delegates from Trades Councils and local Labour Parties in Cardiff. Broxtowe Divisional Labour Party in Nottinghamshire offered support. MPs were supportive along the route and, in London, ten MPs appeared on the platform at the final rally. The *Daily Herald*, previously opposed to the NUWM, became more enthusiastic and the NUWM leaders addressed 200 MPs in the Commons at a meeting convened by Labour.[27] As the number of unemployed fell, so the movement was reduced in scope. Although there was a South Wales miners' march to London in 1937 and there were a number of local marches, the NUWM was moribund by the time of its last National Conference in 1937.

There was one march for jobs which had cross-party support and passed off peacefully. Two hundred men marched behind the Jarrow MP Ellen Wilkinson in what became known as the Jarrow Crusade. The press was sympathetic to the march, which rejected co-operation with the National Unemployed Workers' Movement and was blessed by the Bishop of Jarrow prior to its departure. Along the route Communists and the Labour Party gave support, and in Chesterfield the Conservative Party provided accommodation and food.[28]

Some of the unemployed became politically active. Bob Cooney, an unemployed Aberdonian who had been in the ILP Guild of Youth and then joined the Communist Party recalled how in Spain in 1938:

> I said, 'Remember the hunger marches, lads. If our feet won't get us there, our voices will, and whatever happens we'll bloody sing as if we were one hell of a column marching along.'[29]

According to Reg Underhill and Ted Willis in interviews made in 1976, many members of the League of Youth were unemployed.[30] The League's National Advisory Committee member Will Nally noted in 1933 that 'there are Leagues of Youth in the Manchester Federation [of which he was a member] with a membership composed entirely of unemployed. A while ago I attended a League meeting where only five out of 90 members were in employment.'[31] Probably the most common reaction was that expressed by John Edmonds:

> Hope, in varying degrees, was ever present . . . and with it, a silent resentment at not knowing what or who was really to blame . . . My father read the *Daily Herald*, stoutly supported the Labour Party, and blamed Mr Baldwin [The Conservative P.M.] for every and any thing.[32]

There were many who did not march but who greeted marchers with offers of help or turned out to show their solidarity.

[Hunger marchers] started from all different points, and there was a village next to us, East Calder they called it, and I can remember us going there. The marchers were going through there and were living in the local community hall, and we went down there and seen them off . . . Go down there and give them a bit of encouragement. The people that were nae able to go on the march, it was all the younger lads in their late teens and early twenties that were marching, and everybody just turned out to wish them well.

Alex Kitson, Edinburgh

We walked down with the miners because the big Co-op at Stratford [East London] put on meals. And most of the Women's Section here went to Stratford, which was the Co-op then, and helped take the miners in. All took bowls so they could wash their feet. And then thick lumps of bread and cheese, I can see it now – mugs of tea.

Vi Willis, Ilford

The South Wales hunger marchers take a break on their march to London in 1936

NMPFT/Science & Society Picture Library

I went down to Leith Co-operative Hall one Sunday morning when I was doing my [nursing] training, to dress the hunger marchers' blisters, who came from Fife. And they'd all been given new boots, and by the time they got to Edinburgh they all had blisters, so I think I must have taken the initiative and organised this blister dressing session on the Sunday morning. And they must have stayed overnight in the Co-op Hall and I went down and spent the morning putting sticking plaster on dressings.

Margaret Lawson, Edinburgh

I was down with members of the League of Youth at Trades Hall, Tottenham, which used to be the Labour Party premises, and provided sandwiches for the hunger marchers.

Olive Rainbird, Tottenham

They came from Wigan way, and Manchester, and they stopped at Chorley . . . We had sandwiches and that for them, and we'd a first aid chap, 'cos some of them, their feet were sore walking so far. And I can remember this little Mr Waugh: 'Why didn't we tell him? He'd have given us bread, he'd have given us all sorts from this shop to make a meal . . .' but we'd begged off members. Anyway, we joined this march and we walked to Preston. Well, it's only nine miles. And there were Young Communists walking and all. So they're shouting 'YCL', and we're shouting 'ILP', and I've never forgotten it. Some of them had been hungry properly, some of these men. But there were some women came out, it would have been at Whittle, I think, and they fetched pies, and these men said 'Give it t'young women.' I felt terrible, 'cos I'd never been hungry. 'Cos even that week with no money, I don't think we were ever hungry after, it were just one day. And we got to Preston . . . and the Labour MP [1918–31] would be Tom Shaw. And they took us to; I can't tell you what it were called, but it had been a picture palace, well it still was. So they march in, this would have been the Young Communists, I think . . . So you walked through. There were an audience, they'd have been advertised, and they walked through twice, so it looked like a big procession. But I never forgot that, because they made a tea, and there were no plates, or anything, and it were a mountain of corned beef sandwiches, and Herbert had two.

Betty Crook, Chorley

I can remember the hunger marchers walking when they come through and I can remember a bit of conversation going on then but very little. Most people seemed not to want to think about it.

Frank Booth, Stockport

When [the hunger marchers] came down, and this was down at Marble Arch (we used to sell *Challenge* [the newspaper of the Young Communist League] down at

All over the country, people took to the streets to demand the right to work

NMPFT/Science & Society Picture Library

Marble Arch), the mounted police came along and started to break it up. And they slung marbles, and of course the horses skidded on them. There was a lot of brutality because these mounted police got out their truncheons, walloping.

Dot Welsh, Paddington

I was a NCCL observer when the red-head girl first marched into London, Ellen Wilkinson. She was MP for Jarrow. Clive and I had seen the Jarrow Marchers come in. She only joined them at Shepherd's Bush.

John Platts-Mills, Finsbury

During the 1920s the unions lost some of their influence within the Labour Party. This was partly because the Party's income from the unions was reduced by the 1927 Trade Disputes and Trade Unions Act and partly because, in the face of high unemployment, many union leaders became immersed in their own concerns. After the events of 1926 and 1931 the trade unions began to take more interest in parliamentary politics and less interest in direct action. Ernest Bevin, the General Secretary of the Transport and General Workers Union, and Walter Citrine, the Secretary of the TUC General Council, were particularly keen to be influential within the Labour Party. Those on the

Jarrow MP 'Red Ellen' Wilkinson addressed the crowd at Hyde Park in November 1936
NMPFT/Science & Society Picture Library

left of the party became more hostile to the unions, which were seen as right-wing obstacles, while union leaders were disdainful of intellectuals and the interest in foreign policy. The unions determined that, when Labour was elected, it would repeal the 1927 Act and in 1946 it did so. This led to an increase in both union membership and Party funds. The trade unions were less interested in social and welfare legislation. Some held that benefits undermined bargaining power or working-class collective self-help. Lobbying for changes to improve the lot of the destitute was done by the people who became involved with helping Labour through their own experience of poverty, their fear of poverty or their sympathy with the poverty of others.

VI

Countering Fascism and Racism

In the 1930s, many people in Britain perceived fascism and war to be serious and related threats. Fascists had gained control of Italy in 1922 and Nazis dominated Germany from 1933. In Britain the Conservative-dominated National Government was elected after Labour fell from office in 1931. In 1935 the National Government adopted the policies of the Labour and Liberal Parties and then, within weeks of re-election, returned to appeasement, particularly of Italy's leader, Mussolini, as a central foreign policy. There was no election planned until 1940 and the Conservatives were popular among many of those with jobs. Even after victory in the Second World War, the 'war against fascism', there was violence and prejudice against ethnic communities which many members of the Labour Party strove to combat. That they opposed the scapegoating of new migrants to and within Britain and gave the issue of anti-racism a higher profile than some Party leaders wanted, indicates that activists play other roles besides that of loyal team supporters of the parliamentarians.

Spain

In July 1936, fascist Falangist army commanders of the Spanish Foreign Legion in Morocco initiated a civil war against the left-wing Spanish Republican government, which had been elected to power in 1931. The British government feared the results of a Republican victory and officially stayed neutral, indeed, the only country to support the Spanish government outright was the Soviet Union. Fascist Italy and Nazi Germany supplied the rebels, led by Franco, with arms and troops, which helped to ensure Franco's victory in March 1939. Among the general population of Britain there was widespread support for the Republic. Many collected money, food and clothing for the Republicans or organised the resettlement of refugees. Over £2 million-worth of money and goods were contributed to help the Spanish people. The cause lit a spark within many activists.

> The thing that awoke my political awareness was the Spanish Civil War. I went to a convent and I was in the sixth form and there were a couple of people, I think they were priests, came to tell us about the Spanish Civil War. But it was very biased, and Franco was supposed to be absolutely marvellous, you know, God's gift, and the government of the country was wicked, and so forth. And they were talking about the way Franco took as mercenaries the Algerians and Moroccans, and they said 'Any questions?' So I said 'Yes. I understand that Moroccans are Muslims (or Mohammedans, as we called them then). How is it that they were prepared to fight

for a Catholic cause?' And the headmistress looked at me – I wasn't very popular. I can't remember what reply I got now, but it was something very anodyne, and obviously not particularly honest, and that really started me thinking.

Noreen Law, East Ham

The Spanish Civil War altered me a lot. I felt really bitter. Before I was political but I really began to feel there was evil in these fascists, and even in these Conservatives who supplied arms.

Maurita Matthewson, south London

My best friend who I made at college . . . at that time when I first went to see him and his parents. His father was a shipbuilder on Teesside and I never knew him to be in work. He was always, permanently, on the dole and that was the background to my thinking. It was also a time of the rise of Hitler and Mussolini, Nazism and fascism . . . Our conversations and private debates centred on the rise of fascism . . . Like me he was lucky to have the opportunity to go to college. He realised there was a lot of sacrifice to get him there, and to get me there. We were serious-minded and we thought we could put the world to rights. There were those two things, conditions at home and conditions abroad which fired us. We both pretty well joined the Labour Party together in a sense, but independently. I joined in Redcar. I actually joined the Labour Party in November 1935, at the time of the General Election. My interest and inclination had always been socialist. I hadn't studied it, it was more emotional than academic.

Ted Willis asked me to help with a campaign on behalf of the Spanish people, which I helped with. I happened to be in London with a van that he'd hired. He became secretary of something which was known as the British Youth Peace Assembly and it was under the auspices of the British Youth Peace Assembly that we were going round with this van on behalf of the Spanish people . . . the other aspect of it that I and others thought was very important was the idea of the Popular Front to defeat the National Government. A Popular Front to defeat fascism, which would embrace not only the Labour Party but a whole range of left-wing radical parties. I didn't have a regular job at that time. I was more a Labour Party activist than I was a teacher. I was largely supported by my mother.

Jim Tucker, London

We were terribly concerned about the war in Spain. We read and re-read every pamphlet and article we could. Our heart went out to those who were fighting for the Spanish government . . . What we did was to collect money for milk for Spanish children. This was quite non-political, because children on both sides needed feeding and milk was the best food for them. I gave up a great many Sunday mornings to this work of collecting. How pleased we were when the

Nottingham Co-operative Society decided to pay for an ambulance to send to Spain to pick up the wounded there.

Scott Garnet, Nottingham

People like me did a lot of work in Stockport, supporting the Republican side in the Spanish Civil War. We did send people to fight in the International Brigade. We did concrete things like supplying medical aid. One of the things we did was to equip motorcycles and sidecars; made them into first aid vehicles . . . Another thing we did was to collect money for milk for babies for Spain. That was so widespread that you could have coppers, money, stopped out of your wages.

Aileen Plant, Stockport

We had two garages full of collected goods at one time. We must have had 300 tins of something which could be shipped abroad and endless woolly coats and woolly jackets and thick singlets and shirts and so on.

John Platts-Mills, Finsbury

We were involved in the International Brigade thing. We saved silver paper. We didn't have much money but we saved silver paper for the International Brigade and my father wanted to go but, once again, he had responsibilities here. Spain was a terrible thing to us. We were well aware of it . . . Funnily enough, the other branch of the family, the Campbells, one of them had a medal from Franco for the work that he did.

Martha Feeney, Glasgow

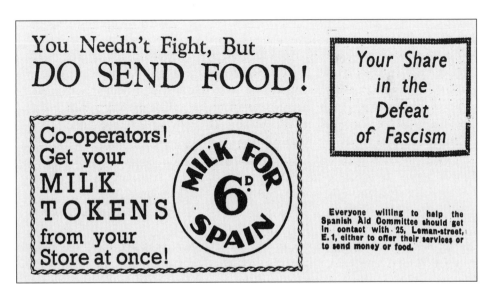

There were many different ways to support the Spanish Republicans

We were collecting food for Spain. We used to go round the Peabody Estate and people used to give us what food they could give us, tins of food, and some of them even apologised that they couldn't give us anything. And we also used to collect money for Spain and then, of course, there were big demos that we used to have, 'Arms for Spain'. And we used to do a lot of whitewashing on the walls, 'Arms for Spain'.

Dot Welsh, Paddington

The cinema, which is now a furnishing shop up towards the existing police station, in 1936 there was a big, successful concert held there with variety artists appearing as local and wider people came – wider in the sense of living outside the district. In 1936 a considerable sum of money was raised in aid of support for the Republican cause in Spain. I had friends a little older than I was who went to Spain. I remember the discussions that took place about the role of the POUM in Spanish affairs. [The Partido Obrero de Unificación Marxista, POUM, with which the ILP had associated itself, was the non-Stalinist Marxist militia]. Because the Communist Party didn't have an enormous influence in the affairs, it was the equivalent to the ILP, if you like. They were the bigger force.

Syd Bidwell, Southall

There was big rallies [for Spain] in the city hall. And it was astounding the amount of money that they could collect. I mean, people would even put in – well, this seems pathetic to you now – but they were putting in pound notes, and there were masses of that audience who would be people that were really unemployed. I used to go to them quite often on a Sunday night, to those rallies.

Helen Cameron, Glasgow

One started collecting money. We were told, did you want to give something to Harry Pollitt's fund? [Pollitt was the General Secretary of the Communist Party.] We didn't know what it was for, but we were told it was something important, and so we started paying money in. Quite large quantities of money were being paid in by all the young people that we knew. This, of course, turned out to be the financial support for the International Brigade which was, of course, run entirely by the Communist Party and I suppose a good percentage, perhaps 50 per cent, of these young graduates from Oxford and Cambridge [working at the British Museum] were at that time actually members of the Communist Party.

Hugh Chaplin, Holborn

Despite the fact that volunteering, recruiting volunteers or aiding them was illegal, over 2,000 British men volunteered to fight for the Republican cause in the International Brigades; 95 per cent of the volunteers came from working-class backgrounds. Approximately 1,200 of them were injured and 500 of them were killed.

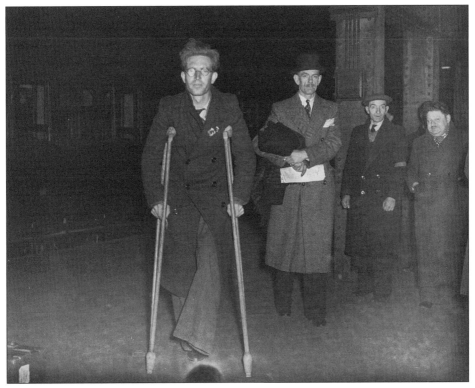

A wounded member of the International Brigade returns to London from Spain

NMPFT/Science & Society Picture Library

I, and many others, decided to go. The Communist Party organised five vans to be driven from London to Madrid and be converted to ambulances, and the drivers then to do whatever they wished. I was one of the drivers and indeed, because of my smattering of French and what-have-you, led the convoy which, going over the Pyrenees at night with my bad eyesight, was not perhaps the most perspicacious decision made by the Communist Party of this country. However, we got there. I was only a member of the Communist Party for an extremely short period of time. I think I joined in about '36 and I left in about '39. We delivered the ambulances and I went down to join the International Brigade . . . Spain was an extraordinary example of mind over matter. The Republican side had no arms, no ammunition, no airforce, no field guns, no tanks . . . Eventually I was invalided out and was arrested in France.

Joe Kahn, Tottenham

Whilst we were in the [Co-operative Society] Comrades Circle, it was the time of the Spanish Civil War. So we used to go out and knock doors and ask for

British socialists volunteered not only to fight but also to aid the wounded in Spain

NMPFT/Science & Society Picture Library

evaporated milk and condensed milk and money for milk, and make tablet and things to send out to Spain. Because there was quite a few lads in Govan went out and joined the International Brigade . . . Some of these boys hadn't worked for a long time, and they all went south and joined the International Brigade.

Helen Cameron, Glasgow

My brother for a time was a member of the Communist Party, and a friend of his, and colleagues of his, and neighbours went to Spain, and one of them, he died in Spain, one of them never came back . . . We were very interested in Spain. We did fund-raising, we marched. I remember one time, at least, we had a big fund-raising in the McLellan Galleries . . . Fund-raising and fund-raising and fund-raising, and seeing people equipped to go out and join the Spanish War.

Isa Paton, Glasgow

One friend went away to fight in the International Brigade, and we all thought he was dead, and we mourned him, and then he turned up again.

Margaret Lawson, Edinburgh

The League of Youth chaps, we were about eighteen, nineteen years of age, being socialists we felt that we ought to be out there fighting amongst them and one or two did actually go and join the International Brigade.

Stanley Bell, Kingston-upon-Thames

I joined the Conservative Club because they had the best dining club in town . . . I was broadly Liberal . . . When the Tories won an election, one of the promises of Sam Hoare [the British Foreign Minister] was that we'd impose every sanction that will drive Musso [lini] out of Abyssinia. The only sanction needed was water, to prevent him getting water down the Suez Canal and land it. Then the Hoare-Laval pact [between Britain and France] said let him have it without any more war. This stopped the war by giving him Abyssinia and that was what first moved [Clive Lewis and I] into more action than Civil Liberties. I got married and joined the Labour Party and he was, within two years, in Spain and fighting. [Clive Lewis died in the anti-fascist struggle in Spain.]

I was much in touch with the headquarters of the International Brigade in London and thought I might go, and they said 'Married? You're out'. Then I applied again

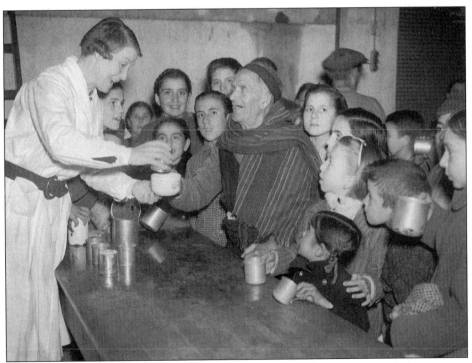

While some activists collected food in Britain, others travelled to Spain to oversee its distribution

105

in a year's time, and they said 'Married and one child? You're out', and so I was struck out.

John Platts-Mills, Finsbury

In October 1936, the Spanish government granted the Basque region a degree of autonomy and the leader of the Basque Nationalist Party pledged support for the Republic. In March 1937, the Germans serving with the Nationalist rebels bombed the small northern town of Durango and, in April 1937, the Nazis bombed Guernica in the Basque region of Spain. *The Times* devoted a whole page to reporting the attack, and many in Britain saw newsreels of the terrible destruction. The British Foreign Secretary Anthony Eden was later to call it 'the first blitz of the Second World War'. The British government, which had previously refused to allow refugees to enter the country in case it was perceived as an infringement of the Non-Intervention Agreement, agreed to the admission of Basque children. Although the Labour Party officially distanced itself from Communist-dominated bodies such as Spanish Medical Aid, there was considerable sympathy for the refugees from the left. An appeal for funds was launched and £12,000 was donated, with another £5,000 given by the TUC and 1,037 pairs of boots and shoes donated by the National Union of Boot and Shoe Operatives. 20,000 children were evacuated from Spain, of whom 3,826 came to Britain.

Jesus Martinez was fourteen years old when he was put on a ship from Bilbao bound for England:

> The boat was full to bursting with children. There were more than 4,000 of us. It was a very trying day's journey with everyone squashed up together and every available space on the boat taken. We arrived at the port of Southampton in the early hours. It was a week after the coronation of George VI. We were very surprised to see the streets decked with bunting and fairy lights. We thought that it had all been done for us. We were taken to a camp near Southampton at a place called Stoneham. The camp was divided into three sections of 200 tents each. Three large tents were used as dining rooms. The first surprise was the food. These little triangular slivers of bread with paste inside! . . . We ate with great gusto – especially the bread which was so white, so delicious and plentiful after the hunger we'd suffered in Bilbao during the blockade.[1]

The campsite was loaned by a local farmer and volunteers, many from the local Co-operative Society had dug the latrines, put up the tents and fence and laid on a water supply. Appeals for specialist help were posted to trade unions and Labour Party wards.

The British carried out medical examinations of all the children prior to their departure. On arrival those suspected of being verminous and those who had suffered severe travel sickness were taken to the Corporation Baths in Southampton.[2]

The whole of the Labour Party were very caring. One of the very, very sad things which sticks in my mind was the time we went to help Spanish refugees. They were children who'd been rescued from Barcelona and they'd been brought to Southampton on a ferry boat and they had been taken to Southampton swimming baths. Now these were very nice swimming baths but I'm sure those little girls who went there are haunted by the awful things that happened to them. Because one of the first things was that they were taken into the cubicles and stripped of their clothing. Well, of course they were riddled with lice, but nobody thought of telling them that, they just undressed them, and then they cut their hair off. Now, to a young Spanish girl, to have her hair cut off is almost as bad as being raped and these girls screamed and screamed and screamed and they came out of these cubicles with the jagged bobbed hair. And then we took them to a camp somewhere near the River Test. We put bell tents up and we filled palliasses with straw and we cooked food and we tried to settle them in and eventually they were moved on to other places, but I often wonder what happened to those little children who came to England as refugees and had this horrible experience.

Patricia Meitlis, Southampton

The camp at North Stoneham was only intended as a temporary measure and it closed in September 1937. Groups of children moved elsewhere. Catholic convents and orphanages took 1,200, and between 400 and 450 went to Congress Hall, a Salvation

In 1937 thousands of young refugees, fleeing fascism in Spain, were welcomed in Britain

Army Hostel in east London. Later, half the children were moved to a Salvation Army orphanage in Brixton. Others went to over seventy hostels run by local voluntary committees. These included a country mansion in Barnet and an empty hotel near the Thames at Maidenhead. Javier Martinez lived in several hostels and then with an English family in Coventry until he was moved to a hostel in Barnet:

> They were a nice couple, socialists, Labour people, and interested in the Spanish children. They didn't have any children themselves – I think that is why they took me. He used to come and visit me in Barnet, and I kept in touch with them till they died.[3]

Rafael Flores lived in a hostel between 1937 and 1939.

> I believe our colony was sponsored by the Labour movement and the Co-operative movement. We were very fortunate in Walsall . . . We were very fashionable at the time, I believe. A lot of the kids weren't treated all that well, but we were; those of us who fell into the hands of the labour movement – they were really concerned about us.[4]

> The Spanish. That, I thought, was dreadful. I marched. 'Arms for Spain! Arms for Spain!' I really marched. And I also became heavily involved when I was in the sixth form. I became heavily involved in the Spanish children that came over during the war. We had them in Richmond. They took over a house in Richmond and Labour people and trade union people, about twenty of them these children, girls and boys, and we looked after them. I used to go down on a Sunday, it was the only time I had. And I felt so bitter against the fascists.
>
> **Maurita Matthewson, south London**

> Quite a lot of the Basque children who had been bombed out and were homeless and we managed to get a very big house in Kingston Hill which was pretty derelict and the women manned this and they were in there and looked after.
>
> **Stanley Bell, Kingston-upon-Thames**

> I remember the Basque refugees came in quite large numbers to England and we had quite a few youngsters in Watford where I lived, so we knew all about the Spanish Civil War at that time.
>
> **Alan Yates, Watford**

A year after they arrived more than half the children were still in Britain. By the time the Second World War prevented further sailings 470 remained, and after the war about 250 remained in Britain.

Five Basque refugees prepare to return to Spain in January 1938

NMPFT/Science & Society Picture Library

Germany

Hitler came to power in Germany in 1933 and refugees fled from the Nazi regime, some of them to Britain. After having been sworn in as the government in 1933 the Nazis suspended basic constitutional rights, took control of most aspects of German life and took Germany out of the League of Nations and the disarmament conference. In 1934 all workers were gathered into the German Workers Front, many high-ranking political opponents were murdered and Hitler became President. In 1935 conscription was reintroduced and the following year the demilitarised zone of the Rhineland was occupied. In 1938 German troops marched into Austria, and the British and French persuaded the Czechs to cede Sudeten German areas to Hitler. Chamberlain famously claimed that this agreement represented 'peace in our time'. In 1939 Hitler invaded Czechoslovakia and then Poland. The British and French presented Hitler with an ultimatum which he ignored and so, on 3 September 1939, the war with Germany began.

In 1934 I went walking in Austria with a New Zealand lawyer. We saw a crowd gathering round a cottage and this fellow, we'd heard of him but no more . . . It was Hitler, and he talked to people. We heard a genuine Hitler speech. It was gentle and appeared to be thoughtful and measured. We didn't understand many of the words, not of the local dialect as it were, and people listened and then clapped. And then he talked louder and he talked faster and he talked with longer pauses and then faster and louder and then he shouted and they cheered and then he raised his arms, both arms, and then he did this [Hitler salute] and they all did it. He said 'Do it! Do it!' and undoubtedly we heard this madman in the height of frenzy and people responding to it.

John Platts-Mills, Finsbury

They had Clarion cyclists, and they had a Clarion Club in Glasgow, and they also had a refugee club at the beginning of the war. And there were a lot of refugees [from Berlin and Vienna] made contact with the Glasgow Labour movement and became our friends . . . A lot of them offered their services to the Labour College as speaker, and they would run day schools . . . They would speak about the dangers of fascism and how it had affected their countries.

Margaret Lawson, Edinburgh

Some of the girls were coming over [refugees from Hitler's Germany], Jewish women, there was a period when we were trying to marry them off to English boys or blokes [so that they could gain citizenship]. I don't think the Labour Party did as much as they ought to have done over that.

Naomi Wolff, Walthamstow

We got very involved with refugees in North Staffordshire at that time. Refugees had been coming over from Germany and Austria but, of course we were in the beginning of the Czech crisis, and so Czechs were also coming over now. Since the Sudeten area was where the pottery came from, quite a number of the potters who wanted to get out who were Jewish or political or both decided they would like to come to north Staffordshire, which is The Potteries, and so two families came and immediately, almost on arrival, said 'Please can you help us to get some more people out?' So we set up a committee. There was already a refugee committee. Colonel Wedgwood, who had been the Labour MP since 1918 for Newcastle-under-Lyme. He was absolutely first class about refugees. Helping them, giving money, going to the Home Office and trying to squeeze more visas or work permits or whatever out of them. But also having them in his house, which is quite an exceptional thing for a rather grand old gentleman. Many refugees living in his house in the country. Really wonderful old boy. We got involved with refugees and helped to get out a whole number of Czech children who came with one or two adults. We utterly failed to get their parents and, of course, they were all murdered. All of them. When the kids went back after the war there was nobody left. That was quite a job. I helped with setting up a home.

Stoke-on-Trent City Council gave us one of their orphanages. Fine old Victorian house. Fiendishly cold and dim and dark and gruesome. We had to collect curtains, we had to collect furniture, we had to get beds, we had to just get everything. There were going to be ten kids and two or three adults, so it was quite a performance really. The Trades Council, the churches all contributed and it was a very, very good effort indeed. Excellent effort. There are still Czechs living up there. The children have gone back and come back to live there. When we went to the Lidice celebrations two years ago, the mayor of Stoke-on-Trent and Newcastle and their wives came over for the celebration, so this link has been kept going.

Anne Swingler, Newcastle-under-Lyme

I went to a very progressive school. I was very fortunate indeed. It was a state secondary school . . . It was the time of the Spanish Civil War, and the persecution of the Jews in Germany. In this school that I was at German was the first foreign language that you learnt, this was one of the unusual things, as opposed to French, which everybody learnt. I used to have terrible rows with my German teacher about what was going on in Germany. I went on a school journey to Austria in 1936 and we went by train to Munich, where one saw the obvious signs, and then through into Austria, and at the frontier there was a big banner which said on it 'Juden Nicht Erwünscht: Jews Not Wanted', so we were all very angry, and then landed up in the most lovely place in the Austrian Tyrol, but I've never been back since. I wouldn't go . . . At the age of seventeen I won a Modern Language Travelling Scholarship. That was one of the progressive things the old London County Council did for its pupils and because it was German speaking I wouldn't go to Germany and so I travelled to Switzerland, to the German-speaking part of Switzerland, where I stayed three months.

Bea Serota, Hackney

We collected against Franco in the Spanish Civil War . . . and we did have refugees over in Hammersmith and we were against Hitler and that sort of thing. I got very much caught up in the racism and fascism rather than the politics. Sydney's two brothers were going to be called up . . . Henry was terrified he was going to be called up and I remember going with him to the West Green station, and the next thing I knew he put his head in a gas oven. This great fear of Hitler and, in a way, because I was married to Sydney who was Jewish, I got very much caught in anti-Hitler racism, away from the domestic political thing which was really the Labour Party, that was the basis of the Labour Party.

Naomi Wolff, Hammersmith

The question was: what on earth are we going to do with Hitler? We were in Canada when the Nazis actually came to power. It seemed very much the other side of the world, not very relevant to Canadian affairs. But in London at that time it was extremely relevant, and this really overshadowed everything else. I don't think one thought about labour problems or whatever.

Anna Clarke, St Pancras

In 1939 I spoke at two meetings, one in Nottingham, one in Hyde Park. By this time I'd left the Communist Party. I made it quite clear that Hitler would invade the rest of Europe and this country unless he was stopped, and that was the tone of both the speeches.

Joe Kahn, Tottenham

Britain

In 1932 Sir Oswald Mosley founded the British Union of Fascists, adopting the Italian fascist black shirt as its uniform. There were soon around 20,000 members. Mosley had entered Parliament as a Conservative in 1918. He was later returned as an Independent, then switched to Labour and won a by-election in 1926. In January 1931 he was expelled from the Labour Party and formed the radical New Party. None of its twenty-four candidates were successful in the 1931 General Election and Mosley left for Rome, where he studied fascism. His socialist past meant that there was some interest in him from a number of Labour Party members. Mosley's first wife was Lady Cynthia Curzon, the granddaughter of a millionaire. She was left-wing and of Jewish descent. Three years after her death in 1933 he married Diana Guinness in Germany at a ceremony attended by the Nazi propaganda minister, Goebbels.

Lady Cynthia Mosley did speak and take part in the socialist movement but as time went on, towards 1930, when we began to be aware of the rise of National Socialist movements on the continent, it started to be realised that probably Lady Cynthia Mosley's husband, Oswald Mosley, was deviating away from straightforward socialist principles. Although he had spoken at the Labour Fellowship in the early twenties; when it was thought that he might be invited again towards 1930 it was realised that probably he wasn't the right person to be invited. So in fact my father and another member of the Labour Fellowship, maybe perhaps even more, they were sent to attend a Mosley meeting somewhere else in the country where Oswald Mosley was speaking, and they were deputised by the Labour Fellowship in Stockport to decide whether or not he was a suitable person to have on their platform, and they rapidly came to the conclusion he wasn't, and so he was never invited to Stockport again and, of course, history itself proved they were right in their decision.

Aileen Plant, Stockport

Oswald Mosley was one of the speakers [at the Guild of Youth] . . . it were 1934 when he came to Chorley . . . I didn't like looks of him, I don't know why. I don't remember a lot of his speech. He were a rabble rouser after, weren't he? But I don't remember to say whether he were a good speaker or not. Funny he turned out bad, 'cos I didn't like the looks of him from beginning. A horrible man. Anti-Jewish an' all, for some unknown reason . . . I can't understand anybody that had been a socialist called could go like that, but he did. He did . . . You can't understand anybody as was socialist being . . . Well, I can't understand anybody really as is like that, you know, against another race. You might be against one or two, but you can't understand 'em being against another race.

Betty Crook, Chorley

We used to go out on demonstrations, mainly against various restrictions that the Tory governments of those days were doing, and against the fascists. Narrow escapes from being caught by the police over scraps with the fascists up on Spouters Corner opposite Wood Green station several times . . . The British Union of Fascists used to meet there every Friday and Saturday evening. We used to go up there to heckle them, and they didn't like us. It was only by having a good pair of boots and a vicious kick that I got away from getting caught on one occasion, 'cos they used to put a ring of Blackshirts round the speaker, and I was shouting at the speaker, and they came behind me and they were going to do me in. The police came the other side of the road, outside the pub, the Nag's Head. Somebody gave a shout that they were coming over to break it up. And there was this one great big fellow, we used to call him Ernie, standing in front of me, and I thought, 'If I don't get away I'm going to get pinched. I'm sorry, Ernie, there's only one way.' And he got one in the shin. I was clear then.

Tom Riley, Tottenham

I was only about eighteen. Trying to get a workmate, a girl, interested in politics. 'You come down to the town hall, so-and-so's speaking tonight'. So when we got home my Dad says, 'Had someone round from the Labour Hall to say be on your toes tonight.' The Communist Party had phoned up the Labour Hall to tell them that the Blackshirts were out, really out – Mosley's – was out to get into the town hall, break up the meeting and do as much damage as they can do. I says 'Of course they won't, Dad.' Dad was steward, and I said I wouldn't do anything 'cos of taking my mate. I dearly wanted to get her interested in politics, so I wanted to sit with her. Anyway, when we got to the town hall, the balcony was full before the rest of the hall, and I remember saying to him, 'Fancy that, they've filled up the balcony'. Anyway, the meeting started, hadn't been going long, when all of a sudden Union Jacks come fluttering out, *Land of Hope and Glory*, oh, that does annoy me, *Land of Hope and Glory*. My friend was next to me, there was shouting and hollering – what a thing to take her to. In come the police. Locked us all in! Dad was saying, 'Vi, you and Sue get in the bandstand'. Like hell I'm going in there. Anyway, they did beat us up. They did beat us up. The police thought they were doing well, like, in controlling it. And we couldn't do anything about it. And my mind goes back to it now that I saw grey-haired women up there shaking the Union Jack, you know, and 'We want Hitler! We want Hitler!' and the fascist salute. And you know it frightened me. Not for the violence, but for people's thoughts . . . That's when I changed my mind about Great Britain. You're not what I thought you were. Because there were these people who were willing to co-operate with Hitler.

Vi Willis, Ilford

In those areas where Mosley was most evident, a considerable amount of opposition was organised by the Communist Party. We are talking of an opposition to Mosley which runs into millions, and we talking about a Communist Party which had effectively very few thousand over the entire country . . . In regard to Mosley and the Blackshirts, I don't believe there was any great conflicts, the mass of opposition to Mosley came from members or supporters of the labour movement and of the Labour Party and of the trade union movement. Very small number would have been Communists. One has to put this whole thing in perspective.

Joe Kahn, Tottenham

Mosley and his Blackshirts parade through the East End of London in 1936

NMPFT/Science & Society Picture Library

Mosley held a large rally in Finsbury Park, north London on 3 June 1934.

Oswald Mosley, he used to march on Sunday mornings to Finsbury Park and hold open-air meetings. A number of us invariably used to go up there and, mostly on a Friday evening, we had a meeting at the corner of St Loys Road in Bruce Grove, Tottenham. And our members (I didn't, Bill did) would get up on the box and give a speech and urge people to join us.

Olive Rainbird, Tottenham

In the East End [the anti-fascists] used to have huge demonstrations, and they used to be hurt, a lot of them. And [my husband] used to go sometimes as Harry Pollitt's guardian with two other people, because they used to throw things at him and knock him down, and all the rest of it.

Olive Parsons, London

I did a hundred [court] cases against Mosley in north London or Old Street magistrates court. Two very busy magistrates courts and Ridley Road [Hackney] was very near to that. Remember that the practice of the police was to keep order during Mosley's speeches and arrest those who made a disturbance, and then to drive the chaps away and arrest anyone who wanted to stay and talk about it all, or argue, or make a fuss, or throw a stone.

John Platts-Mills, Finsbury

The disruption was by no means one-sided. Oswald Mosley asked hecklers at his 1934 Olympia rally 'Can you name any socialist meeting at which Blackshirts have interrupted?' Less than a week later the Home Secretary referred in the Commons to an attempt by fascists to disrupt a meeting in Kilburn. Between 1936 and 1938 the British fascists held 2,108 meetings in the East End of London and frequently attempted to disrupt events organised by churches, the Co-operative movement and their party political opponents.[5]

In 1934 Viscount Rothermere's *Daily Mail* ran the headline 'Hurrah for the Blackshirts!' His *Sunday Dispatch* took a similar view, calling Mosley 'perhaps the greatest political teacher we have produced in this country'.[6] His *Evening News* ran a competition inviting readers to give their reasons why they liked the Blackshirts. A number of interviewees failed to win any of the prizes, which consisted of 250 tickets to a fascist rally at the Albert Hall in April 1934. Nevertheless, they went along.

There was a night when Mosley took over the Albert Hall, and we went with the crowds. A vast crowd assembled all around South Kensington shouting slogans and so on. That was when we were actually involved in a police charge in a place in South Kensington where the police suddenly decided to break up the crowd. We didn't get hurt. The leading person there, who was very tall, imposing looking person on our side, was John Strachey who was, again, never officially a member of the Communist Party but he wrote Marxist books and became a very respectable member of the Labour Party after the war was over. At that time he was the leading figurehead of the crowds that used to gather to protest against Mosley.

Hugh Chaplin, Holborn

We didn't get into the Albert Hall, it was virtually cordoned off by the police. But we gathered with the [ILP] in a mass gathering outside, and some people went inside deliberately to ask polite questions, in other words, to do what was necessary to provoke the fascists, which they did. The Blackshirt stewards were very violent, but what was worse was the police conduct on that occasion, because they started moving the whole crowd from outside the Albert Hall, by foot and mounted police, and they pushed us gradually down Exhibition Road, and across Brompton Road into Thurloe Square, and Thurloe Square was a massacre. Because what they did was they shut off the two exits from Thurloe Square, and we were caught in the middle, and then they attacked with foot and mounted police in the good old traditional way, and a lot of us fled down into the basements and escaped them, and there was a general bundle, and I was one of those in one of the basements for some time with a lot of others, because the horses couldn't get down there. And eventually they were compelled to open up and we escaped, but it was an escape.

Jack Gaster, Marylebone

In June 1934 Mosley held what was presented as a showpiece meeting. 13,000 seats at Olympia were advertised at between 1s and 7s and 6d. A large number of anti-fascists turned up to be greeted by 760 police officers outside and, for those who got in, fascists inside. Hecklers were treated violently. The *Daily Telegraph* reporter wrote:

I saw one man being set on by a gang of Blackshirts who seized him on every side. He flung up his hands to show his willingness to surrender and allow himself to be escorted out of the hall. It was an entirely unequal fight. He was thrown down by a jujitsu trick and kicked in the ribs while unable to move. Having yanked him up again the Blackshirts were not content with leading him away, but others ran up behind him, battering him on the head with bare fists.

Seventeen-year-old Communist Christopher Cornford was at Olympia and remembered that:

I got up and started yelling anti-fascist slogans, and a bunch of these Blackshirts converged on me and yanked me out of my seat and dragged me along the corridor . . . I was thrown down some concrete steps and some of my teeth were loosened in a well-aimed punch from a Blackshirt.[7]

Tottenham had quite a large number of unemployed and a number of these flocked to Mosley's support, and this was true of places like Bethnal Green, Hoxton . . . Mosley had an appeal for these people . . . I was friendly with a family in Hackney named Briar and they had three boys who went in for physical training, and the four of us went to Olympia and we were sitting in a row and Mosley was haranguing the audience and one of the boys said, 'When I give the signal tear up the seat and go for the platform', and my natural instinct was to tear up the seat and go for an exit. However, it was a bit difficult to go the other way, so we went for the platform and I ended up on my head outside Olympia and was taken to a First Aid station, where my mother was working to help the wounded. I have never since thought of anything more absurd than me in glasses and about four foot nine tall rushing towards two or three hundred black-shirted stewards. That was Olympia.

Joe Kahn, Tottenham

Alarm at fascist violence was not confined to its victims. A number of prominent editors, peers and politicians were present and commented on the fascist violence.

Olympia provoked the formation of the National Council for Civil Liberties. There were a number of people, lawyers and others, who were got together to observe what went on in Olympia, inside and out. I was outside with my ILP-ers and party people. By this time I was an admitted lawyer. I was a solicitor, practising, and knew quite a lot of other lawyers with left tendencies, and doctors, with Hugh Faulkner and people of that kind and nurses had organised a first-aid station just off Olympia. And once again the police behaved in the same way, and there were a number of casualties, all on our side. Not a single Blackshirt was arrested, although they physically threw people down the stairs in Olympia, and threw them out in the presence of the police, who did nothing. It was quite apparent, and very shocking. The result was a terrific furore in the press. Stimulated by the people who had been observing, including a lot of prominent people, people like Jack Priestley and, I think, Vera Brittain, and people of that kind. And a number of MPs of all parties were horrified.[8]

Jack Gaster, Marylebone

Initially the BUF denied that it was anti-Semitic but, by 1936, Mosley was arguing that 'it was the intention of British fascism to challenge and break for ever the power of Jews in Britain'. In March 1936 there was an anti-fascist meeting in Thurloe Square, London. The police were called as the meeting was drawing to a close. Most of the observers from the recently-formed National Council for Civil Liberties had gone home. A Unionist MP who was there said that the crowd was 'impassioned' and in an 'ugly mood' when the police cleared the area. His evidence was recorded in *Hansard*. The survival of this source probably determined the reconstruction of the events six years later by Kingsley Martin. In an article in the *New Statesman* he referred to the Thurloe Square 'riot'.[9] According to 113 witnesses who were interviewed by the National Council for Civil Liberties, mounted police attacked the crowd and a number of people were injured. Sylvia Scaffardi of the National Council for Civil Liberties, who did much of the interviewing, summarised the events as not 'a riot but more of a rout' in which the police forced the crowd into a small area and beat them with batons. As has been observed elsewhere, the struggle against power is the struggle of memory against forgetting.[10] Recalling the events almost sixty years later Jack Gaster countered the Conservative version in his testimony and made a more general point about the police. He agreed that the police 'shut off the two exits from Thurloe Square, and we were caught in the middle, and then they attacked with foot and mounted police in the good old traditional way'. A complex picture of the event is provided by analysis of spoken, contemporary accounts, and those recalled retrospectively.[11]

Other interviewees also focused on individual incidents of violence in order to make a more general point about capitalism. Lew Smith emphasised that the issue was one of political control:

The police were more blatantly – were trained that anything, picketing or marching, that they were there, but they were your enemy. They were controlling you . . . It's the other way round actually because, after all, we employ the police. I mean, we pay taxes and rates and we keeps saying, 'So why the blinking hell, why are they being called out against us?' And the miners experienced it, and experienced it in any disputes. But I don't want to say they, the individual copper, was necessarily a nasty bloke.

Olive Rainbird said that her presence as a witness at a demonstration was a formative moment. She too employed rhetoric and hindsight:

There used to be the horse-back police who took men and women, dragging them. Two horses, with a man or woman, dragging them on their heels, backwards. And I do remember one black horse in Whitehall, losing his feet with all the scramble, and the horse went down. I don't think I've ever been so angry as I was then.

Subsequent events may have modified people's interpretation, attitude and values, but the memories can be used as a prism through which we can view class and community relations. Within each person are all the connections between the social and the individual. Individuals form society and society forms individuals. Each individual's testimony reveals the history of a period through the relationship of the individual with others, and how people are both constrained by, and create, economic and social relationships. Even if memory is reshaped through time, and in response to received images about the past, people live within the material and cultural boundaries of their time-span, and their life histories can reveal relations between individuals and social forces and changes in experience over time. Each life is a unique sensory and psychological entity but its social determinations are shared by others.

In September 1936 the BUF announced that it intended to march through Stepney. At this time it had as many as 40,000 members, mostly from lower middle-class backgrounds. Approximately 110,000 Jews lived in the East End of London. A petition signed by 100,000 people, including local Labour MP George Lansbury and four local mayors, called upon the Home Secretary to ban the march. He refused. The Communist Party had arranged a rally in support of Republican Spain for the same day, 4 October 1936, but transferred the meeting from Trafalgar Square to the East End. Joe Jacobs recalled that:

> The whole area seemed to be alive. Squads of whitewashers seemed to be everywhere. We didn't get to bed until after 4 a.m. I was so tired I must have fallen asleep the minute my head hit the pillow. My mother had a hard job getting me up for work on Thursday morning.[12]

When Mosley went to march, 6,000 police were on duty, but they were unable to clear the way as it was blocked by thousands of people, immobilised trams, an overturned lorry and numerous other items. Charlie Goodman said

> It was not just a case of Jews being there on 4th October, the most amazing thing was to see a silk-coated Orthodox Jew standing next to an Irish docker with a grappling iron . . . the people understood what fascism was and, in my case, it meant the continuation of the struggle in Spain.[13]

Mosley and his 3,000 fascists were forced to abandon their march. Alan Yates lived with his parents in Watford and studied in London. He recalled the atmosphere of that time and place:

> Nobody had ever been to University on either side of my family. I was at Queen Mary College, London, in the East End. You can't be in the East End without becoming aware of politics. It was the Thirties when the Jewish population were in dire difficulties with the Nazis, Mosley and that sort of thing . . . I voted for the first time in 1935 and I voted Labour then.
>
> **Alan Yates, Watford**

> I was in the Cable Street events, when we all went over to join in the protest against the Mosley movement and the anti-semitism in the East End of London. I recall that very vividly . . . my memory of that is the barricades put up in the streets – They Shall Not Pass. Also because there was arguments about whether Mosley was really anti-semitic, and of course his followers certainly were, I think

his first wife was of Jewish origin. I remember them chanting, walking the street: 'The Yids. The Yids. We gotta get rid of the Yids.' I don't remember marches so much in Southall as street corner meetings with Blackshirt people trying it out.

Syd Bidwell, Southall

The battle with Mosley. We were in the thick of that. I remember that very well. We weren't actually in Cable Street, but we spent most of the day round about Gardner's Corner. That was one of the centres. And then we finished up in Shoreditch town hall, where there was a big meeting in the late evening after the battle was over, packed with people . . . I can remember the crowd. I don't think I ever saw any of the fascists. The whole streets were packed with people. What happened was they tried to march down Cable Street. The police were willing to let them go, but people just blocked it, made barricades in the street and so on. And in the end Mosley's people just turned round and went back. And then there was this great jubilation. I've never known anything else like it in my life, not having been brought up in Paris I hadn't seen similar events before or since.

Hugh Chaplin, Holborn

You've heard of the famous Mosley march in the East End? Well that was on the Sunday and we got married on the Saturday. I came off duty at 9 o'clock on the Saturday morning and we got married at Epping Registry Office on the Saturday. But on the Sunday Mosley was trying to march through the East End. Should we join the demonstration? It was our honeymoon. Our honeymoon consisted of a short weekend. I had to be back on duty on the Monday morning at 9 o'clock, so should we spend the Sunday up in Cable Street, Aldgate? We decided to spend it on Hampstead Heath. This has troubled us ever since [laughter]. 'Where were you,' they said, 'on Cable Street?' I wasn't on Cable Street at all. I'd just got married.

John Horner, Walthamstow

We did have street corner meetings, with quite a number of people, I don't know where they all came from, dressed up as Blackshirts. They wore a uniform that was inspired by Mussolini's fascist movement in Italy, rather than Germany at the time. But they didn't have much joy. Of course, really the coming of the war knocked that on the head . . . Mosley, this former bright spark in the Labour Party, was a key figure in all that.

Syd Bidwell, Southall

There used to be a lot of soapbox meetings then. When [the BUF] had a soapbox meeting, we used to stand round by them selling the [Young Communist League newspaper] *Challenge*, you see, and then when we had a meeting, they used to come round selling theirs, so we didn't actually get to fisticuffs, but it got quite near it. And then, of course, there were all those big dos. I wasn't there. The fascists had a big meeting and there was some brutality there and some [Communist] Party members went there and started challenging and they got walloped. And then there was all the stuff over at the East End, when the fascists were marching down in Brick Lane, but I didn't go there. Just as well, because there was a lot of fighting there then, down in Brick Lane.

Dot Welsh, Paddington

In 1937 huge crowds erected barricades to stop 3,000 fascists marching through Bermondsey, and the marchers had to be re-routed through a deserted area.[14] There was another rally there in May 1938:

The League of Youth, we used to chivvy [the Blackshirts]. They had a march going through Brixton and there was us on all the pavements. And when we got to the headquarters one of them said to us, 'Would you like to come in?' 'Yes, all right.' In we went . . . it was really military.

Fred Combes, London

In 1936, '37 I was responsible for organising a meeting in Redcar based on the Spanish relief campaign and we featured a film, I think it was called *The Relief of Madrid*, some sort of Spanish propaganda film in the Republican cause, and it was billed with special speakers, We put out special posters and issued special leaflets and someone went round and put on the posters 'Meeting cancelled' in the form of a stamp. At the same time on my front window was pasted on some small leaflets, small posters, 'Mosley Will Win'. Obviously I was being pinpointed as an opponent of the Mosleyites, which of course I was. Thinking about it now I'm lucky there wasn't a brick on it. We turned that to an advantage. I'd formed by then a relationship with the local press and I immediately contacted the local evening paper so that the following evening the front page news was about the posters and the attempted disruption and what had appeared on my window. The local printer who'd produced the leaflets turned out a leaflet with a little bit posted on the bottom. The handbill postscript said 'The meeting goes on in spite of Mosley and his gang'.

Jim Tucker, Redcar

In 1938, it looked as if Britain and the Germans were going to be very friendly with one another, and my father had to burn all his books. And I remember, he got word from the Communist Party to burn all his books and prepare to go underground. So I remember him burning all his books. He had endless pamphlets – *The Irish Struggle* and Lenin, all the things that Lenin had written, and he had *Utopia* by Karl Kautsky and he had to burn that too. And he was very upset at that. And that was because we didn't know which way Britain was going tae jump.

Martha Feeney, Glasgow

121

—— : 0 : ——

LEAGUE OF YOUTH MEETING.

The Redcar Labour League of Youth held a very successful film show and meeting in the New Pavilion, Redcar, on Sunday night, when Mr. Charles Gibson, assistant national secretary to the Labour League of Youth, deputised for Mr. Ted Willis, the National Secretary, who was unable to the present. Alderman W. Mansfield, prospective Labour candidate for Cleveland, was also unable to be present.

Mr. Harry Rigg, Stockton Labour League of Youth secretary for Stockton, also spoke. The films "Youth" and "Unite" were shown to a large audience.

Despite the attempts of Fascists to put a stop to the meeting by the sticking of the word "Cancelled" over the organisation's bills announcing the event, there was a large attendance.

The local newspaper in Redcar reports on unsuccessful fascist disinformation
South Bank Standard & Express, 23 October 1937

After the war more refugees arrived, there was little unity between the Communist and Labour Parties and fascism re-emerged on the streets of Britain. In 1946 the 43 Group was formed in London to oppose fascists. Many of its members were left-wing Jewish former Servicemen. It was this latter element of his identity which aided Morris Beckman when he was stopped.

At a riot in Ridley Road I was grabbed by a policeman about my age whose ribbons included the North Atlantic Star. I pointed to it:
'Convoy duty?'
'Yes.'
'What were you on – Corvettes? Destroyers? Armed merchant cruisers?'
'Corvettes. Why?'
'I was picked up by the *Dianella* off Iceland: we were hammered on the way back from Halifax, Nova Scotia.'
'The *Dianella*,' he recollected, 'that was one of the flower class.'
'That's right,' I said 'Are you still going to hang on to me?'
'Go on,' he released my arm, 'You'd better beat it fast before the marias get here from Dalston Lane and Stoke Newington stations.'[15]

Joe Kahn was treated somewhat differently:

You did have the rebirth of the Blackshirt movement and this did arouse a certain amount of feeling amongst the people of Hackney with very few exceptions. The mass of people were very anti-Mosley . . . He continued to hold meetings in the Hackney area, his favourite place was the Ridley Road. These were frequently the cause of a fair amount of arrests and fights. The police who were, I suppose, bound to ensure that he had free speech, were, in Hackney, led by one or two officers who had a more partisan approach to the question. I attended some of these meetings. Although they aroused a fair amount of interest and excitement at the time, in retrospect they are of little significance and, even at the time, I have to say that the numbers of people involved were very small. You had 160,000 people living in Hackney at that time and if you had a couple of hundred people this could produce police protection and so on but we're really talking relatively small numbers . . .

I attended a Mosley meeting at Dalston, Ridley Road, a favourite meeting place and was arrested and charged with assaulting five police officers. As I was being taken by a couple of the policemen to the car the only Communist on the council came running across the road demanding to be taken too because he thought it was an absolute shame for the Communist not to be arrested. When they phoned my wife and told her that I had been charged with assaulting five police officers I'm afraid that she fell about laughing and said 'What? Him? He couldn't assault a policewoman.'

Joe Kahn, Hackney

Since the Second World War, Labour Party activists have continued to support those fleeing oppression. Between 1959 and 1975 Vietnam was dominated by war. Afterwards many people fled from the victorious Communist forces and some came to Britain:

We had the people from Vietnam here, right after the war ended. We had them here and they came for a Burns Night. And one woman was telling us that she worked in a paddy field and she gathered grain. She was now a doctor in Vietnam. A very well educated woman but, I think, self-educated more than anything else. During the Vietnam thing she had been doing her nursing and fixing people up and all that, and they trained her to be a doctor.

Martha Feeney, Glasgow

Migrants included people from Britain as well as other countries. Between 1920 and 1936, 145,000 miners in South Wales lost their jobs. Before 1926 there was noticeable migration. After defeat in the 1926 General Strike there was a flight, principally of those without families or mortgages. Mining was a skilled occupation, but the skills could not be applied to other work, and most of those leaving were classified as unskilled. The process has been described as 'the uprooting of Welsh youths to become waiters in London', while miners' daughters sought work as domestic servants, or as shop assistants. Wal Hannington, the leader of the National Unemployed Workers' Movement, claimed that these new recruits undercut wages in the building and furniture trades and that 'in some London localities where large numbers of South Wales workers have settled, rivalry has expressed itself in street fights between groups of young men'. In 1929 a meeting of former miners was addressed in London by the miners' union leaders A.J. Cook and Arthur Horner and by former dock union leader Tom Mann. In 1938, in a survey of workers in newer industries, Michael Daly concluded that 'the most difficult people to organise are the Welsh transferees'.[16] Syd Bidwell noted the continuities between the pre-war situation and that which occurred after the war.

> We had workers coming from South Wales in search of employment. They'd been out of work for two or three years, and I can remember the top of Trinity Road, whitewashed on the wall was 'Go Home Welshers', on the very spot where I was later to see 'Go Home Blacks'. The very spot. I took Neil Kinnock over there to see the actual wall where I remembered that.

Syd Bidwell, Southall

George A. Pargiter was the Labour MP for Middlesex Spelthorne 1945–50 and then MP for Southall, in west London, 1950–66. In 1963 the Palgrave Residents' Association became concerned that Asians might purchase a house which was for sale in Palgrave Avenue, Southall. The Association successfully petitioned the Labour council to purchase the property, which then remained in white hands. In the local elections of that year the racist British National Party, founded in 1960, came second to Labour, ahead of the Conservatives, in a safe Labour ward. In 1964 Pargiter called for 'a complete ban on immigration to Southall', and the British National Party leader stood in the General Election. He called for a ban on all further 'coloured immigration' and no National Assistance for unemployed immigrants unless they applied for repatriation. He received 9 per cent of the vote, the highest percentage yet won by a blatant racist in a British parliamentary election. In 1966 the Conservatives on Southall council called for a fifteen-year qualification period before immigrant families could go on to the council's housing list, and two Labour councillors were expelled for voting with the Tories. This was the situation in which the new Labour candidate, who had already fought seats twice before, found himself. In 1966 Syd Bidwell was returned to the Commons for Southall with a majority of 5,347. He gained 14.2 per cent more of the vote than the runner-up. In 1970 his majority was 4,223, and he gained 11.6 per cent more votes than the second candidate. Bidwell made an effort to help his Asian constituents, and became a member of the Commons Select Committee on Race Relations and Immigration. Even when, in the 1980s, there were threats to depose him, this was recognised. Mahdar Patil, an Asian councillor and chair of the Southall black section, said that 'the older generation of black people in this community are subservient to Bidwell. He does everything for them.'[17] The former MP explained his views:

I was elected as MP in 1966. The seat had been nearly lost by Pargiter in 1964. He didn't know how to handle the coming of the immigrants, substantially from the Punjab part of India, where I visited, of course, several times in subsequent years. He ended up by calling for a dispersal of people – there were too many congregated in Southall, he claimed. I don't think he really knew how to confront it, but it was getting well-established by the time that I was on the scene as a Member of Parliament in 1966 with a fair majority, which I increased election after election.

Syd Bidwell, Southall

Although Labour won the largest number of seats in the 1964 General Election, there was a swing to the Conservatives in Smethwick, Birmingham, where the prospective Labour Foreign Secretary, Patrick Gordon-Walker, lost the seat to a Conservative who called for strict immigration controls. A number of leading anti-immigration campaigners were members of the Conservative Party in Smethwick, where the Conservatives won three council seats in 1962 after they promised to evict immigrants from overcrowded houses and not rehouse them. However, racism did not go unopposed. In the course of the 1966 General Election, former Conservative Minister of Health Enoch Powell proposed voluntary repatriation and further immigration controls, and saw his majority cut by 3,271 votes. In Southall the British National Party candidate's vote fell from 9.1 per cent to 7.4 per cent and in Smethwick the party received just 1.5 per cent of the vote.

The Member of Parliament [for Brixton 1945–70] was Marcus Lipton, who was a tremendous character. He used to ask questions all the time and, at the annual dinners of the Brixton Labour Party his speeches really had us all rocking in the aisle. He could have been on the music hall. He was so funny. Very much loved. He did a surgery every Friday night in Lambeth and then the LCC members on rota used to do it with him. I used to go down to either the GMC or do a surgery every week. I used to do the housing or the education cases. The local government cases, in fact. It was a fairly traditional Labour Party, not as stuck in the 1920s or Thirties as other local Labour Parties in that area, because Brixton always had a slightly different population to say Lambeth, Vauxhall or Southwark. It had been the centre of music hall. Artists used to live along the Brixton Road. Charlie Chaplin was born in Brixton. There was a slightly different atmosphere there as between the Brixton Party and the Vauxhall Party, which were always at each others' throats, in Labour Party terms. Slightly cosmopolitan feel about the party there. From the middle Fifties onwards you had the problems of West Indian immigration . . . These were people recruited by London Transport and the hospitals to fill the labour gaps in our services, generally the low-paid jobs. This undoubtedly caused problems in housing where some of the large houses in Brixton went into multi-family occupation with absent landlords and all the problems of multi-occupation in unconverted premises. Until it got to the point, quite frankly, in the 1967 election that if I was canvassing a road and realised from the exterior that there were black families on each side I didn't bother even to knock on the door in the middle. It was as bad as that. [She lost her seat in 1967.]

Bea Serota, Hampstead

Jimmy Allison was concerned at the views of a leading member of the Parliamentary Labour Party, known for his support of Spain's General Franco, Bob Mellish.

I managed to go as a delegate from my union to the National Conference of the Labour Party. Now that was 1965, and that was my first annual conference as a Labour Party delegate. What appalled me was the racist attitude of that conference. At that time Bob Mellish and people like that would not want to

All over Britain Labour activists like Irene Wagner (in glasses) campaigned agaist racism

Irene Wagner's private collection

126

allow immigrants into this country and, of course, the National Union of Dyers and Bleachers and Textile Workers was very much based in Yorkshire, which is a high textile industry area and a high Muslim community and I discovered that our delegation was very racist, and I was appalled.

Jimmy Allison, Paisley

In 1968 Powell campaigned against the right of Kenyan Asians, with British passports, to come to Britain. The government introduced vouchers and the passports became invalid. Powell made a number of other speeches against immigration and received widespread publicity and support. An opinion poll held immediately after the 1970 General Election found that 25 per cent thought that he was the only admirable British politician. This figure rose to 42 per cent in the West Midlands. In that area the swing to the Conservatives was not 4.7 per cent as it was nationwide, but the highest of any region: 6.1 per cent. It was 9 per cent in Powell's constituency of Wolverhampton. John Horner remembered the atmosphere and his own opponent, John Stokes, who had twice unsuccessfully contested seats, beat Horner, gaining 5.2 per cent more of the votes cast.

To the north my neighbour was Enoch Powell. I was strategically ill-placed. I hadn't got the votes [of the Afro-Caribbeans who lived in neighbouring Smethwick]. I'd got the backwash and, of course, I'd got Enoch. When I lost the constituency it was very tough. Enoch, not in any way responsible, except in an indirect fashion, gathered around him a gang of thugs . . . My lads around the Midlands area, the firemen, they worked for me, worked very hard and every night we'd go canvassing and then we'd all gather after canvassing time was over in this pub, and this night the tail of Enoch activities turned up, they were thugs, they looked at my firemen and decided they wouldn't stay. They would break up meetings. There were two things; blacks and hanging . . . My opponent in 1970 was the most objectionable man that I've ever come across, Sir John Stokes. He guaranteed to serve all true-born Englishmen. I get on well with people but I never spoke to Stokes.

John Horner, Oldbury and Halesowen

In the 1930s, campaigning against fascism involved more than the conventional political activities of demonstrations and lobbying. It included collecting money and goods, helping refugees, providing medical aid and fighting in Spain and within British cities. There have rarely been votes in foreign policy or anti-racism, and the leadership of the Labour Party has tended to focus on immediate economic concerns. Nevertheless, among members there has been fierce personal commitment to the eradication of prejudice. In the post-war years Labour activists have campaigned against racist immigration legislation and prejudice, not just within the government, but also against fascists and racists within the electorate and sometimes even within the Labour Party. This has led to divisions and to extra-party alliances, the subjects of the next two chapters.

VII

Cross-Party Links

Since its earliest years Labour's success in Parliament and on many local councils has been partly attributable to pacts with Liberals, Communists and others. Ideological and personal differences notwithstanding, in those areas where activists know members of other parties and there is clear recognition of common enemies and the benefits of unity, links have been made. Sometimes these links have been attempts at destabilisation or infiltration, or have been perceived as such. Labour has had less interest in such arrangements since 1945, when it dominated in the Commons, and these issues are considered in the next chapter. Here the focus is on the 1930s and 1940s, when alliances were struck in order to promote peace or anti-fascism.

The complexity of the relationships between the Communist Party, the Labour Party and the ILP has led some people to misremember the events of over half a century ago. In a study of Labour Party activists in the 1950s, 94 per cent of those questioned initially said that they had supported the Labour Party all their lives. In fact 17 per cent had been members of either the Communist Party, the ILP, Common Wealth (all three were left-wing parties) or the Conservatives.[1] People crossed from one party to another and, although the Communist Party was never affiliated to the Labour Party, some people held membership of both simultaneously. Others were influenced, while in the youth section of the Labour Party, by the Communist Party or by other left-wing organisations. Often left-wing activists made little distinction between the Co-operative, Labour, Independent Labour and Communist Parties; 'seeing them as different branches of the socialist family'.[2] As these are memories of time spent outside the corridors of power, mostly by those who have remained in such a position, simply forgetfulness is more likely to be the cause of inconsistencies than any attempt at manipulation.[3]

The peace movement
In the 1930s, when it appeared to many in Britain that a major war with fascists loomed, some people campaigned for peace. In 1933, two weeks after Hitler became German Chancellor, the students of the Oxford Union resolved: 'This House will in no circumstances fight for its King and Country'. That autumn the Labour Party conference unanimously passed a motion committing the party to opposing war, including supporting a general strike against war. The following January, a leading member of the Ilford Branch of the League of Nations Union organised 500 volunteers to test local public opinion on peace and disarmament. The results impressed Lord

Robert Cecil, the President of the League of Nations Union since its inception. The Union decided to run a nation-wide ballot, and drafted five questions. This was before the days of public opinion polling, and the intention of the ballot was to counter the propaganda of the Conservative press. At the time, this was the largest-ever effort in doorstep campaigning. In November the Peace Ballot was launched, with the approval of the TUC, the Co-operative movement, many churches and the Labour and Liberal Parties. By June 1935, 11.6 million people's opinions had been recorded.

On average each worker called on 30–40 houses, sometimes several times. Scott Garnet gathered signatures in Birmingham which boasted, in 1936, 40 different peace societies and 6,500 canvassers: 38 per cent of the electorate offered their opinions. There was opposition to rearmament, but not everybody was against the government. Some sought to appease the Germans, while others wanted collective security against fascist aggression, and others argued that the defeat of fascism in Spain would check the advance of fascism and prevent a larger war. Strategies of the left varied. When in 1935 the Italians bombed and gassed Abyssinians, the grouping on the left of the Labour Party, the Socialist League, and the ILP opposed the call for sanctions against Mussolini. The Communists, opposed to the League of Nations until Russia joined in 1934, supported sanctions.

I belonged to a discussion group in the period '31–'35 and we used to invite people to talk to us. We invited a Marxist, and his arguments intrigued me greatly. We had also a Quaker. Egalitarian views impressed most of us very favourably . . . We were a fairly lively, faintly progressive movement, some of us were very left-wing indeed, and undoubtedly the left-wingers in it influenced me more than the others. We were all anti-war . . . This discovery that the experts, the people who ought to know, including even the chairman of the Bank of England could be so terribly wrong [in 1931], and the discovery at the same time, because I'd just left school and was looking for a job and I combed Birmingham, round and through and through, and couldn't find work, brought home to me how important the economy was . . . I became very interested in economics and very shortly afterwards very interested in politics.

I joined a discussion group and from there it was suggested to me that I should help the League of Nations [Union] in its ballot, which actually took place in 1934 . . . I was given two streets in a slum in Birmingham, two desperately poor streets, and I went round with the ballot papers. Housewives came to the door, 'I can't afford to buy anything. I don't want to buy anything.' As I went round on this quite difficult job in this terribly poor area I thought how people were living on the very edge of subsistence, undergoing terrible nerve strain. I saw how normal relations between parents and their children, husband and wife were constantly under strain because of the difficulties they were facing in day-to-day living. I saw too the terribly poverty-stricken four-roomed houses that they had to

Trade unionists and socialists lined up to support the peace movement on May Day 1936

NMPFT/Science & Society Picture Library

live in, small rooms, nowhere for the air to go through and poverty-stricken furniture and clothing. I saw all of this and it made me determined to take the side of the 'have-nots' against the 'haves'. 'Have-nots'? A very popular cliché of the Thirties.

There were other factors which hurried me along the path to socialism. Books, I think. I read a great deal at that time. Shortly after leaving school I read the novelist H.G. Wells and I read a great deal of George Bernard Shaw. Later on I read Upton Sinclair. Right through the Thirties I was a great admirer of Beatrice and Sidney Webb, and all that they wrote inclined me towards the Fabian view and towards a clear socialist path. [H.G. Wells, G.B. Shaw and the Webbs were all Fabians]. Early on I read Reed's *Ten Days that Shook the World*, and this probably misled me somewhat into thinking that the Soviet Union would perform more than it ever did . . .[4] I read the *Reynolds' News*, I occasionally took a copy of [the Communist Party] *Labour Monthly* edited by Palme Dutt. I wanted to settle for myself, 'What is this socialism? Should I become a socialist?' I was brought up in a very Conservative family, and I took out of the public library a book by a back-bench Tory MP and a book by Bertrand Russell. It didn't occur to me at the time what a very strong imbalance this was. The Tory MP didn't impress me greatly, but Bertrand Russell did. I sat down with a pad of paper to criticise the argument that he made, possibly to plan a pamphlet in defence of Conservatism, even then I was hanging on to my Conservative upbringing, and before I'd finished scribbling a dozen pages I had been converted by Bertrand Russell's arguments. I was a socialist.

Scott Garnet, Nottingham

In 1934 the Labour Party and the TUC affirmed their commitment to 'preventing War by organising Peace' and a vicar, Dick Sheppard, wrote to the press asking people to sign a statement saying 'I renounce war and never again, directly or indirectly will I support or sanction another'. Fifty thousand people signed and the Peace Pledge Union was formed in 1935.

In 1935 I can remember the Peace Pledge Union and the League of Nations Union running a peace ballot. We carried it door to door. I was living in Watford. I was at the University. We had to answer questions which got an 80 or 90 per cent 'yes'. 'Do you approve of collective security?' Of course we all did. The last question was the only one which divided the country then. 'Would you be prepared to fight if necessary to sustain peace?' It split the country about half and half. You remember the Oxford Union said they wouldn't fight for King and Country . . . There was a general feeling, following the Peace Pledge Union ballot that we really ought to have collective security.

Alan Yates, Watford

The first time I started knocking on doors was the Peace Ballot. What we had to do was to deliver a form for people to fill in and answer questions, and then we had to go and collect it again. It was as simple as that. In Redcar a committee was formed in order to organise the Peace Ballot, and they held a series of meetings throughout the whole of the town, and I attended all of them in order to interest people locally and also to recruit assistance in order to get down to the job of delivering and collecting. I've only got a vague recollection of what the questions were now but it was based on the League of Nations Union.

Jim Tucker, Redcar

United and Popular Fronts

The Communist Party sought affiliation to the Labour Party soon after its foundation in 1920. Its application was rejected, and in 1921 the Communists stood a candidate against Labour Party leader Ramsay MacDonald in a by-election. The following year the Communist Party called for a united front and showed some support for Labour. Labour barred Communist Party delegates from the 1922 party conference, but two members of the Communist Party were returned to Parliament with Labour support in the General Election that year, and the Communist Party ran only six candidates of its own. Links between the two parties continued at local level, and six official Labour candidates who were in the Communist Party, and two other Communist Party members, stood in the 1923 General Election. The following year, in which Labour formed a minority government with the support of the Liberals, it initiated a prosecution against the editor of a Communist Party journal. Communist Party affiliation was rejected more decisively, and Communist Party members became ineligible for Labour Party membership. Despite protests there were expulsions and, by 1927, thirteen local Labour Parties had been disbanded over this issue. In 1928 the Communist Party decided to spurn the Labour Party as a capitalist party. The 1929 Communist manifesto defined the new policy as that of 'Class against Class'.

In the face of the threat posed by fascism, left-wing activists were divided as to tactics. In 1932 the ILP voted to disaffiliate from the Labour Party following an argument about the party to which the ILP MPs were answerable. The ILP moved leftwards and, by 1935, the number of members had declined by 60 per cent. Isa Paton remembers the effect on her household:

About the middle of the 1930s there was a kind of break-up of the ILP, and my father joined the Labour Party. Both my father and mother, from 1914, right on to the time they died were members of either the ILP or the Labour Party, and my mother lived to be ninety-three.

The alleged inconsistency, that the left-wing ILP could be affiliated to the Labour Party but the Communist Party could not, was removed. In 1933 a campaign for a united front against fascism began when the Communist Party ceased to vilify the

Labour Party and attempted to interest the ILP and Labour in joint activity. The ILP accepted the invitation. Labour rejected the idea of affiliation and was uneasy about joint action.[5] In 1935 the Communist Party decided to support the formation of a Popular Front of all anti-fascists, as opposed to a United Front only of socialists. However, the broader Popular Front had to be preceded by a United Front. The Communist Party once again sought affiliation to Labour and was rejected.

Although some people were openly in both parties, such as Denis Healey, who was both chair of the Oxford University Labour Club and a Communist, the official Communist Party policy was to infiltrate the Labour Party secretly.[6] Communist Douglas Hyde described how he gradually recruited members of the local Labour Party and sought to get likely converts on to the executive. He called a meeting, and only then

revealed that everyone present was already a Communist Party member, and suddenly they realised what had happened and just what strength the party already had in the local Labour movement. Then we got down to business . . . we functioned as a Communist Party group, continuing to keep our membership secret and working inside the Labour party and Trades Council . . . We decided it would be a good idea to have a local Labour Party paper, which would in fact reflect Communist Party policy . . . It was of course published as a Labour Party organ. . . .

The ILP joined the Communists in a United Front – but this was not popular with many members

[After Chamberlain returned from Munich, the decision was made that Communists should publicly leave the Labour Party.] Almost the whole of our group resigned from the Labour Party, getting maximum publicity for their action . . . The Labour Party in that Division was all but wrecked, losing all its active and leading members at one move, and a brand 'new' Communist Party branch appeared on the scene.[7]

The ambivalence about the relationship between the two parties in Manchester and Glasgow was echoed in Ilford, where Vi Willis also noticed a blurring of the edges.

We had two headmasters. The Green brothers. And they were – don't say, 'cos they were headmasters – daren't say they were communists. So we just used to say they were very red. They were practically communist. And they used to get all the literature, all the pictures and everything. Come and speak at the meetings. The chairman used to put it over as, they've come to let us know how other people in the world live . . . Then they'd pass all, mostly Russians in their national costumes, doing the dances and the schools, education, and we got it in that way. Let people see that you can do these things. You haven't got to have a revolution – there was no need for revolution here. You put your cross on a paper and eventually you get this.

Vi Willis, Ilford

[My mother] in 1931 went on a delegation to Russia . . . I think it was organised by, possibly by the Communist Party. I don't know. But my mother was a very active co-operator, as was my father, and the Co-operative movement came into it, and I think they were perhaps asked. And the position would be, men wouldn't be able to get time off their work, and they would be looking for women to swell the delegation. I can only make that assumption, but she certainly went to Russia for six weeks in the early Thirties.

Isa Paton, Glasgow

I joined the YCL, which was the youth wing of the Communist Party. I continued my Labour Party membership. From 1936 onwards, at least in south Manchester, there was an increasing number of Communist Party members who were members of the local Labour Party branches. We never had any fiat from on high saying we must throw out any Communist Party members. It must have been suspected, if not definitely known to the local organiser, but he never took any action.

We did have faction meetings, so that before a meeting of the Labour Party organisation there would be a separate meeting of the Communist Party members, who would be attending that Labour Party meeting, for us to decide what line we were going to take at the Labour Party meeting. It was rather like a Labour group

SUBSCRIPTIONS do not count for membership UNLESS
a stamp is affixed for every month's subscription paid.

Manchester Central .... *Branch*

| Member's Name | *H. O. Heather* | *Roll No.* |

Address ....

Branch meets at ....

on .... *Monthly Subscription*

Secretary .... *F. Lewis* *1/4*

| | April | May | June | July | August | *Card Issued* |
| I.L.P. One Month Sub. paid | | | | | | *March* 1940 |

NOTICE — Members 2 months in arrears

Members two months in arrears of
contributions will be reported to the
branch committee. If such members do
not then clear their arrears they will be
lapsed from membership of the Y.C.L.

Regular payment of contributions is
the first obligation of every member of
the Y.C.L.

CARD No.
B 3139   *Secretary*

Printed by the Marston Printing Co. (T.U.
throughout), Nelson Place, Oxytan St., London.

Young Communist League
of Great Britain

16, King St., Covent Garden, London,
W.C.2

The holder of
this card is a
Champion of Unity

1937

Owen Heather's membership cards show that he was a member of several left-wing parties

Owen Heather's private collection

on the council meeting to decide what line they were going to take at the council committee or full council meeting.

Owen Heather, Withington

Membership of the Communist Party did not rise above 11,000 until the late 1930s when it rose to around 18,000 as middle-class intellectuals joined. Labour's organiser for the Home and Southern Counties argued that the Communists were influential in his area because:

> Party experience is briefer and the steadying influence of historical background is more scanty than in any other district. The immigration of a huge population, most of it young, whose roots have been torn from their natural soil and have not yet taken hold of the new, predisposes the acceptance of what is presented as a new and challenging, though old and spurious, doctrine.

Labour's leader of the London County Council, Herbert Morrison, added:

> When one looks at the names of London local Labour Parties which are for the Popular Front, one notices the predominance of parties which are notably deficient in the carrying through of real Labour Party work.[8]

In those middle-class areas where support for Labour was limited, an alliance with another left-wing party appeared to be a more valid option than it did in those areas where alliances seemed unnecessary. The Labour leaders were uneasy about such close links, and some members recalled their distrust of the Communists:

> We argued about the Russian trials and their theoretical authenticity. My husband was very logical, and he was very sceptical about all the claims that Russia put out.
>
> **Margaret Lawson, Edinburgh**

> During the course of my membership of the Party I've had to fight Communists who'd infiltrated the party, and afterwards the Militants. And the Communists, they used to affiliate to the party, and this was quite an important problem as far as the question of one member one vote is concerned. They would pay their political levy and be involved in the workings of the party, and they used to be active members of the Communist Party. This was in the 1930s, 1940s and so on.
>
> **Fred Combes, Southwark**

Many Labour Party members supported joint action against fascism. Hugh Chaplin explained how those around him felt then, adding that some have tried to marginalise that part of their lives:

It was the air you breathed, it's all round you. And all those people, whatever they may say now, were very influenced, very much influenced by Marxism, by the Russian Revolution and so on . . . Everybody who was against Franco was working together – we didn't make political distinctions – Liberals, Communists, Labour Party, whatever it was, we were anti-fascist and, of course, we campaigned hard against Chamberlain at the time of Munich.

Hugh Chaplin, Holborn

In 1936 a group within the Labour Party, the Socialist League, supported the Communist Party's application for affiliation to the Labour Party. The League was largely made up of members of the ILP who did not wish to leave Labour.[9] The ILP, and most of the Labour left, supported the United Front but at first rejected the Popular Front, arguing that, as fascism was a form of capitalism and that capitalism had to be dismantled in order to stop it, it followed that only socialism could stop fascism. The Communist Party sought affiliation to the Labour Party as a phase in its Popular Front strategy. The Popular Front strategy assumed that fascism was a choice made by capitalists, and that an alliance with supporters of capitalism, such as Liberals, would not be harmful. The ILP and the Labour left supported the United Front as an end in itself. Some constituencies which supported united action with the Communist Party were disciplined by the national leadership. Hampstead supported the United Peace Alliance, a *Reynolds' News*-sponsored grouping, and joint Communist Party and Labour Party Councils of Action to promote the United Peace Alliance were established in some areas.[10]

On going to Manchester University in 1936 I became a member of the Communist Group there; about a dozen of us used to meet weekly and discuss how to influence our fellow students. Each read out a list of his contacts, with a report of progress made. I retained my membership of the Withington Labour Party. I was living at home and cycling each day to the University. We had, each year, a mock election there, followed by a mock Parliament. In 1937 the election was won by the United Front, and I was Home Secretary in the mock Parliament. In 1938 the election was won by the Popular Front by about 136 votes to 40 for a non-political candidate and 16 for the Conservative . . . At that time the CP members who were members also of the Labour Party (as most of them were) were organised in order to have the greatest possible influence on the Labour Party. Those in each section of the Party, whether ward branch, League of Youth branch, Divisional Party (later renamed Constituency) and so on, formed a faction and met together before each Labour Party meeting to decide what line to take at that meeting, what resolutions to propose, who to support in election of officers.[11]

Owen Heather, Withington

In May 1938, after suggesting that there be an investigation into the Communist Party in

Russia and calling for a United Front rather than a Popular Front when the party line was the reverse, Owen Heather was expelled from the Communist Party. He joined the ILP.

When it were this United Front there was Stafford Cripps. I've forgotten who it was from th'ILP, but there was a Communist. You know, there were three. They had a collection, but it would be before [the war] when there were talk of there might be war. And it were against war, really, in a sense, th'United Front. I've never seen as much money in my life. There were £5 notes floating about in this collection.

Betty Crook, Chorley

Already one or two of our League of Youth had volunteered for the Spanish Civil War, so we knew what to expect. It was probably because of all this that we got the constituency party to support the Popular Front against war led by Sir Stafford Cripps, and he came and addressed another mass rally at the New Coronation Baths Hall. Great publicity, high drama. I remember a coffin being carried by the League of Youth, presumably to denote death as not far away. This all got to the notice of Head Office at Transport House and they even sent two leading officials to live, one in Malvern and the other in Kingston, to spy out the land. The leading culprits of course included Stanley Bell and Dora Berry and we were suspended, as was the executive committee. So they formed a new replacement one, and the first resolution they passed was to lift the ban on the suspension and its members. This was too much for Head Office, who completely closed down the party and no activity took place until towards the end of the war. There were lighter moments – when the spy from Head Office in Kingston woke up one morning to find all his windows plastered with Popular Front posters. Was the League of Youth responsible?

Stanley Bell, Kingston-upon-Thames

It was suggested to four or five of us that the Party would do better for our absence. I was about nineteen. It reminded me very much in later life when we had the Militant Tendency, the awful nuisance they were in the LP. We were much the same, except we weren't so large in numbers. We were preaching a Popular Front, which was not unfashionable in those days. We had the temerity, and this is what riled the party in Chester, and very rightly of course I understand now, to approach someone we thought would be a good Popular Front candidate in Chester. We also approached the Young Liberals and they agreed on this person. When we then put it up as a proposal to the Party in Chester they were absolutely furious. We'd gone behind their backs. The upshot was that they said 'We think you people had better cool your heels for a bit. Stay away for about 12 months.' So we did.

John Crawford, Chester

Douglas Hawkins recalled that: 'as is frequent with young people, we had differences of opinion with our parent party, which ultimately led to the Labour League being changed to the Barry Young Socialist League'. The Labour Party conference of 1936 reiterated the ban on links with the Communist Party, but in 1937 the Socialist League, ILP and Communist Party published a joint 'Unity Manifesto', calling upon 'the whole Labour Movement . . . to oppose fascism in all its forms'. As a result the Socialist League was disaffiliated from the Labour Party in 1937 and dissolved itself. After Germany annexed Austria in 1938, Cripps began to advocate a Popular Front of opposition to the government's policy of appeasement. For this he was expelled.

Those with roots within the trade union movement were often disinclined to support the Popular Front. They saw parallels between Cripps, a disloyal middle-class intellectual who expected to lead, and Oswald Mosley, and noted that most of the Labour Ministers who had joined the National Government in 1931 had been middle class. George Ridley, a trade unionist on the Labour Party National Executive Committee, complained about these 'Bloomsbury revolutionaries'.[12] Bloomsbury resident and librarian Hugh Chaplin said:

The Popular Front was started in France, and there was an attempt to start up a Popular Front in England, and there was a thing called the Popular Front Committee, which we joined . . . It was a national organisation, the aim of which was to form a political anti-fascist front of Labour and Liberals. We both joined the local branch of this organisation. Before I'd been in it very long I decided to join the local Labour Party. My wife didn't want to join the Labour Party, she thought the Labour Party was a stick-in-the-mud organisation. At that point the next thing that happened politically was the United Front between the left wing of the Labour Party and the Communists, run by Stafford Cripps, Aneurin Bevan and a journalist. This was the movement that we supported, and we were active members of it. I didn't persuade my wife to join the Labour Party until about a year after I joined it.

The outstanding thing about the local party I was in and, I'm sure, a very large number of other local Labour parties, was that we were supporters of this United Front and we were the Labour Party people and the Communist Party people locally were working together co-operating on local problems, local issues. In fact, very often one didn't know which of the two parties the people one knew belonged to. I can remember one person I knew well, who was a colleague of mine at the British Museum, who told me that she was a member of the local Labour Party where she lived and also a member of the local branch of the Communist Party. And she seemed to think it was the most natural thing in the world to belong to both parties. Although she knew it was against the rules of the Labour Party to belong to the Communist Party. People weren't deterred by rules of that sort, and so we worked together.

Hugh Chaplin, Holborn

Violent disputes undermined unity in Spain and led to bitterness in Britain. In March

1937 the leaders of the Spanish Partido Obrero de Unificación Marxista, the POUM militia, were denounced as agents of fascism by the Communists. Two months later in Barcelona there was fighting between the Communists and the POUM and some ILP members who were serving with the latter. In June the POUM was declared illegal. Its leaders were imprisoned, tortured and killed by the Communists. Bob Smillie, a former chair of the ILP Guild of Youth, died in a Communist gaol in Valencia. The ILP leader Fenner Brockway recalled that he and the Communist Party General Secretary Harry Pollitt 'spoke together from the same platform and were scrupulously careful not to reflect our Party differences, but the inner spirit of unity was dead'.[13]

Cripps was supported in his calls for unity by a faction inside the Labour League of Youth. The League was led by Ted Willis, who edited a newspaper, *Advance*, which took a different line to that of the official Labour Party youth newspaper, *New Nation*. Willis also wrote for the Young Communists' *Challenge*, a newspaper almost identical in tone and policy to *Advance*. Jim Tucker remembered how he and Willis campaigned under the auspices of the Communist-dominated group, the British Youth Peace Assembly for Aid to Spain, for a 'Popular Front to defeat fascism which would embrace not only the Labour Party but a whole range of left-wing radical parties'. In 1936 Willis's branch of the League proposed a motion to the League's conference which was critical of Labour's international policies and, by 1937, the League was so critical of Labour that the conference was abandoned. Bromley League was disbanded for supporting affiliation to the Communist Party, Islington's branch was suspended *en masse*, and Deptford Labour Party refused to allow a League to be formed. Elsewhere the League and the Young Communist League worked together. Willis remembered how the League

> rallied, we campaigned, and our activities reached a climax in February 1939, when we organised a great Youth Pilgrimage to London. It succeeded beyond our expectations: thousands of young people from all over Britain, travelling by train, bus, bicycles and on foot descended on Trafalgar Square. Morrison was shouted down with a chorus of 'We want Cripps.'[14]

Aileen Plant also remembered the atmosphere:

> I belonged to the Labour League of Youth, again it was propaganda meetings, all the time trying to alert people that there was a fascist menace, because it was denied, it was denied, it was denied.

The party acted to silence its youthful critics through reorganisation of the League, and in 1939 Willis left for the Young Communist League. He invited others to follow him and most of the leaders and some of the branches did so.

In September 1939 Britain entered the Second World War. Labour supported the war effort and soon wartime industrial and military conscription extinguished interest

The campaign against fascism and anti-semitism united people from all parties

National Museum of Labour History

in the League. The Communist Party initially opposed the war and, in 1940, D.N. Pritt MP was expelled from the Labour Party for his views about Russia, and Hampstead Labour Party was disaffiliated for the same reason. After the Communists decided to support the war effort there was some co-operation between the two parties.

By this time my membership of the Labour Party must have lapsed, because I think I went along offering assistance as a member of the Communist Party. It possibly reflects the sort of atmosphere that there was at the time that I was called upon to chair a large public meeting in a local cinema. It was partly because Russia and Britain had been allies during the war that there was definitely friendly feeling between Labour Party and Communist Party members.

Owen Heather, Withington

While I was at school I went to various lectures on Russia, when Russia became our ally.

Maureen Dewar, Tottenham

One day I bumped into some refugees and for two or three years, well for most of the war, I was very involved with refugee organisations, helping with English. We had a theatre group and we used to go down into the Underground shelters in the East End of London and put on plays and sing. There again we came across these poor little, poverty-stricken little children, filthy dirty. They did have plimsolls on, but most of them had great big holes in them and little worn-out jumpers covered in holes and down in these deep, deep shelters. Eventually Russia came into the war and, like many many people in my age group and during that time, I joined the Communist Party. Many many people who subsequently worked for the Labour party joined the Communist Party. I remember being caught by the police painting slogans on a bridge in Paddington 'Second Front Now' and, not many people know this, but there were a group of us who were being taught by an older member of the Spanish Civil War, whose name was Morgan Jones. We were being taught to shoot and use hand grenades. We went to this fantastic garden in a house in Maida Vale and there we learnt to crawl on our tummies and learnt how to pull out the pin of Mills Bombs with our teeth and duck and throw it over our shoulders. We were going to be the equivalent of the Marquis, to be the Communist resistance.

Patricia Meitlis, London

Because I'd belonged to the Junior League of Nations and because my whole outlook was against war and particularly imperialist wars, it was very hard for me, personally, at the beginning of the war, to change. Now my mother, being much older, much wiser, it was difficult for her, but it was almost like St Paul on the road to Damascus. She had to struggle with it in her soul. In fact, she was rather poorly one weekend and stayed in bed and she was wrestling with could she support the war . . . She had to support the war because it was against fascism. It took me longer to arrive at that but, because I'd always been passionately interested in the Russian experiment, when Hitler invaded Russia I was so anxious that Russia shouldn't be defeated that I could support it wholeheartedly. In fact I became very much involved in the Stockport Anglo-Russian Friendship Council . . . We collected enough money to endow a bed in the new Stalingrad hospital.

Aileen Plant, Stockport

Common Wealth

In 1942 some of those who opposed wartime unity and, after the fall of Tobruk in Libya, were anxious about the way in which the war was being conducted, organised a new party, Common Wealth. It was not a signatory of the war-time truce between the major political parties and so stood candidates at by-elections. Three MPs were returned on its platform of 'common ownership' of land and industry, 'vital democracy' in elections and industrial relations, and 'morality in politics'. It was a mainly middle-class party with 300 branches and 12,000 members by 1944. By 1945 many branches were seeking affiliation to Labour and Common Wealth had, in effect, brought a section of the otherwise non-political middle class into Labour's camp.

There were Common Wealth Party, weren't there, then? I can remember a fellow, I think his name were Acland, and he were famous.[15] And they were all really after the same thing, in a sense.

Betty Crook, Chorley

The Labour Party had a pact with the Tories that there would be no elections. And I was in Midlothian at the time, north Midlothian they called it. And the MP had been the owner of Coalhole steelworks in Motherwell, a real right-wing Tory and the Labour Party, a section of the Labour Party, wanted to put up a candidate against the proposed candidate of the Tories. The Labour candidate had been selected in 1939 and we wanted him to stand but, because of this pact, the Tories were allowed to select. And a party had been set up, the Common Wealth Party, and they decided to fight. So it was a man and wife, Tom Wintringham, and I forget her name, and one of the Wintringhams stood and a group of us decided to go and work for them. And we got into bad breed with the Labour Party and were sidelined and werenae expelled, but we were excluded, and that wasn't raised until 1945. The end of the war they gave us all amnesty and we were all back in.[16]

Alex Kitson, Edinburgh

Communists

The Communist Party vigorously opposed fascism until the Soviet Union and the Nazis signed a pact in September 1939. The Party then characterised war with Germany as an imperialist conflict. A third of the membership left in the next two years. The Germans then invaded Russia, and the Communist Party changed its view. It sought to cooperate in order to win the war. Across Britain there was widespread support for the Soviet Union, which bore the brunt of the war against Hitler. In February 1942 an intelligence report for the government recorded: '"Thank God for Russia" is a frequent expression of the very deep and fervent feeling for that country which permeates wide sections of the public.' The Foreign Office supported the establishment of a left-dominated Anglo-Soviet Public Relations Committee and, to mark the first anniversary of the alliance between Britain and the USSR, a demonstration and pageant was organised at Earls Court. Although most of the organisation was done by Communists, the meeting was chaired by the Bishop of Chelmsford who broadened the Popular Front by praying, 'May God Bless Russia'. Communist Party membership increased fivefold to over 64,000 by late 1942.[17] Alan Yates recalled the atmosphere:

We formed an Anglo-Soviet Committee in Farnborough as soon as the Soviet

Union came into the war in 1941. I became secretary. We organised an Anglo-Soviet week which was, of course, partly collecting money for Mrs Churchill's 'Aid to Russia' Fund, but of course we used it as a political opportunity to talk about the Soviet Union, which was then attracting a tremendous interest. I ran a series of lectures, bringing speakers down from London in my flat. I had an upstairs, very large room, but I noticed that I had thirty-five people in it on one occasion and people downstairs naturally complained. This series of lectures enabled me to meet all sorts of people like Professor [Hyman] Levy, [of Imperial College] and Alan Bush, the musician [and founder of the Workers' Musical Association in 1936]. The Anglo-Soviet Committee was an Aldershot plus Farnborough affair and, of course, Aldershot was a military centre so we aroused a bit of suspicion, but as long as you were collecting money for the Soviet Union it didn't matter. I went up and down on the organ at the cinema for a week before the films making appeals. I stood beside the organists as we rose out of the bowels of the earth.

But even more exciting was the theatre, which had a sort of series of strip-tease shows for soldiers. As soon as the curtain went down at the end of the first part, I appeared on the stage. I used to make an appeal for aid for Russia. The last turn on the stage before the interval was Fifi the French fan dancer. She had to subside on to the stage in a series of feathers and there was a blackout then and she rushed into the wings past me and then I followed her out on to the stage and made my appeal. One night I was busy talking to the lighting chap, probably about the Soviet Union or something, and he pulled all the lights out except one leaving a single light so that she had, rather ignominiously, to come into the wings past me. Expressing herself in French she said, 'Forgot my bloody blackout'. Those were exciting days and we did a good job I think politically and raising money too.

Alan Yates, Farnborough

During the war the Communist Party had got highly organised in this country, and had got control of some of the trade unions, from the management point of view, and were able to propagate, through their monthly magazines and their meetings, messages to working people: 'You have rights. Fight for them!' And I think this stimulated people who had no knowledge of politics or trade unionism to become more active.

Mike Turner, Ruislip

After the war the Labour Party gained power at national level without forming any alliances. It rejected the Communist Party's application for affiliation in 1946 and characterised Communists as conspirators when the Party supported the 1948 Dock Strike. However, some supporters still showed interest in the Communists.

I've always voted Labour except once. In a local election in the borough of Walthamstow. It was probably about 1949, or early Fifties there was a Labour candidate, there was a Conservative candidate and there was a Communist candidate, and the Communist candidate was a man of some distinction whose name was Alan Winnington and he was the brother of the famous *News Chronicle* film critic, Richard Winnington. Alan Winnington himself was an intellectual of considerable distinction and not the sort of man normally one would find in a local council, so a friend of mine on the [school] staff and I both thought, 'Well, we're not Communists and this man is a Communist, but none the less it looks as if he might put a bit of ginger into the council in many ways,' so we voted he and I for Alan Winnington. And the result? I do not swear to the exact figures but I do swear to the gaps between the parties. The result was Conservatives 752, Labour one behind 751, Communist two more behind 749. So the only time I did not vote Labour I got the Tories in.

Jack Lodge, Walthamstow

The Communist Party then decided to establish, or take over, organisations which would attract sympathisers. These included the British-China Friendship Committee and the World Peace Council. The Labour Party issued a list of Proscribed Organisations to which Labour party members were not allowed to belong. Jim Mortimer, vice-chair of the British-China Friendship Association, was forced to leave the party. He remembers how, as a supporter of Bevan, 'Recognition of China, that was another main issue. The Chinese Communist government, should it be able to take its seat in the United Nations?' However, he returned and later became the Labour Party General Secretary 1982–85.

The uneven electoral and ideological development of the Labour Party has led to a varied policy on pacts. It has benefited from them at both local and national level and also scorned them, sometimes simultaneously. Activists have sought to find common cause with Liberals, Communists and others over particular policies and also sought electoral advantage over them in order to aid the Labour Party. These ambiguities have led to rows and expulsions and it is to this aspect of party life that we now turn.

VIII
Party Debates

Interviewees did not only relate their own successes or talk about achievements. They recognised that tense negotiations and power struggles are also part of the Labour Party. Social events can lead to fellowship but also to people feeling burdened by the need for organisation. Publicising socialism through flyposting or the production of a local newspaper can be expensive, time-consuming and not lead to any obvious shifts of local opinion. Lack of success in an election can lead to acrimony and disillusion, and success to a broadening of membership which includes those fundamentally at odds with the party leadership. Discussions can lead to squabbles and divisions between factions within the Party, while the stifling of debate can lead to frustration and a sense among some activists that membership is futile. Some of the divisions are institutionalised into organisations and, in this chapter, attention is initially focused on some of the factions in the Labour Party since the Second World War. In the later section the spotlight is on the discriminatory attitudes of some Labour Party members. These reflect divisions in society between men and women and between Christian denominations. As social attitudes and awareness have changed, so has the Labour Party. Some Labour Party members find sects or tendencies easier to deal with than more ingrained attitudes. Nottingham Constituency Party chair Hassan Ahmed found that:

> My black consciousness sharpened more and more as a result of my and others' experiences in the Labour Party . . . I heard many stories of how black people had tried to get nominated for the council but they never got through . . . They were never looked at as political equals.[1]

In London there was a Labour Party chair of housing who boasted of how he discriminated against black people, while a colleague on the same council mentioned the racism of councillors.[2] When a new group came to dominate that particular party it ensured that the Labour council became the first local authority to evict a white family for racial harassment, abolished the residential requirement for housing and the practice of demanding to see black people's passports before considering their housing applications.

Bevan and the left

In order to recruit younger members, those in positions of authority have often promised opportunities for debate and a degree of autonomy. However, perhaps because they do not have the responsibilities of office, the younger members have often moved leftwards and embarrassed those who initially welcomed them into the party. Despite the pre-war problems with radical young members, in 1945 the Labour Party National Executive Committee relaunched a youth section with a new journal: *Young Socialist*. Within six years there were 806 branches, 2,500 members of the renewed League of Youth and it had its own publication: *Socialist Advance*. However, the organisation soon collapsed and in 1955, as it had in 1936 and 1940, the Labour Party closed down its youth section at national level because it had fallen into the hands of Marxists. The remaining branches of the League reverted to being Youth Sections in 1956.

The decline in interest from the young continued, and by 1959 there were only 262 sections. The Labour Party once again organised a relaunch and the Young Socialists was formed, with its first national committee elected at a conference in 1961. This organisation was also taken over, and in 1965 it was relaunched as the Labour Party Young Socialists. Although in the past the infiltration had been by Stalinists, there had always been other currents. In the 1930s there was a Trotskyist group called the Militant Labour League within the Labour League of Youth. A sect broke away from this and became the Workers' International League. In August 1941, on the anniversary of the assassination of Trotsky, its leaders Ted Grant and Gerry Healy addressed a meeting at which the chair was Syd Bidwell. The two groups merged again in 1944 and became a separate party which was formally disbanded in 1950. Syd Bidwell recalled that period:

> The Communist Party members didn't like me because I was a Trotskyist and they were basically Stalinists, they thought Russia could do no wrong. Later their attitudes were to evolve and change, of course, in the light of greater knowledge, but at that particular time I was caught between two schools. I wasn't loved by the right wing of the Labour Party and I wasn't loved by the Stalinists either, although we did have a presence, and the Revolutionary Communist Party came into being as a result of the merger of four Trotskyist organisations. We did have delegates, we were a very lively grouping, we did have many delegates to the local Trades Council. But the Stalinists were gunning for me, they wanted to shove me out. I was the treasurer then of the local Trades Council. But that's all water under the bridge, and many of these people who were going for me then ended up as quite good friends in the light of the experiences of the subsequent working-class struggle after the war.

> Morgan Phillips, General Secretary of the Labour Party, was able to say that the fact that I was a member, or had been a member, of the Revolutionary Communist Party, which stayed in existence for two or three or four years after the war, didn't matter, because they'd never got round to putting the organisation on the proscribed list of organisations that would disqualify me if I wanted to become a member of the Labour Party.

Syd Bidwell, Southall

Syd was one of the many former RCP members who joined the Labour Party. Some, including Healy, were expelled but others, including John Lawrence, continued to be members. In his case this was despite the fact that in 1954 the Labour Party banned the Trotskyist *Socialist Outlook* newspaper which he edited. He became a councillor in St Pancras in 1953 and was council leader from 1956–8. He was supported by fellow Trotskyists and the left of the local party, who were opposed to the cooperation between the orthodox Labour leadership on the council and the Tories.[3] Once in control of the council the left reduced the mayoral allowance by 83 per cent, broke the agreement with the Tories over aldermanic seats and twinned with an East German town. A £300 grant was made to Unity Theatre and the red flag flew over the Town Hall on May Day, when all the council staff were given a holiday. The council defied the 1948 Civil Defence Act by refusing to make provision for 'civil defence' in case of nuclear war. It reduced rents, increased the building programme and paid some of the rents of private tenants. Lawrence became involved with a Communist-dominated umbrella tenants group and was expelled along with fourteen other councillors. He later joined the Communist Party.[4] Hugh Chaplin remembers John Lawrence:

We didn't object to people because they were left-wing people, but we got a bit fed up with John because he overdid things and he used to do the most extraordinary things. He first was famous for fastening himself to the railings outside Camden Town Hall, when he was on the council. And they used to fly the Red Flag over the old town hall. One way he lost a lot of support was the 'Ban the Bomb' movement, which was very strong, and most of our friends were supporting it and John Lawrence made a speech saying that he did not agree with unilateral nuclear disarmament, and everybody thought that it was very wrong that he didn't. And what was the reason? Because we might need the bomb if Labour won and we had a socialist government in Britain, we might need a bomb to defend ourselves against the United States. A wonderful piece of reasoning. But that was typical of John.

There were other left-wingers in the Party, many of them grouped around Aneurin Bevan. Often at odds with the leaders, they were sometimes called Bevanites or, in Parliament, the Tribune Group, *Tribune* being the newspaper of the left-wing of the Labour Party which was edited by Bevan from 1941. There was also an internal party group called Victory for Socialism. Unlike the Trotskyists, these groupings were relatively informal and open. The leadership knew who was involved and sometimes took action against them. John Platts-Mills was on the left of the party. There was little enthusiasm for him within the party leadership and he was later expelled from the Labour Party. During the war he served in the coal mines of Yorkshire. He recalled the action of the leadership of the Labour Party to keep him in line:

Krishnan Menon said to me in the pits, he said to me, 'Come to London, I've got a job for you'. [The Labour Party was unhappy about Platts Mills' candidature.] The agent conceded to me that his job was to spend so much that first that I couldn't meet the expenses and next that I would be sacked if I won. I would be turned out of Parliament for exceeding expenses. He kept two books. There was the rightful book and we were vastly overspent . . . Will Webster [the agent] agreed to destroy the honest books, so I was in the clear.

John Platts-Mills, Finsbury

Although John Platts-Mills was often isolated, there were other prominent, well-organised and long-established left-wingers in the Labour Party.

At various times I was member of left-wing groups. I can't remember the years now, but I was a member of Victory for Socialism – that wasn't proscribed. I was a member of what we privately called the Bevanite Second Eleven, which was a group of people, who some of them subsequently became quite prominent. We used to meet and we supported the Bevanite line, Aneurin Bevan. But we weren't the front rank of Aneurin Bevan and Barbara Castle, and Crossman, and so on. We used to meet in the House of Commons. Victory for Socialism, I think that was a little later, but I was a member of the executive of Victory for Socialism. We had Sidney Silverman, of course, Fred Messer MP, Steven Swingler, I think. And then, on the Second Eleven, I can't remember how closely associated they were at the time but there was a whole group which used to move around which included Betty Boothroyd, who's now the Speaker, she was sympathetic. Jo Richardson, who's on the Labour Party Executive. I don't know whether we had formal membership, I don't think we had, just people who would get together because we were sympathetic, to do what we could to help the Bevanite movement and, of course, the Bevanites took all the seats on the National Executive for the constituency section. Every seat was occupied by a Bevanite.[5]

[Within the Bevanite Second Eleven] we were united on the main issues. We weren't ranging over the whole philosophy of the left. The big issue at that time was German rearmament, the European defence community, our attitude to rearmament. After all, this was the issue on which Aneurin Bevan and Harold Wilson and John Freeman had resigned. Recognition of China, that was another main issue, the Chinese Communist government, should it be able to take its seat in the United Nations? There was our opposition to rearmament, our support for Clause Four and, I suppose at that time, the beginnings, the stirrings of the discussions about nuclear armament and nuclear weapons. It attracted a lot of people who, perhaps, if you'd had a much fuller philosophical discussion would have found areas of difference, but I don't remember any problems at all because we were united on the things that we wanted.[6]

Jim Mortimer, London

I was associated with the Tribune Group. Things began to form right after the '45 election. I was always a great supporter, even during the war, of Nye Bevan and he had a great influence on my thinking. Well, I was a *Tribune* subscriber and that became the sort of Bible, when we were getting things that we couldnae agree with in the party. And the *Tribune* was the vehicle that I used and, of course, the New Left and all that, all spun off from *Tribune*. There's no doubt about that. These organisations felt that *Tribune* wasnae doing the job.

Alex Kitson, Edinburgh

There were other divisions within the party. In 1947 three Labour MPs: Richard Crossman, Ian Mikardo and Michael Foot, with the support of twelve others, launched a manifesto, *Keep Left*. This was critical of Britain's relationship with the USA and its hostility towards the Soviet Union. It proposed closer collaboration with Europe and the Commonwealth. It was not supported by Platts-Mills, who was closer to the USSR, or most of those involved in 'Socialist Fellowship'. The Keep Left group grew to absorb the Bevanites four years later. David Coates has argued that 'the Bevanites had no organised working-class roots'.[7] However, there is evidence that Bevanism was 'a mass current rooted in the ready-organised party mass'.[8] Three interviewees suggested that the ideas were attractive to activists around the country:

There was a national movement, Keep Left. We set up a branch in Ealing which involved members of the Labour Party, members of the Communist Party and anyone else that was interested. I went as a delegate from the Trades Council. Everything went along swimmingly. It really was marvellous, the co-operation that could take place. It all broke up when there was a General Election. That was it. A General Election took place and immediately polarised all. Communists were Communists and Labour Party were Labour Party and that was it. It all smashed up and never really resumed after that, not properly.

Lex Diamond, Ealing

I gave up the chairman of the party when I went on the LCC [London County Council] in 1954, so I had two or three years as chairman of the Constituency Party at a very difficult time during the Bevanite period. 1950 it was that Bevan and the other two [Harold Wilson and John Freeman] left the government over charges for teeth and specs, prescription charges. There were great divisions within the Hampstead Labour Party between the Bevanites and the others. Holding the party together at that time was my main task as chairman. There was always trouble at the GMC, because you'd have a resolution or they'd want to send a resolution to party conference, either one side or the other, and there was very strong feeling, I mean disillusionment, of those who were on the Bevanite side, and it extended into foreign policy as well as into teeth and specs. It was a time when conference after conference there were rows. [In Hampstead] there was a very strong Bevanite stream, even if it wasn't the dominant one and, of course, they were the most vocal . . . There were these terrible rows between Bevin and Bevan and Morrison and Bevan.

Bea Serota, Hampstead

There were witch hunts on various things in the party. The trade union officials were dominating. I mean the Deacons of this world, and the Lawthers and these people were dominating the National Executive, practically blackmailing them. I mean, that was the 1960 annual conference in Scarborough. Well, you've seen the divide there. Gaitskell just got beat. But the organisation of the Tribune group at that time was fantastic. But it was in the constituencies, mainly.

Alex Kitson, Edinburgh

Trade unions

The trade unions' control of party funds and votes gives them considerable significance within the Labour Party. This is the case both at local level and at national level. Although they were often supportive of the unemployed and others outside their ranks, their principal concern is the defence of the interests of their members. When other claims on the Labour Party are made some trade unionists are aggrieved. On the other hand union attempts at domination within their own industries, improving, or at least preventing, the depression of their members' income and preserving differentials in pay have made some individual members of the Party feel that other issues have been undermined.

It's an odd situation about the unions. As Labour Party members we regarded unions as the great obstacle. We said this ought to be done, that ought to be done, this is what we favour and so on, but of course it's no good because the unions won't support it. We regarded the unions as the great brake on the Labour Party in those days. It was only Frank Cousins who altered that.[9]

Hugh Chaplin, Holborn

Trades unionism, for all the good it has done, has major shortcomings. No trade union in the British Isles has ever written into its aims and objects an intention to change society. All they ever do is cut a larger slice of the capitalist cake. They do not reason that the capitalist system is the root cause of all problems. The market economy is the driving power behind the organised greed of all humans. The market economy is essentially a process of imbibing human effort and defecating shorter lives and bankruptcy.

Douglas Hawkins, Barry

At one time we had to be members of a trade union to be a member of the Labour Party. That seems to have gone out the window. Things have become a little bit more distinct. The party is in the process of being what they call modernised, and so we have a lot of things that fall by the wayside. Whether that proves to be a good point in the end or not I don't know. I'm very dubious about it. I always feel that it isn't the party I joined originally.

Maureen Dewar, Tottenham

Harry McNeill and Joe Kahn realised that trade unionists were not always Labour supporters and, like other members of the electorate, had to be won over to the Labour Party:

You didn't have to be an individual member of the Labour Party to be a delegate to the constituency and a number of trade union delegates to the constituency weren't members of the Labour Party.

Harry McNeill, Glasgow

The Labour Party was split into regions and wards. The wards were all local people and there was a fair spread, that is to say there were workers like myself, trade unionists, there were small shop keepers, there were factory workers, the ward was never very large. Most of the wards in the country were fairly small . . . The work of activists like myself was recruiting, helping trade unionists and trade unionism, canvassing both for the Labour Party and at election times, and sending delegates to national conference.

Joe Kahn, Tottenham

The General Management Committee of the Labour Party was about fifty strong then, and all the trade unions were affiliated to it, so it was a platform for good political action. Today it consists of about twelve people and hardly any trade unionists at all. The trade unions have lost so much power and shut all their branches down. But in those days it campaigned for things like transport, housing, all the sort of things that were badly needed at the end of the war.

Mike Turner, Ruislip

One of the reasons I left the Labour Party, who were so rabidly anti-trade union that I just couldn't see eye to eye to them, having had a trade union background and having always been a loyal member and I will always continue to be. I can think of no occasion of a General Election, or any kind of election when I wouldn't support the Labour candidate.

Lex Diamond, Ealing

I had attended local Labour Party meetings and there was a vacancy in Westborough Ward and Westborough Ward was certain for Labour and I was interviewed by the ward committee at Westborough, but they chose as their candidate somebody from Dennis Works who'd got trade union backing, who was relatively new in the area but never turned up at any Labour Party meetings. I was furious at this and thought 'What the hell, you work like blazes for the local party and do a lot of work and when there is a reasonable seat they do not give you a chance of standing for it'.

Edward Britton, Guildford

I had been General Secretary [of the Fire Brigades Union] for twenty-five years and I felt that somebody else should move in . . . but I was not of that retiring age which applied generally throughout the trade union movement. After my experience in the Communist Party I'd been ten years signed up officially, although I'd been a fellow traveller for a number of years. I'd come out [in 1956], as did many others, feeling 'what did the future hold?' and my decision to go into Parliament sprang not wholly from a desire to rebuild Britain but partially to rebuild John Horner's life . . . People were leaving the Communist Party and their lives were ruined. I had another life ahead of me . . . I was invited by a Black Country constituency [Oldbury and Halesowen, now West Warley]. A short list was drawn up, I was nominated by London union branches. Of course I had the trade union votes cooked, ready in the oven, so I became their candidate.

John Horner, Kingston

Providing support for striking trade unionists has frequently given an impetus to Labour Party activists. During the 1984–5 pits dispute, activists had something important to do and felt empowered. According to a member of the Woking Constituency Labour Party: 'The party came to life: we had something practical to work on, we had a cause'. Brighton Labour Party reported that 'many inactive members got involved in our collections and started coming to meetings again, and new members joined' and this was echoed in Hull: 'We reached out to people in a way we never have before'.[10]

We were very active in the miners' strike. We adopted a village in Derbyshire. I got given a little black badge that the Derbyshire Mineworkers issued for assistance during the strike. I chaired a meeting in support of the miners, and the main speaker was Paul Foot. I did the collection and I thought, I'll start off high up on the scale and I said, 'Well, I don't want to scare you, but who's going to give £50?' And a couple of old ladies from Bramhall on the front of the auditorium said: 'We'd like to give £100.'

John Broome, Cheadle

Sheffield's Lord Mayor in the early 1980s, Bill Owen, a former President of the Trades and Labour Council, spoke of the links in his city: 'The trades unions had built up the Labour Party; it was our party. We never had much of a middle class like they did in Leeds, where the Jewish community and others contributed a lot to the Labour Party.' Local Labour Party secretary and NUPE activist Steven Walmsley explained how the tradition was maintained during a sixteen-week-long engineers' strike in Sheffield in which 'People actually went out doing street collections, producing leaflets explaining the case, it was a new thing that, since the miners' strike'.[11]

Militant

Opposition to the Labour leadership also came from Trotskyists. In 1955 Ted Grant formed a new organisation within the Labour Party which, in 1964, started to produce the newspaper *Militant*. By 1967 other Trotskyist groups had left the Labour Party, and a member of what became known as the Militant Tendency was elected to the National Committee of the Labour Party Young Socialists, gaining a majority there by the end of the decade. Life within the Tendency was at least as intense as that of any of those groupings described in the 1930s. David Mason joined the Labour Party in October 1974 and spent about eighteen months in Militant:

> One day I suddenly realised that after a year my social circle had totally drifted. I only had my political friends left, simply because of the lack of time. There'd be the Militant branch on Monday evening, the Young Socialists meeting another evening, 'contact' [ie recruitment for Militant] work on Friday night, selling papers on Sunday afternoon and on top of that, to prove to the local Labour Party we were good party members, we went canvassing for them every week and worked like hell in the local elections.[12]

Mike Barnes joined the Labour Party Young Socialists in the 1970s and was soon recruited into 'a secret spy-like world'. He too found it a strain. 'If you were even moderately active, you would be asked to attend up to six or seven boring meetings in one week'.[13]

> We had a Militant cell of about twelve and people left the Labour Party rather than stay and fight because they were extremely unpleasant. I've been driven into a corner by them with demands that we were not able to meet . . . Eventually the ringleaders were expelled which took a very long time because, of course, we had expelled them, but there was that ridiculous ruling by the judge (whose wife, incidentally, was the Liberal candidate here) and we had to have them back again which, of course, made them very triumphant. We survived and we've now a membership of well over 100.
>
> **Josie Tipple, Winsford**

> In the old days we'd have political discussions, the cut-and-thrust of debate, we'd really go for each other, the old Tribune left and us, arguing and carrying on there, but we'd leave the hall with our arms round each other, metaphorically, you

know, and go to the pub and continue the debate and really enjoy it. This Militant lot, they were dreadful. They didn't agree with anything, they'd throw all their papers in the air and we were upstairs with just a wooden floor. They used to jump up and down, and the dust used to fly everywhere. And the noise! And we had to take the older people, we had to take them out. They were like wild beasts. It was terrible.

Maurita Matthewson, Cardiff

There was certainly quite a strong Militant influence [within the Govan constituency] which was, to my mind, totally disruptive because they just drove people away, and it ended up that they practically destroyed the local party. They were down to selecting a candidate for Parliament with about twenty members.

Harry McNeill, Glasgow

Then we had the Militants. God, did we have the Militants. We went through an extremely choppy period with them. Then we had the friends of the Militants, and then we had the friends of the friends of the Militants, and then we had the friends of the friends of the friends of the Militants. But no Co-op Women's Guild people, no people coming up through the women's section. Young Socialists, of course, oh yes, but there was a heavy overlap with the Militants and the friends of the Militants and the like. Trade union content, so far as skilled trade unions are concerned, has virtually gone, reflecting I suppose the erosion of the manufacturing base but also reflecting, I think, the changing attitude of many of the people who are still members of these craft unions. The trade union content that is there is nearly all white-collar public sector stuff. Things like COHSE, in its day, General and Municipal, Transport and General, of course. And there is no debate of an intellectual nature. You get what we did get in Cathcart, great set-tos with Militant over whatever Militant chose to regard as the issue of the day. Be it defence policy, be it Nicaragua, be it the Royal Family, be it some tree felling in the local area. But whatever they chose to treat as the agenda item well, of course, it suffers does the agenda item. So one's overall impression, I think, of a constituency party meeting these days is that it's either lively or it's not lively. If it's lively it's acrimonious and, at times, quite distressing, and if it's not lively it's an absolute bore.

Tom Carbery, Glasgow

I will never forgive the Militant Tendency for what they did. The people who came into our movement who were renegades, who were mavericks. They were terrible years, but we fought, and we fought, and we won . . . I'd like to think that I played some small part in putting down forever the Militant Tendency, who played so much havoc in our movement during the years. I saw decent, good

155

people, Labour Party supporters, activists, who cried with their antics at GMC meetings, at ward meetings. But, thank God, they're gone, and let's hope they're never resurrected.

Ricky Ormonde, Cardiff

At first I found many of these young [members of the Militant Tendency] excellent because they had brains, they could speak publicly and they were keen to have schools where we got them to put the two sides of an argument. And they were very good at it. And a number of the very able came from Paisley, needless to say. But then they moved away from that and it became the straight Peter Taffe, Ted Grant doctrine. That is that, that's the line and you spout the line and nothing else.

Jimmy Allison, Paisley

All young people on the left of the party are susceptible to the more extreme views. But as you get older, you mellow. And most of them went into the main party and they by and large became good party members. Some of them held a bit extreme views, but not the same kind of extreme views that they used to hold. This was the mellowing process.

Fred Combes, Southwark

In the 1980s, the Conservative government replaced local council rates with the Community Charge. Militant supported those who did not pay this 'Poll Tax', which was based on those whose names appeared on the electoral register, and this gained them some support.

Inside the Labour Party you came across people who were left-wing in one way and not left-wing in another. And I feel sometimes, if you're left-wing, be left-wing . . . I'll give you an instance. I was talking about the Poll Tax. Now I said 'People shouldn't pay the Poll Tax', and the councillor says to me, 'But it's the law, it's the law', and I said, 'It was a law to murder young kids in Germany just because they were Jews. A bad bloody law has got to be fought. And this is a bad law.'

Martha Feeney, Glasgow

In the early 1980s there was great trouble in Northern Ireland and we were going off to America to our holidays, and the night before we were due to go off the chairman of our CLP, who was a nice bloke, phoned up to ask Alec, how about us convening a meeting to help Bobby Sands? Well, the last thing we were concerned about was a meeting to help Bobby Sands in Northern Ireland. [An imprisoned Irish republican who refused to eat. He was elected as an MP. He died in prison.] And he was so persistent about the whole thing that Alec said, 'That's

156

it, we're finished, we're fed up with the clenched fists, we're fed up with Bobby Sands' and we decided that, the way the Labour Party was going we weren't interested, and we left.

Helen Cameron, Crieff

You always found that when people joined the Labour Party from the Communist Party they were very good at being disciplined and doing what you asked them to do in the Party and they were some of them very good members of the Labour Party. Some of them, of course, have moved to the far right, as is not uncommon. You also discover that quite a few of the former supporters of the Militant Tendency viewpoint who are in the Labour Party have moved further and further to the right. It's not an uncommon thing.

Jimmy Allison, Paisley

Although it has been argued that Labour Party members are in general well to the left of Labour voters, there is some evidence that activists recognise that divisions about policies can lead to members becoming diverted from the central aims of the party: recruitment and electoral success.[14]

It really was, I would say, an excellent Labour Party. There was left-wing people and middle-of-the-road people, but there was no real ill feeling that I hear about in other places. The criterion, as far as I was concerned as an election agent, was the members that were willing to do the work and go out.

Helen Cameron, Glasgow

Any faction, to me, was something the party would be better without. I think we should be broad enough to accept one another's views and embrace them and come to a collective decision on most of it.

John Uzzell, Swindon

These are the left-wing wards, which have always been kept small by intention, so that it would be controlled, but now that so many people are joining it's not possible for them to do so.

Irene Wagner, Holborn

The role of women
In 1918 the Women's Labour League, a separate, affiliated organisation, merged with the Labour Party. Its groups became women's sections with no formal power within the party. There were 650 by 1922. In the 1920s Winnie Smith noticed that 'Men were the masters and women were left to do the soppy things'. She started a local women's section:

Then I found out the women's section were just expected to do the drying-up, the washing-up, run the raffles, but they were never involved in politics at all, and they were never given the freedom so to do. They could never come out canvassing and they were not allowed to speak. Men looked down on them as idiots or just women for the kitchen only.[15]

Margaret Lloyd spoke of the importance of a space for women within the Labour Party and, in Newham, Councillor Annie Taylor, active in the 1930s, was remembered for her involvement in the establishment of a women's section.[16]

I started a little, well, we had a few up and down, just a home meeting. We didn't call it political, we was just, every week, about a dozen people came to visit me. Stayed with us. Made it more a little saving club, I think, more than anything. We would all put half a crown a week in a box and then, after that, we'd another tin. We had a raffle and each one of us in turn made sandwiches, and I made tea . . . anything that went on at Labour Club, we none of us went in a club but only for these Ladies Meetings. And Mrs Shard was there. She was another born organiser and she could get us to do anything. And we'd big meetings. And there'd be a Labour Party Women's Rally all from the North West. And it would be held here and in the Co-op. And it would only cost us a few shillings. People paid in to me and we paid for that as we went along, so it cost them nothing. They all gave me money to pay for the Women's Section and the Labour Party money, so it was all collected weekly and it was done with. No trouble. We'd a marvellous section.

Margaret Lloyd, St Helens

It was more on the social side but, of course, the important thing to the officers of the ward was votes, getting these women together, getting them interested enough; getting them to want to have an election.

There was men round here who was in the Labour Party, who didn't like their wives voting. 'What do they want to go and vote for? What do they know?' . . . She [councillor Annie Taylor] got hit over the head with a broom. 'Cos, being a woman, you see. I always remember, down Alverstone Road – a good road too. The man came to the door 'Bloody woman, coming here, telling me how to vote.' Anyway, it ended up by Annie got hit over the head by a broom.

Sid and Vi Willis, Ilford

A few years later there was evidence of misogyny directed at other woman candidates. Barbara Castle recalls being told by a colleague that: "I think you'd make a very good MP but, unfortunately, women won't vote for women", and that was their great alibi for years'. She gave a well-received speech at a Party conference, 'that gave me my chance' and, after the women in Blackburn Labour Party women's section threatened to stop making the tea for the men if a woman was not placed on the short list, she was selected. Barbara Castle became one of the twenty-four women elected to the Commons in 1945. It was not until 1958 that women were allowed to sit as peers, and she went on to become Lady Castle.[17]

> In Cheadle in the Fifties they were discussing the selection of a candidate who wouldn't stand a cat in hell's chance of getting in. There was a very able woman interviewed and the attitude was well, she was very good, but she was a woman. It really did make you livid because it was so wrong and, of course, that did last for a long time. It was subtle. And I don't think a lot of men realised. They used to say things like: 'Well, of course, if she was as good as . . .' But, in fact, what you found was it would be all very well, but here in Cheadle you've got to put somebody who can increase the vote, not a woman, I'm afraid.
>
> **Tessa Broome, Cheadle**

Another interviewee recalled being the subject of similar views about the role of women.

> I remember canvassing with Oliver in a pushchair [in 1948] and frequently being told, because by now we were less popular, people were a bit hostile, that I should go home. Wasn't this my fourth child? I should surely go home and look after the children?
>
> **Anne Swingler, Stafford**

Local activist Annie Taylor's contribution to the Party was recognised in this 1949 *Citizen* article

On some occasions women's political involvement was presented as entertainment. Leslie Hilliard recalled the importance, to his mind, of a pretty candidate. In 1937 he was involved in Edith Summerskill's by-election victory in West Fulham, and after the war he worked for her re-election. Although there were no formal membership records, a ward secretary had records of 130 people who became the basis for activity. There was little by way of equipment: a typewriter and 'we had a rusty old duplicator . . . about 1908 model. It was not workable.' Hilliard went on, 'I decided we'd have to fight the campaign on the street'. The Conservative candidate, Wing Commander Laddie Lucas, persuaded Churchill and Douglas Bader to speak on his behalf:

> It was an extraordinary campaign . . . Beaverbrook came down to speak for me twice and I could always get these first-class names because it was so close to Westminster.[18]

In response Hilliard purchased an old taxi, fitted it with a trailer and made this into mobile committee rooms. After considerable efforts (in postwar Britain there was scarcity of many items) he arranged the printing of a sepia-tinted picture of the red-haired candidate. During the campaign membership grew three-fold and soon there were 14,000 individuals and affiliates. Summerskill increased her majority from 1,000 to 7,000.[19]

> Carole Tonge started there. Carole Tonge, our MEP. She was Miss Havering Socialists. 'Go on. Go on! You put yourself forward.' So she put a nice bikini on and she got her Miss Havering Socialist award . . . She was our first winner of it. She held that trophy for a few years, and then she didn't go in for it any more.
>
> **Ron Whitworth, Havering**

A number of women recalled the division of labour within the Labour Party.

> We had a postal strike that year, 1972, and the regional organiser used to dump all the correspondence on me and I used to take them round. In the snow sometimes.
>
> **Josie Tipple, Winsford**

> I did the lot: canvassing, leaflet distribution, election work, all the old donkey work; addressing envelopes – we hadn't got computers then – stuffing envelopes.
>
> **Noreen Law, Ealing**

> Women did the mundane things like sales of work, jumble sales and coffee mornings, well we didn't have coffee mornings, we had whist drives, and we'd bus runs. All to raise a few pounds at a time.
>
> **Isa Paton, Glasgow**

Despite sex discrimination, women often played key roles in Labour Party campaigns

National Museum of Labour History

Men in Scotland are very Andy Capp, working men. And they think that their wives – thought, not now – they thought that their wives should be at home, not worrying about nursery school places.

Margaret Lawson, Edinburgh

I was more in the background. I was more the doer for the workers. I had open house and I fed them and did all sorts of things, and they came to my house maybe to have a meeting if the hall wasn't available and things like that. So I was more involved that way, doing things, going to jumble sales, sales of work, getting these things organised, bus runs organised. All that sort of thing. I did most of the background work and let my husband get on with the political side.

Helen McElhone, Glasgow

Things are altering. They're not quite so bad now. But in the old days men were very domineering and patting you on the head, dear little woman, go and make a cup of tea and that sort of thing, and I resented that bitterly. Whereas, when I was with the women we were nearly always in agreement. We worked together and we wanted women to get on. The men were so patronising and macho.

Maurita Matthewson, Cardiff

We used to have a women's group, the Labour Party Women, but I wasn't very happy in it because I felt that really, although I'm sure that the leaders didn't feel this, it was very much making tea for the men and baking the buns. That is what did happen in the past with a lot of political women's groups, and that wasn't the purpose of it.

Tessa Broome, Cheadle

The Scottish Office of the Labour Party were very keen that we would set up a Women's Section [in the early 1960s]. Well, I was never keen on a Women's Section, but we were bullied into having a Women's Section, which I found a bit of a pest, because we didn't recruit anybody. Young women were either out working or had children to look after. I was probably about forty at that time. People of my age were spending all morning baking for the old dears about eighty coming down to sit and have tea. I didn't care for it. But, however, I was made a delegate to the Women's Advisory Committee from this Women's Section and, from that, I got on as a women's delegate to the Scottish Executive. And there were two women from Scotland on the National Women's Advisory

Margaret Lawson, pictured outside parliament with her family, was far more than just an MP's wife

Margaret Lawson's private collection

162

Committee and I was fortunate enough to be one of them. Which involved going down to meetings at Transport House once a month and being involved in the Women's Conference, which was only an advisory body. We couldn't make resolutions at the conference that were going to be taken up by the Labour Party. It was only suggestions. And I know lots of resolutions which were made, both in the Glasgow Women's Advisory committee and nationally are only being talked about in the Labour Party today, in recent years. Nothing was done before that. Also, when I was in the Women's Advisory Committee we started up, I didn't work at that time, I'd plenty of time, and we started a Women's Club for the West of Scotland and I was secretary. It involved an awful lot of work, writing to all the Labour Parties within a radius of about thirty miles. We'd women from Ayrshire came up. And we had this club, the Trade Unions had a club in the centre of Glasgow, and we had use of their premises one night a month and the women used to come up, and we really had excellent speakers. I felt that a lot of the educational part of the Labour Party was in the women's groups because branch meetings in the main or ward meetings were taken up with discussing letters and minutes and quarrelling, and the same with the CLP.

Helen Cameron, Glasgow

I was fortunate because my aunt, who was a maiden lady, used to come and help with my son (she ruined him, incidentally) and I was to get out to Labour meetings. And at election time there were always ladies in the party who would say: 'We can't speak, but we'll baby-sit while you go'.

Josie Tipple, Acton Bridge

I remember having tea at work and going straight to a meeting and it would be ten or eleven o'clock at night when we got home . . . You have to have a wife that's keen to be able to do all those things, for them to put up with it.

Frank Booth, Stockport

I don't approve of this business of women's lists. This is where I think the Labour Party are not being quite honest or, at least, they're having two standards. Discrimination. Now, they're against discrimination for colour, creed, sex, disability, what have you. But they then introduce discrimination in favour.

Isa Paton, Glasgow

I know lots of people don't believe in Women's Sections, but I think it's a way of encouraging women to become political and to take office and eventually stand for parliament, so I've always believed in training women.

Maurita Matthewson, Cardiff

The role of religion

Two Glaswegians spoke of divisions within the party on ethnic and religious lines. As with the limitations placed upon women, such constrictions have not always been acknowledged in print because of their informal nature.

> Another person we had with us was Shirley Williams' father [Professor George Caitlin] . . . He was a candidate and there was eight standing at that time. And there was an interval, and when they went into the cloakrooms the whisper went round 'He's a Roman Catholic'. And if he'd any chance that jiggered him . . . It wasn't a case of Roman Catholics couldn't stand, it's just in Scotland there's this Catholic/Protestant thing, and if they heard you were a Catholic some people, not everybody, some people would say, 'We're not having a Roman Catholic here.'
>
> **Helen Cameron, Glasgow**

> If I look back to the Gorbals situation, there were only three of us that were under forty-five years of age . . . The three of us would go for a coffee after the CLP meeting, and we were clearly regarded as Young Turks and three damn pests that prevented the neat Tammany Hall, well-oiled organisation from rolling along.

> As for the composition of the [local] party, it was predominantly male. There were one or two doctrinaire socialists. There were one or two people who were extremely clever (they were Jewish). There was a high content of Trade Union people, mainly men in dark, sober suits with trade union badges and Masonic pins somewhere, either in their tie or in their lapel and then another group of trade union people, generally from unskilled or semi-skilled unions, and they tended to be Irish-Catholic in their background. There were one or two professional people. I remember there was a doctor who hovered around the place. And then there were the women, and the women came from two contributory streams, one was the women's section of the Labour Party, the other was the Co-operative Women's Guild. They were well-nigh indistinguishable, they did not contribute very substantially to debate. In fact, there was very little debate. I think things were pretty well steam-rollered through.

> What has changed [since the 1940s]? Well, there is no Jewish content at all in Cathcart Constituency Labour Party. I mean, to me, it's one of the tragedies of the Labour Party that any Jewish member who recognised the state of Israel would almost certainly never get near the selection conference, such has been the intrusion of militants and pro-PLO elements within the party.

> There was one medical practitioner who used to come, but he has ceased attending. For a while, I think I'd be right in saying, (and this is a heavily owner-occupier area, although it's also got a large council estate) that the chairman of long standing and myself were the only two graduates in the whole place.

Although the trade union movement is there, although the Labour Party is there, although the Co-op is there, and it's a shadow of its former self . . . of course the bodies are there, but they are not the strong, virile bodies that they were and there is not, at grass-roots level, the thrust and counter-thrust of debate and counter debate that there was. It's been driven out. It's been driven out partly by socio-economic forces and, not insubstantially, by intolerance: like the driving out of the Jewish community. I cannot think of a single constituency in this area which would let an intellectual Jew, or even a non-intellectual Jew through to a representative post. I think that's absolutely intolerable.

Tom Carbery, Glasgow

Whether people despaired at, or revelled in, internal disputes, the evidence suggests that they have existed since the Labour Party was founded. Trotskyists, Communists and other, less well-organised groupings have sought power. These differences, and those caused by disagreements between the trade unions and others within the party, have generally been evident to the public gaze as such factions are formally constituted and recognised. Oral evidence throws some light upon these but it also indicates other pertinent but hidden fissures within the Party along ethnic, religious and gender lines.

IX
Elections

In the late nineteenth century Britain had, by ratio, a larger industrial and urban population than any other European country. However, only one in ten adult men in manual occupations belonged to a trade union. In 1900 the Labour Representation Committee was formed in order to promote the aims of trade unions in Parliament. In 1906 it changed its name to the Labour Party. Despite an electoral system which made it difficult for a third party to be represented fairly, and the limitations on the franchise (only about half the male population and almost no women were allowed to vote prior to 1918), Labour displaced the Liberal Party. It became the party of national government twice before the Second World War, from October 1923 to December 1924 and again from May 1929 to October 1931. In both cases it was only able to form a minority government, and had to rely on support from the Liberals. In 1945 Labour achieved a majority of 146 MPs over other parties, though among the voters the Liberals still held the balance. Labour won again in 1950 but lost in 1951, returning to power between 1964 and 1970, and between 1974 and 1979.

Street campaigning

Although committed to enacting socialist legislation through Parliament, the Labour Party, unlike the other two major national parties, developed outside Parliament. It was 'a working-class attempt to break into political life'.[1] This has meant that the party carries what historian Kenneth Morgan has called a 'necessary mythology' that it is a 'crusade . . . a coalition with uncertainty and ambiguity surrounding the ultimate source of power'.[2] Although activists became involved for a variety of reasons, not all of them overtly party political, and although a sense of a party which had grown up on the streets and in local communities is often reflected in people's accounts of the rise of Labour, they frequently emphasised their role in persuading people to vote Labour. They also make clear the inherent diversity of approaches to the promotion of socialism which the use of street meetings for the propagation of ideas involved.

Percy Redfern remembered listening to Margaret MacMillan in 1893 in Nottingham market place. 'She came with a vision of health, joy and beauty in working lives to be demanded and created by the people themselves . . . We listened with respect, touched by something vaguely, unattainably fine, and then we went back to the [miners'] strike'.[3] There was an echo of this feeling at the 1949 Labour Party conference where a delegate called for 'the old evangelical spirit', for the party 'to go back to the street corner where we came from, to go back to the doorstep, to the factory gate, and to express what is truly within us'.[4] The notion was perpetuated by Jack Dash, the Communist London dockers' leader. He reminisced about the 'working-class fighters' of Stepney in the 1930s and how:

> Every night at familiar street corners you could stand and listen to them speaking at meetings, Labour men, and Communists and leaders of the Unemployed Workers' Movement – that was the way to learn politics! . . . It would do the leadership of the Labour Party good to remember that its growth and development into the largest single working-class party in Britain began with street-corner meetings.[5]

Writing in the late 1930s, Labour Party activist Mary Agnes Hamilton called local parties 'the living and growing units of the steadily advancing strength of Labour in the nation. They are the great training schools of service and of idea.' They enabled Labour, 'a Party poor in money to contend on equal terms with its older, richer, fellows.' She went on to explain that, although headquarters supplied advice and literature and organised campaigns,

> it is in the localities, however, that enthusiasm thus generated has to be translated into solid and sustained loyalty; it is there that elections are won and there gains consolidated. It is there, above all, that the Socialist personnel is created on which the working-out of large-scale plans for social transformation depends.

Through activists' contribution of time and money 'is born a sense of comradeship in a great common effort, as well as a new and vigorous kind of citizenship'. She argued:

> Elections are won by the work done in the intervening period . . . Very effective often is the small and homely cottage meeting, for which some woman member will lend a room and often provide a cup of tea. Meetings, especially public meetings, are often linked on to some local issue, keenly interesting to citizens . . . keen minds can be roused, and gradually directed to the larger national policies for which Labour stands.[6]

Historian Neville Kirk has suggested Labour's rise was often due to a combination of three elements: the development of an industrial or municipal 'issue', such as housing, education or deskilling; a seeming inability of other parties to address such issues; and, 'perhaps above all, the ability of extremely talented and skilful socialists and Labourites not only to identify such key issues but to offer effective solutions (especially in terms of municipal socialism)'. He also noted that in 'boom' towns, such as West Ham from the 1880s or much of interwar Greater London, 'skilful political agency, the careful nurturing of a constituency, by political and other means, assumed paramount importance'.[7]

A number of people recalled meetings before the war, and Marianne Elliott and Harry McNeill spoke of how the traditions were maintained in the 1950s and 1960s. Owen Heather recalled his first involvement in electioneering.

> I can't honestly say that in 1934, 1935 or 1936 there was very much of the nature of political activity. What there was, apart from my going round with leaflets, was confined to the November council elections. Then there was a certain amount of door-to-door canvassing, distribution of election addresses and public meetings addressed by the candidate . . . The 1935 General Election came along and I was very busy delivering leaflets, chalking slogans on the roadway and tearing down Conservative posters (we couldn't afford much in the way of posters and redressed the balance by removing Conservative ones).[8]
>
> **Owen Heather, Withington**

> There were more street corner meetings, soap boxes. The candidates would come round with us and gather a little gang of people, whichever party it was. Not just Labour, Tories would do the same. In Birkenhead at the park gates, big strong park gates, much the same as Hyde Park, when I was a lad there used to be the Communists on one side and the fascist party on the other side. And who was in the middle? The Salvation Army, always in the middle.
>
> **Walter White, Birkenhead**

> The only way that the party got to the people was by having street corner meetings. There's traditional places in the constituency and in the ward. It starts in the ward because in these days each ward, in a parliamentary election, each ward was held responsible for its organisation. There was a general organisation but each ward was responsible for their organisation and meetings and pamphleteering and that kind of thing and you had just traditional spots, in Parkers Corner and the Grass Market and Toll Cross . . . [The chair would] have an attack on the other party and the candidate or anything you knew that was going to deface the opposition, you used it. Then you introduced the candidate, 'This is the man that you should be electing to represent you'. And then he would take off then and then you tried to have a collection, told them how you had no money and all that kind of stuff and you'd mebbe end up with about half a crown or something like that.
>
> **Alex Kitson, Edinburgh**

> [Bill Shebbeare] demonstrated to us how to run an open-air meeting. I remember going with him to Red Lion Square and in the corner, outside the Conway Hall, he set up the stand. He just got up and started speaking. There was no one in sight so, as loudly as he could, he started speaking. And just went on speaking. And gradually people began to assemble and listen.
>
> **Hugh Chaplin, Holborn**

I've voted Labour all my life. I joined the Labour Party in 1937, the year I married. It was very good . . . We used to have large meetings everywhere. Outdoor meetings. It's a pity we don't maintain those meetings outside. I think we'd be far better if we had more outdoor meetings. There are plenty of spaces around and they have carnivals and meetings in parks and what not. I don't see why Labour shouldn't participate in these kind of meetings. I think indoor meetings only attract a few people, whereas you attract the public when you're outside which would then give a fuller membership, maybe, of the Labour Party.

Miriam Crook, Ealing

There would be great public meetings, which you don't have today, and everybody would go. They weren't ticket meetings. Anyone who had a vote would be circularised. Leaflets would go out, so you'd have huge crowded meetings before Labour, in fact, were the MPs. That's how I heard Ramsay MacDonald speaking in the borough of Stepney.

Lew Smith, Stepney

We used to have early-morning factory-gate meetings at Hoovers. I remember going to Hoovers with Bill Molley at about quarter-past six in the morning so that we would meet the night shift coming off the work. There were large factories; we used to have factory-gate meetings at Lyons and in the Greenford area, on the Perivale estate, lunch-time meetings. Because there were large numbers of people working in factories all around that area, which of course are all now sadly gone. Trade union involvement was really much higher. We had a large number of trade union reps on the GMC, and they were also quite generous to the party . . . The party was very sort of buoyant . . . Ealing North was a thriving constituency . . . The party used to have mass canvasses in those days and Sunday morning was devoted to a given area. Probably twenty people even would converge on an area and canvass, which doesn't happen now. We used to have a lot of public meetings, a large number of public meetings at that time and always got good attendances.

Marianne Elliott, Perivale

I was a councillor in Glasgow for eight years and I used to have meetings every Saturday morning at a central point in the area where there was at that time a lot of shops, there was a Woolworths and there was a lot of people about and I used to go out with a loudhailer and do a half hour there, just reminding people that I was their local councillor and I was there, and exhorting them on whatever was the current thing . . . I stood on the ground. But I wouldn't be doing it alone. Some of the members would be with me when I did that.

Harry McNeill, Glasgow

In the face of poverty, high unemployment and lack of power in Westminster, Labour's street meetings and other public events sometimes took a more dramatic turn. Poplar Labour Party held frequent mass meetings and marches which 'served as a crucial means of communication'. When, in 1923, Poplar's Labour council was surcharged by the government, one of its responses was to call a special meeting at which 'no attempt was made to restrain the crowd which packed the gallery and the body of the hall [and which sang] not only *The Red Flag* but also a popular song, *I Want Some Money*'.[9] In West Ham Labour recognised the importance of bawdy street entertainment and gave it a party political meaning. It provided drama and excitement, both during the election and at the count. Chas Parish recalled that 'Us kids would be allowed to ride on the back of the motor, provided that we sang out suitable slogans', and Riva Stanton mentioned the 'big banner – the crowds of kids singing *Vote, Vote, Vote for Jack Jones*'. Listeners recalled other elements of street performances. George and Fred Stokes recalled that Jack Jones was a 'marvellous orator, one of the finest speakers you ever heard in your life. He could have them falling about laughing and then crying.' According to the local paper, when the 1919 election results became known 'Councillor Godbold saluted Mr Groves with a hearty kiss and later danced a "bunny hug" with Councillor J. Jones MP.'[10] There were similar recollections from the north west of England:

> Politics seemed more exciting in those days. When it came to voting times, *Vote, vote, vote for Mr Whoever-it-was*. A lot more people put placards in the window.
>
> **Jean White, Wallasey**

> I remember there was songs at the time [1955], *Vote, vote, vote for Georgie Duckett*. As I keep saying, the noise, the movement and the colour, that's what is missing now.
>
> **John Morris Clarke, Liverpool**

When the Labour victory was announced in Winchester in 1945, there was dancing in the Guildhall and a parade in the streets. Thomas Cole, who took part in the procession, recalled how some people drew their blinds when it passed by because 'it was unthinkable that Labour should win Winchester'.[11] In Edmonton in 1945 a lecturer at the LSE, Evan Durbin, was elected as Labour MP. Fifty years later his widow, Marjorie, recalled the importance to the Labour council of good organisation and street campaigning:

> You can't see Edmonton now as it was. It was long streets of working-class houses, and a lot of them had been put up by the borough. It was Labour, and they knew how to run their local community, they were very efficient . . . Ted Cole, the agent, arranged that my husband should be shown to the electorate, and that he should get to as many of the thoroughfares and side streets as he could . . .

We mapped out exactly which area we would go to. We had some of Evan's students down from London to help. With the Labour ladies and the LSE students it was quite a mixture. On election day itself they got a truck and they painted it all red. Evan and I went round his constituency all day long, standing on this truck . . . My husband didn't like any of this activity, he called it just cheering and wasting time . . . We'd say 'Have you voted, have you voted?' We were pushing them to vote and, the poor things, they didn't want to chase up to the Town Hall to vote. They thought it was enough to shout 'Good Old Labour.' It was great fun but Evan kept saying, 'Oh my God, they haven't voted yet.'[12]

An important element of street campaigning was going door to door. Harold Edwards recalled the local elections of 1919 and Fred Combes, although eight years younger, also has experience of many elections. For Olive Rainbird, elections gave her a reason to call on people and talk about socialism. Frank Booth and John Crawford mentioned that elections were an opportunity to find the most efficient method of getting as many people as possible to the ballot boxes.

I did my first canvas, actually canvassed for a person, Jim Phoenix, that was in the [council] election immediately after the First World War. Previously I'd been canvassing for a party and there hadn't been the same sort of personal contact. Our activity was in the Co-op Party and in USDAW . . . The [MP then a] candidate was not a person for whom I'd any personal respect. While I never voted against the Labour Party and I voted for the Labour Party while he was candidate, I couldn't sincerely canvas for him and work for him. I canvassed and worked for the Labour Party. He was a conscientious objector during the First World War and I respected him for it, but later on he criticised the churches and Christians in every way.

Harold Edwards, Warrington

I've been involved in every campaign in this constituency since I joined the party sixty years ago.

Fred Combes, Southwark

It was such a compact ward that, if you got six people, you could leaflet the whole ward in one night. They had it worked out in walks, like a postman, so you never double back on yourself. That was the same for General Elections and local elections.

Frank Booth, Stockport

There's heaps of places in London that I've fought, or helped fight, at by-elections on behalf of umpteen members. I've been a doer, not a talker . . . I worked in elections in all parts of London. There's literally hundreds of election results and election nights that I had played a part in. I've canvassed, and I still do canvas, and I think that knocking on doors and talking to people, not necessarily about what they want, they will often say, 'They don't do anything for me', and I'll always say, 'Well, it isn't what they do for you, it's what they do for the people as a whole and that are most in need.'

I don't hesitate to tell people that it's the greatest good for the greatest need that should be uppermost in people's mind.

Olive Rainbird, Tottenham

If you get on your feet and you get on the doorstep there is no other answer and there never will be.

John Uzzell, Swindon

When we came to this house one of the first people who called was a chap I knew because he too worked for the city council in the engineers' department. He came with another chap and knocked on the door, and he was delighted to see me because he knew how I felt about things through NALGO. He said 'We're recruiting for the Labour Party'. I said 'Oh, great. You can put us down, put us both down.' He said 'We've got the parish council'. I said, 'How do you mean?' They'd had a parish assembly to elect a parish council, and in those days the parish council was elected by a show of hands, and these chaps had been recruiting for the Labour Party and they'd got a membership of about fifty in a very small area, basically two streets, and he said we went round and spoke to all our people and told them that they'd definitely got to be there, so they were there, and when the voting came up they'd got seven Labour parish councillors there, that was the lot the whole lot, and they'd been all Tory or Independent before. That was a good start to the Labour Party in Huntington. I was co-opted on about three months later. We lost that majority after legislation was brought in, by Labour, to say it should be all secret ballot.

John Crawford, Chester

We could go on the doorstep and people would raise matters of a political nature. And instead of saying, 'Oh, all right them,' and going away, you used to talk. You used to stand there and talk to them. In some cases try to convince them that what you'd got to say was right, and your candidate or your party had got the answers to those problems and explain it. In other words, it was a political discussion situation. It wasn't a case of 'Are you for or against? Well, I'll put you down as doubtful then', and walk away. You had discussions on the doorstep. And basically, it was at times when you were on the council this was very important. They got a chance, not just to see somebody interviewing, saying, 'Vote for Bloggs', but there's a councillor on the door.

Ron Whitworth, Havering

I went to the houses on the outskirts of the ward, that was not reckoned to be a favourable area. My wife had the idea that if you picked up ten good ones from an unfavourable area, you possibly had a little bit of groundwork. It was a theory of hers. You didn't go for the easy meat, you played deep. And the first house I went to, he shook my hand and he said 'I'm delighted that you've called', he said. 'I admire you and your team', he said, 'cos he recognised me. He was one of the managers of the company that I worked for, Plessey, and he came round to me at the factory and signed my nomination papers, so her theories paid off.

John Uzzell, Swindon

He said: 'I don't agree with any of your politics, but you walked up the lane and stopped at my door and I'm going to vote for you'.

Mervyn Jones, Chichester

I lost that seat. I deserved to lose that seat . . . I detest organised sport . . . West Bromwich, which is their football team, was in the Cup Final. Every Saturday I'd visit the constituency and I'd have a long list of visits. That would be my

Mervyn Jones went beyond door-stepping to window-sill campaigning

Mervyn Jones' private collection

173

Saturday's work, round and round these back streets. My agent said 'Well, you can't come next Saturday'. 'Why not?' He said, 'West Bromwich in the Cup.' 'Bugger that,' I said, 'Football!' I don't know how many votes I lost that day by knocking at the doors in the middle of the television match. Every shop shut. The only car moving in the constituency was that of the prospective Member of Parliament. 'It's Mr Horner, Mum.' 'Well, tell him to come back next week, we're watching the Cup.'

John Horner, Oldbury and Halesowen

Although research suggests that many people prefer talking on the telephone to answering the door to an unknown canvasser, and that it is easier for canvassers to ring households than to be fobbed off at an entry phone, there is scepticism about this new development.[13]

The idea of telephone canvassing would have been, firstly, useless because not many people had phones. People of my generation would have said 'You're doing it all wrong. The essential thing is to speak to people and to see them face to face.' Except now you call and there is nobody in and you never get to people, so the only way you can get to talk to them is over the phone. Perhaps that's moving ahead, but it isn't something I particularly care for. Similarly, one could say about canvassing, now in Chester we do it a lot on computers. In the old days in parliamentary elections people would do their bit by writing envelopes and things of that sort and that sort of work isn't required nowadays. People feel a little bit left out, that there isn't a function for them, which I think is a great pity. It's the same with money raising. I understand they don't bother very much about collections at meetings these days. We used to make a thing of it. We had one or two people who were very good at making collections, could stir the meetings up and get a good collection going. I wish we could go back to that and I hope we will.

John Crawford, Chester

Nowadays this house is still a committee room at election time, but nowadays you've got sheets coming off a computer, haven't you, and everything's done that way. But you had to go and bang on doors. You had to go and speak to people, and talk to them, and convince them that what you were saying was right. Canvassing now isn't like that at all. Canvassing now is going out: 'Are you for or against?' and tick, tick. It was a damn sight more interesting, to be honest.

Ron Whitworth, Romford

They don't canvas no more. They arrive in a room with a lot of telephones and they telephone and call that canvassing. It's nothing of the bloody sort. So people never see their candidates. They just get a phone call. And the Tories have been doing that for a long time. It hasn't done them any good. It won't do us any good, either.

Lew Smith, Tottenham

Gradually I got people interested in canvassing for membership. But it was always a hard job to get somebody canvassing for membership. They don't mind going out when there's an election on, when they've got some excuse to call on people. But, very often, I got the answer from people, 'Well, you only call on us when there's an election on'. Which is something we had to avoid, and call on people in between. So I organised area stewards so that they could go round at least once a month. Well, at that time it was very easy, because membership was only 6d a month and they had to collect the 6d, so they had some excuse for going up to people.

Fred Neuner, Hornsey

It depended on how well local wards were organised. I always tried to insist that we had regular meetings, that we had issued regular notices to members. That notices were not notes but also to be informative in the form of a newsletter, no matter how brief, but something which had some humanity about it, not just a formal thing. I used to be quite proud of the fact that people would say 'Davenport's one of the best organised wards in the town'. As far as membership was concerned it was as much a matter of organisation, of being prepared to go and get them as soon as you knew that there was someone who was interested, to go face to face and say, 'Will you join us?' It's as simple as that. In many many cases, if you don't have the right people in the right place as far as the sec or chairman of the ward is concerned, who are slipshod about it and don't pay sufficient interest. If you can get someone writing down on a piece of paper, 'I want to join the Labour Party', and handing it in to the officer and then nothing happen about it. It is the follow up that counts. I've seen those pieces of paper and I've had them and one of those pieces of paper I went round and he was on holiday and I went round again and there I recruited to Davenport a member who, along with his wife, ultimately became the secretary of the ward, became the chairman of the ward, became a councillor and his wife became a JP and I always said, 'The day I went round there I struck gold.'. . . I used to see different ward secretaries changing time after time after time. I felt that the longer you could keep your secretary the better. Two or three years wasn't enough. I was one of those who could keep going. I could stay the course and I have stayed the course and I've proved that. I handed over to a new secretary when I knew that we had someone who could do the job and I then became chairman, so that helps a lot.

Jim Tucker, Davenport

Interest in street meetings has gradually declined. There has been a growth of interest in other leisure activities and forms of political participation. Alan Yates realised this and adapted his style.

In 1951 I wasn't the agent, but the candidate lost his voice a week before the election, so I had to take all his meetings, and usually they were in the village hall or pub. We often breezed into the pub in the village and I'd say, 'I'm here to speak for our candidate', and so on. That was when I became thoroughly familiar with pub politics. I would address them on education, the health service and then there would come a voice from the back, 'And what about ground nuts?' You'd switch in a bewildering way from one topic to another. The great thing was to show yourself.

Alan Yates, Cranfield

For the first time we had got a sponsored candidate, a union-sponsored candidate from the Transport and General Workers Union and we had more money, we had more activists, and we did all sorts of gimmicks that we tried out on people. At that time, in '55, rationing of some stuffs was still on and we did a gimmick for the old age pensioners. I packed two halls. I got a couple of comedians, Labour supporters, to come, and we had 1,000 at one meeting and about 1,200 at the other. Pensioners. And our majority was really slim. We won the '45 election with just over 2,500. We won the '50 election wi' about 1,500. We won the '51 election wi' about 1,200. And Labour representation was disappearing like snow off a dyke. And '55 came and everybody was on edge in the party, and our majority was 1,200 or something, so these gimmicks did a lot for us . . . It was worth it. We won.

Alex Kitson, Edinburgh

Impromptu carnivals were never central to Labour's strategy. Stanley Bell spoke about the transition from League of Youth frolics to more mainstream electioneering and Jim Tucker stressed the importance of maintaining good organisation and a high profile between elections. In the 1950s Labour had over a million individual members and was well served with agents. As numbers began to fall in the 1960s, the administrative burden fell on those left behind, many of whom had less time for political education and agitation.

We became a strong and forceful part of the Kingston Constituency Labour Party, which embraced Kingston, Malvern and Surbiton. We led demonstrations, canvassing, trips to Labour Party rallies, and had one at the old Crystal Palace just before it went up in flames, no fault of ours. Many of us held lots of offices in the constituency and local parties and, on one occasion when there was a by-election in the Surbiton division of the Surrey county council, we were given the

Labour keeps its promises

BEDFORDSHIRE COUNTY COUNCIL ELECTION — CRANFIELD DIVISION

VOTE FOR

YATES

on APRIL 8th

Alan Yates campaigned for many people and was also a candidate in several elections

Alan Yates' private collection

job of running the thing entirely on our own . . . In 1937 we had a by-election, parliamentary, due to the elevation to the peerage of Sir George Penny. We were asked to steward a mass rally at the Old Baths Hall where Clement Attlee came to address the meeting. In the November I was persuaded to stand as a Labour candidate for Norbiton and, together with a good local trade union secretary and in spite of another great fight, we lost by about fifty votes. But this time we forced the opposition to come out as Tories, thus ending the farce of 'No party politics.' I stood again in 1938, this time with a local teacher and lay preacher, but again just failed to win. The tide hadn't quite turned.

Stanley Bell, Kingston-upon-Thames

Candidates

Making friends in the area and being accessible to constituents made for popular candidates, as a number of interviewees noted. In Newham Riva Stanton recalled that: 'you could get hold of [Councillor] Tommy [Groves] at any time of the day or night. If he was out in the street he'd talk to you. If you went to his house, no matter what he was doing, he'd take you in.'[14] Labour activist Vi Willis said councillors 'were always walking round'. She focused on the importance of immediacy in the appeal of Councillor Annie Taylor and how, although she represented the Labour Party, 'she was more of a woman for deprived children, deprived wives, that kind of thing than she was for politics'. A number of activists mentioned the importance of candidates being seen.

We had a wonderful young and handsome candidate who also happened to be a jeweller from Hatton Garden. You can imagine the charm and charisma, especially from the young females to our popular candidate.[15]

Stanley Bell, Kingston-upon-Thames

I met some Labour Party members in the village who approached me to stand for the county council . . . I led a campaign straight away to try and get the county council to provide a school. The village I was in had a few people who went to work in the brick works about two miles away, otherwise we were agricultural. Two neighbouring villages had almost 100 per cent brickwork labourers. These three villages were grouped together for the county council as a sort of mini-constituency and, in 1949, I got approached 'Would I fight the seat for the county council?' They'd never had a Labour candidate before. I was put up against a local squire who had perhaps rather blotted his copybook by being head of the Home Guard in the village during the war and perhaps got rather unpopular. Anyway, I managed to beat him in the election. But I was astounded at the reactions. I ran village meetings. I clearly realised that they'd never seen me in the village and the other two villages a few miles away didn't know me from Adam, so I announced that I was coming to speak at the village meeting. We had

150 people. I realised there was quite a lot of political interest. I think they were tickled pink that somebody had condescended to come to a meeting, so I got elected. I served five years in all, being re-elected after three years on an increased majority.

Alan Yates, Cranfield

I made speeches in almost all the villages. The purpose of the speeches, of course, was to be reported in the local press, and a reporter on the local paper, the *Chichester Observer* I think it was, was a strong sympathiser with Labour and guaranteed to get me good space in this, and so I used to write the report, which also saved him a bit of work. The report would begin 'Speaking on Wednesday night at Yapton, Labour candidate Mervyn Jones said . . .' and so on. I would actually type it out and give it to him beforehand. On one occasion I had done that. I was speaking at Yapton. In the morning I had given this reporter a copy of my speech, 'Speaking at Yapton, Mervyn Jones said . . .' and then it came on to rain and it rained heavily the rest of the day, and when I got to Yapton there was

Just one of the Labour Party's nine *Practical Illustrations of Election Committee Rooms* (1951)
Simon Fowler's private collection

179

nobody at the meeting except the chairman. There were no members of the public at all and I felt, 'I can't tell a lie. I can't just get in my car and go home', so I stood on the platform and made my speech.

Mervyn Jones, Chichester

This chap, Eddie Owen, who I knew, was a staunch socialist, and we got talking and he came round one day and one way and another he enthused us to join the party . . . He wasn't a councillor and we went to a few meetings, only a handful of people were at these meetings in his house . . . Eventually we got a little room . . . There were no Labour councillors in the area . . . It was because of Eddie Owen and his enthusiasm and his drive we eventually kicked out three Tory councillors, one, two, three – just like that and put Labour people in. Eddie used to go round, he was one of the best councillors I've known and he used to spend a lot of his own time, especially weekends, and go round the estates and round various places and if you saw him he'd say, 'Got any complaints?' He was interested to know all that was going on. He used to say, 'My door's always open. Come and knock on the door, give me a ring and I'll see what I can do for you.' He was like that with everybody.

Walter White, Long Sutton

Frank McElhone knew as he walked along the street, he'd be talking to old people and weans, what the political temperature was. Now, that may well be dismissed on a political signs basis but, whether people like it or no, some people have that knack.[16]

Jimmy Allison, Paisley

Agents

A number of agents mentioned the importance of preparation.[17] They stressed that organisational skills, local knowledge, and recognition as an active member of community, cannot be gained in a few weeks prior to an election.

The Labour Party agent came into Warrington. He was a very active sort of fellow, and he rode his bike, and he stopped me in the street one day and said 'Aye, you're not a member of ours.' I said, 'I am', and he said, 'Come on, give me your subscription'. And he took the money in the street there, and that's how we used to keep our membership up. He used to make up his mind that he hadn't seen me for a day or two and he came round and maintained the membership in that way.

Harold Edwards, Warrington

The duties of an agent ought to be to make sure that there is a plan at all times. Not only when there's elections on, but at other times. Because if you don't plan for the intervening years, then elections will come as a surprise to people and a big yawn. Whereas if you plan that there's always something political that can be organised between elections, then the election itself becomes more smoothly run because you've already got a staff in place. Most of your staffing with the Labour Party now, for example, it's somebody to deliver materials and somebody to be secretary and organiser in an area. It's got to be political as well. I think the stuff that gets put around nowadays is too inhibited, it's too careful. It doesn't want to upset anybody.

Ron Whitworth, Romford

I was parliamentary agent for twenty-one years, and the first election I fought [1954] we were defeated by 11,002, the majority of the Conservative candidate. After that I managed to whittle the majority down to 2,400 before I sought nomination as a parliamentary candidate, and when I didn't get the nomination I decided well, twenty-one years as party agent was enough, and they appointed someone else to do the job. I threw my hat in the ring because I thought 'I've been the handmaiden long enough', and it was time I was involved in taking some of the kudos and be the party candidate.

Harold Tomlins, Chester

I was a county councillor and reckoned I had quite enough work there, when suddenly the 1950 election was announced. It was the end of the first Labour government. It had been a great success but of course there was still rationing and we were a bit worried about what was going to happen in the election. The local councillor came to me and said, 'Look, we've got a Parliamentary election for mid-Bedfordshire which includes your seat on the county council. We want you to be agent.' 'I've never been an agent; I don't know anything about it.' 'It's all right, you'll get a complete book from Transport House telling you exactly how to run a general election.' And this was three weeks before the General Election. The main job, of course, was to print 50,000 election addresses and distribute them. I took that on and worked full-time for three weeks . . . I planned meetings all over the place, and when the count came Lennox-Boyd's majority was down to 1,800. This was the time when Labour did rather poorly, still remained just in power. The seat has never been held by Labour . . . I remember being rung by Barbara Cartland, very upset about her election address. I said 'What's worrying you, Mrs Cartland?' and she said 'There is a picture of your candidate and his daughter, and she is wearing a Red Cross uniform.' I said, 'She's a child of nine, isn't she?' 'Yes, that's right.' 'Well, shouldn't she be wearing the Red Cross uniform? I understood she was in the Junior Red Cross.' 'Yes, I think she is, but she shouldn't be wearing it on a Labour pamphlet.'[18]

Alan Yates, Cranfield

When I was made the election agent for '55, I started to work on the '55 election in 1953. The machine started to work then, how we were going to divide up the constituency. Who was going to take charge of this and who was going to do this job. Well, there's all types of jobs. Started to write up election envelopes in 1953.

Had them all done by the end of 1954, so that all that had to happen . . . was to get the election address, which was the last thing to be done. You had to go as near the wire as possible to make sure you'd no got anything in the election address that wasnae factual. And so, whenever you got them, you had the envelopes all ready, and you'd arrangements with the Post Office to make and that kind of thing. A hundred and one jobs. When the election was declared I would be, right I've got leave from the union [his employer] to go and work there, and I was there for six weeks, half past six in the morning to half past twelve at night.

Alex Kitson, Edinburgh

[As agent] you'd an election once a year, really, and basically you got an election address printed, usually compiled basically by the city Labour Party, but we ordered a supply for our area and then delivered them to all the houses in the area. And at that time we used to hold public meetings, so we'd book a room in a local school, maybe twice, either end of the ward, you'd book a room in the school and have a meeting. And we'd also take our room in the local town hall and have that as a committee room where you would be every night in the week, just the week before the election. And that was it. And on polling day you were out there, at the school, trying to get people to come and vote for us . . . We didn't have that much of a system because there weren't all that many of us and there was times when we didn't have a car. Well, if you knew somebody was a member or something who hadn't voted you would probably go and try and dig them out.

Harry McNeill, Glasgow

We attended meetings and weekend schools on election procedure and then we got all this bumf out from Transport House and they told you the last day for nominations and the last day for paying your election fees, and how much you were allowed to spend. It really was spelled out if you took the trouble to look up the information. There was a lot of information sent out to the committee rooms – to the agent.

Helen Cameron, Glasgow

How To Win an Election. Win in Wales. Who is this by? It's by Plaid Cymru. I've used this religiously. There's more information in this: canvassing, getting the vote, mobilising the workers. How many people in the party, down in the rank and file, are aware of how to set about doing this today? Very, very few, you know. Everything is in this little booklet and I got this many years ago. It was priced ten shillings in those days.

Bill Herbert, Cardiff

Committee rooms

Most activists realised the need for organisation in order to make the most of the canvassing returns and the street meetings. Some also were able to make use of younger family members:

When I was a very small boy I was doing some work on polling day in elections, mainly just running messages from one committee room to another or going to collect numbers from number takers at school, that kind of thing. I was doing that at the 1924 General Election, which I remember quite well.

John Crawford, Chester

[My children] are all right. They're out knocking up on election day . . . They saw what was going on in the home and I think they tended to support most of what I was doing. They got a bit fed up at times with it, but they accepted it, and when their mother became involved they more than accepted it.

Harold Tomlins, Chester

When it came to elections everything was dropped at our house. The room where we voted, the church, was just opposite. We'd got a committee room quite close to us. We'd always committee rooms. And we did all our canvassing beforehand. We went to every place and they all dropped on me.

Margaret Lloyd, St Helens

We always had a committee room at election times, and I always tried to arrange that I had time off so that I could help on election day, and I could also help at other times when I was at home.

Doris Ashby, Perivale

Josie Tipple and colleagues hard at work in an election committee room

Josie Tipple's private collection

I got all the canvas cards sent, so I had to get all these women (we got women, more or less, we did, not so many men with us) and we did all the canvassing. When we'd done it all we used to take them all in on the day. In between you'd have them marked so you'd know who'd voted, then we didn't need to bother them again. But with me knowing everyone round there, I knew the women who'd come in the morning. And my brother had a car, he'd send us one up there, and I could get these women out. And I'd only need say to one, when Mrs So-and-so's coming she'd come. I'd say 'Such-and-such a body's coming'. I knew who their friends were, you see. We'd get them all in. And at night time, what we did, we'd get 'em, only one car then, and I'd ask them to come to a certain spot and the car would drop them off there and pick the next lot up.

Margaret Lloyd, St Helens

The Reading system involved using marked cards which have carbon copies underneath which you tear off at various times of the day, having cancelled out the ones which have voted. And so you're left with the residue of the people who haven't voted.

Margaret Lawson, Edinburgh

Right from the very beginning I was always involved in taking the numbers, polling numbers, at the polling station, because everybody had to vote in the school, there was only one polling station, but various classrooms, and it was useful to have somebody who was able to run about to catch people as they came out. And we had boys on bikes going backwards and forwards to the one committee room that we had, with the numbers. It was all highly organised.

Doris Ashby, Perivale

Isa Paton and her sister Helen Cameron recalled how, during the 1959 General Election they were two of the four people who spent six weeks running a constituency campaign.

My sister and I manned these rooms and another two people, another lady and another gentleman, manned these rooms from half past nine in the morning until half past ten at night for about six weeks. It was a wonderful campaign, the 1959 campaign. We had canvas cards and my brother, he set it out that we had to call back, really the Reading System as we now hear about it. But this was his own devising, and we worked it out. And I think why we got such a good response was, when people were canvassing, too often in an election rooms it's, 'That's the canvas card. How did you get on? All right. Goodnight.' But we didn't. We had to go through every canvas card and say to the canvasser: 'Right. What was your response?' And so on, and so on. 'Car calls? Postal votes?' So on. 'Wanted to see the candidate? Wanted the candidate to call?' And we took all that and noted it after the canvas was over. And the canvassers saw that and they appreciated that their work wasn't just a nameless knocking at doors, it was purposeful. And we had people like the Fire Brigade Union, whose men were on shift duty and they could come during the day. And these men turned up, with a team of men every day, and I used to wonder at their enthusiasm. But then I saw what it was, because they felt it was being used, it wasn't just an exercise or keeping them out of the committee rooms, it was purposeful. And we worked at it, and we worked at it, and we called back and we called back. And we succeeded then, and we pulled it off, and we got a majority of 600 and it went on then from strength to strength.

Isa Paton, Glasgow

Her analysis as to the importance of activists is bolstered by a study of party membership in 1960. This concluded that activists were of significance.

The usual reason for a big membership is not the character of the area nor the size of the Labour vote, but the presence of either a good full-time agent or a group of hard-working and efficient members . . . The existence of big and well-organised parties may have stopped certain seats going Conservative in 1959; Faversham (Labour majority 253) and Lanark (Labour majority 540) both had memberships of over 4,000.[19]

The people went out with the cards, and we asked them every part of that constituency was canvassed. We didn't have any no-go areas and said that they all voted Tory. We felt, at that time, that the young middle class, that was the Gaitskell period, 1959, we felt that the young, so-called middle class would be quite interested in the Labour Party's policy on education for their family and we thought there would be ones that would vote Labour this time that hadn't in the past. Everybody was canvassed. And they came in with these canvas cards. Well, when they brought these canvas cards in to the rooms they were all checked and we spoke to the people about them. They weren't thrown aside. We had notes down that they'd to ask for cars if they wanted cars, that they'd to put notes down if they wanted a postal vote and if somebody said doubtful, or they wanted to speak to the candidate, that had to go down. And we recorded all these things. And there was a system of committee rooms in every polling area and what happened was that they all got a folder, a big cardboard thing, and each of their canvas cards were put out individually for that. And they knew the number of Labour votes there should be in that area. And, in the morning, each person had to phone in at a certain time. One on the hour, one five past the hour. So it meant that all the time we were having phone calls from committee rooms to see how many people had voted at that time. So that if there was a very poor poll in one of the schools we could send more people in to bring voters out of that area. And that went on every two hours. And then, from about five o'clock, it was every hour they were to phone in. That was the system. And it really worked beautifully . . . We won that seat by 709.[20]

Helen Cameron, Glasgow

The night we won the election . . . we could see that we were home and dry and I went off to the phone to tell [my mother]. She wasn't the least interested. 'We've won. We've won, Mum.' Wasn't the least interested. 'Poor Mr Gaitskell. Poor Mr Gaitskell. He's just conceded the election. I'll never live to see another Labour Government.' She was so sorry for the whole thing. Well she did. She did . . . By a strange coincidence she lived not only to see a Labour Government, but to see her own MP as Secretary of State for Scotland.

Isa Paton, Glasgow

We werenae organised at all [in 1959] and it was just taking everything for granted, and we sent out an election address written on an envelope to the electors and that was it. That was the way it was done in safe seats in Paisley and elsewhere. And it was the same in '64 and '66. They didnae do any canvassing in the General Election. The Young Socialists wanted to do it.

Jimmy Allison, Paisley

I went along [in 1964] and the women were all sitting writing the envelopes and making the tea and doing all the tremendously good work. They made me very, very welcome. 'Come in and sit down.' And all chatted to me. And it was like coming home. It was fantastic.

Jean Goldie, Paisley

[In 1966 one agent] had a squad of young men on motorbikes who went to each polling station at five minutes to the hour, and the agent at the polling station gave them a figure as to how many people had voted in that area. And they then got on their motorbikes (it was like the TT on the Isle of Man), and they raced to a telephone box to phone this information. In one particular part of the constituency, so I'm told, three bikes would converge on the same phone and the boys would fight with one another to see who was phoning first. There was no idea of saying 'Give me your numbers and I'll phone for all three.' And then it was like a bookmakers. She had guys taking down these numbers, and they passed them up to her, and she had a massive blackboard, which had the hours of the day, along one side and all the polling stations down the other. She had the previous year's vote in for each hour. And she would then, in a different colour chalk, write in the vote for that hour. And after we had seen this till about three in the afternoon I said to her 'Why are we doing this?' And she said: 'To see how our vote's going' . . . 'And if you feel that a place is doing badly, what do you do about it?' 'What can I do about it?' she said. 'Well,' I said, 'do you have reserve battalions, that you can call in and put them into the fray?' 'Oh, no,' she said, 'everybody's out working.' I said 'OK, do you have some device to take them from some areas that are doing well anyway and put them into areas where the poll's not coming in but where you think that so to do would be to our benefit?' 'Oh, they wouldnae move,' she said. 'Well,' I said, 'if you've got no reserve battalions and you are not prepared to move your divisions, why the hell are we doing this?' And she said 'Don't be stupid: so that at the next election we can see how the vote compares with this election.'

Tom Carbery, Glasgow

In 1972 during a local government election, a team intensively canvassed and leafleted a block of flats in a strong Labour ward in Dundee and left a similar block untouched. A post-election survey showed that there was a 10 per cent difference in the turn-out of Labour voters. Other evidence indicates that turnout is higher in marginal seats, and this could well be due to the more intensive canvassing which occurs there.[21] Other surveys show that there is a lower proportion of working-class Tories in working-class constituencies than the average, and this might be due to a local political culture. Where voters have more contact with the Labour Party they are influenced to conform to the dominant local norm and vote Labour.

By 1984 Labour Party membership had fallen to its lowest level for forty years. Since then it has climbed once again. In 1989 individual membership stood at just under 30,000, about 5 per cent of Labour voters. In the late 1980s the average constituency had about 300 Labour Party members within it. A survey which questioned between ten and eleven members in each constituency indicated that 'party activism and to a lesser extent, membership have a significant impact on the change in the Labour vote in 1987'. It showed that if the party had been a third larger, (assuming the new members had been as active as the old ones) then Labour would have gained nearly 35.7 per cent of the poll rather than the 30.8 per cent which the party actually received. The conclusion was that 'a strong sense of personal efficacy is very important to political involvement and that is likely to be strongest at the level of the local community', and that 'an active party membership is absolutely vital to the electoral performance of the Labour Party'.[22]

As it is difficult to prove how far Britain has advanced towards socialism under Labour, elections are a more concrete measure of the success of the Party. They feature prominently in people's stories. There are tasks to be performed, rules to be observed and a date on which the results can be seen. For three weeks in approximately every 260 there is an increased interest in politics among the general population and the many routes to success and opportunities to promote the cause can be exploited by activists on soapboxes, on the doorsteps of strangers or in the workplace. An election can be the culmination of years of nurturing constituencies, leafleting in the streets and seeking publicity in numerous localities. When, after a ten-year gap between elections, the first-ever majority Labour government came to power, the excitement was intense.

The Electoral Victory of 1945

On 5 July 1945, the British electorate went to the polls in order to vote in a General Election for the first time in ten years. The results were declared on 26 July, after the Service votes had been collected. The result was a triumph for the Labour Party. Overall, the party gained a total of 393 seats, giving it a majority of 148 seats and 48 per cent of the poll. The Conservatives suffered their greatest reverse since the Liberal landslide of 1906. The Conservative-dominated National coalition had won 429 seats in 1935, but in 1945 the Tories won only 210 seats.[1]

Opponents

The dislocation caused by the Blitz, general mobilisation, overtime, evacuation, shift-work and the black-out had made it very difficult to run the party while the Second World War was on, and the wartime political truce undermined its *raison d'être*. In May 1945 the war in Europe came to an end. In contradiction to the wishes of his Cabinet colleagues from the Labour Party, Prime Minister Winston Churchill requested, and received, a dissolution of Parliament. Left-wing activists gathered to campaign, canvass, flypost, heckle Tories and convince those around them of the value of a vote for Labour. There were many similarities between the two major parties in terms of the literature they produced for the election, though with important differences in emphases. The Conservative manifesto was a sober restatement of the wartime consensus, entitled *Mr Churchill's declaration of policy to the electors*. It focused on foreign policy and the Prime Minister, as Syd Bidwell and Donald Matheson recalled:

> My understanding was that Nye Bevan, who became one of the favourite political activists (also a member of the Labour College Movement, by the way, from South Wales), was very optimistic about there being a Labour Government, but many other sceptics didn't think there would, they thought Churchill would win the election. In the election of 1945, Tory candidates would go round saying 'If you like Winston Churchill, vote for me' – they didn't seem to have many other ideas in the locker.
>
> **Syd Bidwell, Southall**

> Just after the war, when I was still a schoolboy, we came to the 1945 election, and that was just wonderful. It was amazing. There was no television, of course, so

political meetings were huge meetings – crowded out. All out into the street. There was a huge interest in it . . . Nobody expected it. There were no polls. No polls that anybody knew of and no television, not much coverage. Churchill's big photo was everywhere on billboards. The Tory campaign was Churchill's face, and 'Say thank you very much.'

Donald Matheson, Liverpool

There were vague promises to maintain high employment levels, but also attacks on planning and state intervention. The Conservatives produced a poster of Churchill with a cigar and the slogan: 'Vote National – Help Him Finish the Job'. However, Conservative broadcasts concentrated on portraying Labour as left-wing extremists. Churchill said in one broadcast that 'no socialist system can be established without a political police . . . some form of Gestapo', and that Labour would erode the value of people's savings. The next morning the *Daily Express* headline was 'Gestapo in Britain if Socialists Win'. One Conservative candidate claimed: 'Mosley and Cripps have the same policy. The socialist state of Cripps is to be the same as the fascist state of the Blackshirts', and Harold Macmillan referred to the left-wing political theorist Harold Laski as 'Gauleiter Laski'.[2] Tom Carbery and Magda Clarke recalled the effect of this sort of propaganda:

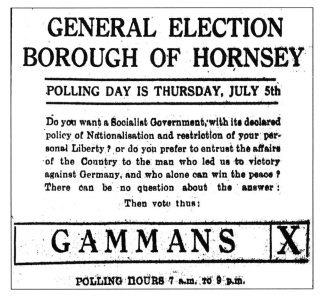

Tory candidate Gammans based his 1945 election campaign on the appeal of Churchill

Hampstead and Highgate Express, 29 June 1945

We never thought we were going to win like that. And it came over the radio. Labour elected. Labour elected. Labour elected. And the Tory girl was getting more and more panicky, and I couldn't resist it, because of all this silly talk of red revolution, I said 'Look out, you're all going to be hanged from lamp posts.' And she went, 'Ooooh!' And I thought, 'Little fool. If you don't know your fellow countrymen better than that.'

Magda Clarke, London

By the time I got into work at my RAF station in the Midlands and they had the radio on, it was pretty clear that Labour was winning. And I remember that most of the people were appalled. There was one girl, she was in tears, who said that she would give herself to the first American who dated her in the hope that he would do the honourable thing after she became pregnant and he would marry her and take her to America and therefore help her escape from this country that was clearly going to lapse into Bolshevism.

Tom Carbery, Glasgow

Alan Brownjohn thought that dissatisfaction with the Tories was a central element of Labour's victory. He was at secondary school where

some classrooms had been a riot of Labour election material, not interfered with or removed by the staff; the eye wandered from maths problem to slogans like 'Let's Face the Future!' or 'Straight Left!' Defaced Conservative leaflets presented the features of Churchill given hair and spectacles or obliterated with Plasticine. [When the Tory candidate stood up he gave] an uneasy, apologetic performance and he never finished it. From out of a knot of grim-faced people in standing room at the back of the hall came a perfectly pitched, very slow bass growl, booming forward over the heads of the seated audience and reaching the platform with an almost physical effect: 'Leopards Don't Change Their Spots!'[3]

Even though most unemployed people were not politically active, Syd Bidwell indicated his view that resentment of unemployment was burnt into working-class consciousness:

People were very friendly [during the Second World War], they were all in the same boat, and these wartime experiences brought people together. I think it had a great deal to do with the ultimate consequences of the 1945 General Election, when Labour had a landslide victory. But it had a great deal too to do with the unemployment background of the Thirties and people, even many middle-class people, moved over towards socialist ideas.

Syd Bidwell, Southall

Policies

Labour's *Let Us Face the Future* put domestic policies first and promised nationalisation of finance, transport, iron and steel, coal and power. Lyndal Evans spoke about planning for government, but the 1945 programme actually contained much that had been in the 1937 *Immediate Programme*. The important differences lay in the new commitment to full employment, a National Health Service, a major house-building programme and price controls.

> During the War the Fabians had wonderful summer schools in Dartington, and there we put the world to rights. We solved every possible difficulty for an incoming Labour government. Goodness, that was exciting. We decided that there shouldn't be advertisements in the press, that it was advertising that controlled the press and therefore this should be banned. All sorts of things like that. The excitement of listening and discussing with people who were going to be Members of Parliament in '45, it really was like changing the world.
>
> **Lyndal Evans, London**

How many people read these manifestos is unclear. Anne Swingler indicated that her husband, Labour's successful candidate in Stafford, did not have ready access to them and he may not have been alone. 253 of the 393 Labour MPs had never sat in the Commons before, and most did not know each other or the party leaders. Lieutenant James Callaghan, Labour's successful candidate in Cardiff South, said:

> I was selected in 1943 and I went away the same night to join a convoy in Liverpool, and I didn't get back to the constituency until the campaign was well on its way in 1945, because when the election was called I was serving in the Indian Ocean. [He eventually got home] . . . There is an extraordinary difference between campaigns then and now. I was not conscious of any interference from Transport House. We fought our own election. We were isolated. There weren't all these quantities of leaflets or instructions or things you ought to concentrate on. I came back from the Navy from a fleet where there was some disgruntlement because people had forgotten in Europe that we were fighting the Japanese. I didn't know what the domestic issues were and I thought up my own slogan for the election which I plastered around the place, 'We built the Spitfires. Now we can build the houses.'[4]

Aileen Plant also stressed the general nature of Labour's appeal which was made at the time, and Bea Serota suggested that wartime social mixing led many people to vote Labour:

All through the war you were talking about what it was you were trying to save, a democratic way of deciding things and you believed in the values for which so much of Britain stood and you hoped it would be a better Britain, not so much a class-ridden Britain with very established upper classes and working classes. If you were all required to fight for this Britain it had to be a Britain that was of value and gave opportunities to all its citizens. You were preaching that.

Aileen Plant, Stockport

We did quite well. It was exalting. Absolutely overwhelming. I mean, it was beyond one's wildest dreams, really, the outcome of the '45 election. We all hoped that it would be good for us but I don't think anyone realised, I don't think anyone in the country realised what the movement of opinion would be. This was really the Forces' vote that brought enormous swing. I think it was this feeling people had that the war had revealed so many social injustices. [My husband] Stanley's group went in to do air crew training. The top of the class – and it was a highly technical training – was a young man who'd joined the post office at fourteen. People realised the tremendous waste of ability that there'd been. When I helped with the evacuation of schoolchildren, people in the country saw poverty for the first time. Six out of eight children in my carriage had never been in a train before, and it wasn't that poor an area that they came from. I think it was all these things which brought this great upswing to the Labour movement, and the feeling that people wanted change.

Bea Serota, Hampstead

Fabian writer Margaret Cole also believed that evacuation made the 'comfortable classes suddenly and painfully aware' of poverty, but a Fabian study made in 1940 found that evacuees and their hosts resented one another and that class prejudices were often reinforced. The public opinion surveyers, Mass-Observation, analysed the election: 'Politically, the undoubted leftward swing is essentially away from old beliefs, not yet clearly or enthusiastically directed towards a new source.'[5] Echoing this, Joe Kahn made the point that people voted for immediate material changes rather than for an ideal of socialism.

I don't really believe that there was any great political fervour amongst the people of Hackney, or indeed any other area that I knew reasonably well. There was a general discontent with Tory policy, which had first expressed itself in 1945. There was a pathetic attempt by masses of people who were homeless and if not homeless living in appalling conditions to improve their lot. There was feverish activity on the part of the council to try and build as many homes as possible. There was a hatred of Mosley's fascism and this dislike spread to certain individuals who were either politically important in the Tory Party or financially important and who were backing Mosley but I think politically the people of Hackney were not terribly involved or concerned. They would vote Labour for local elections, they would vote Labour for general elections, but apart from that they were intent on going about their own affairs. Life was very difficult and at the same time it was a rebuilding time because we were very close to the end of the war. We really were at the bottom end, and I think if you are in that position you don't have a great deal of political ideology generally . . . You have a number of people who are politically conscious, who have political aims if not ambitions, but the mass of the people I don't think were permanently concerned with politics as such.

Joe Kahn, Hackney

Jim Mortimer agreed with Joe Kahn that housing was an important issue at the election, as was welfare provision. In December 1942, after a long career as an advisor to government on social policy planning, William Beveridge produced a plan to establish full social security for all from the cradle to the grave. He stressed three assumptions of that which was required for a comprehensive social insurance system: children's allowances, health and rehabilitation services available to all and the maintenance of employment. The report declared: 'Want is only one of the Five Giants on the road to reconstruction and in some ways the easiest to attack. The others are Disease, Ignorance, Squalor and Idleness.' In October 1944 he entered Parliament as a Liberal, following a by-election, and in November he published his *Full Employment in a Free Society*, which advocated central direction of the economy. He lost his seat in the 1945 General Election but Labour took up his ideas.

I do remember, in Oxford, going to a meeting at the Town Hall when Beveridge spoke. That was absolutely wonderful. This was the first outline. Funny-looking guy, but he was precise, sensible, very realistic, down to earth. He knew what he was saying.

Anna Clarke, Oxford

The issues which we were discussing at the time were: one, that there should be full employment; two, that there should be social security; three that we should have international co-operation in the post-war period between Britain and the Soviet Union and the United States. Those were the three main issues. Oh, and housing, of course. Social services and housing. The interesting thing at that time was that, even among people with whom I was working, who may have said that they were going to vote Conservative, there was no real opposition to those points. Those who were Conservative were more inclined to say, 'Well, Mr Churchill has led us during the war, and it's not right that he should be cast aside, and therefore I'm going to vote Conservative.' But if you asked them: 'Look, do you think we should be pledged to a full employment policy?' they said 'Yes.' If you said: 'Do you think we should plan a very ambitious housing programme?'

they said 'Yes.' 'Do you think we should have social security?' they said 'Yes.' 'Do you think we should continue with international co-operation, with the Grand Alliance?' they said 'Yes.' So, the mood, even among those who voted Conservative, was sympathetic to a planned economy.

Jim Mortimer, Hounslow

Campaigning

The Party won the support of those who wanted change, but many were not interested in public affairs. In 1941 the Army Bureau of Current Affairs was founded under the direction of W.E. Williams, who had important roles in both the creation of Penguin Specials and the adult education movement. The ABCA produced pamphlets for those officers who had to lead the compulsory weekly talks and discussions which were supposed to counter cynicism and ignorance among service personnel. Churchill argued that the ABCA was run by left-wingers and, two days after Beveridge published a ABCA pamphlet explaining his report, the War Office withdrew it. Although it is not clear that the ABCA had much effect, it did give those with left-wing views an opportunity to air them.[6] There were also attempts by some servicemen to establish their own forums for discussion. These included a mock election in Cairo in 1944.

The atmosphere was for change, of course, definitely, and I think there had been a Forces Parliament in the Middle East, but there was a movement, because being in the armed forces was a leveller in many ways, not all the middle class become army officers, or officers in the air force or navy, and that had a profound effect on the shift to the left – a shift, if you like, to socialist appreciation and determination.

Syd Bidwell, Southall

I was very active in the Army Bureau of Current Affairs debates and we had the, for want of a better word, the fag-end of the Middle East Parliament, the Cairo Parliament . . . They tried to supersede it by the Army Bureau of Current Affairs debates, and I have attended many of those in Cairo and obtained great pleasure from them. I was also a technical assistant and, up in the observation post, on the training ranges and that, there was a couple of officers who were favourably disposed, and we had many, many conversations, and books and pamphlets were exchanged.

John Uzzell, Swindon

[Being in the army in Egypt] wasn't a political blank as far as I was concerned because Nan [his wife] used to send me out political newspapers and so on. I kept up to date in that way. I did spend a very short period going to the Forces Parliament that was set up in Cairo and that was interesting, but it didn't last very long.

John Crawford, Chester

I was in Italy at the time of the 1945 General Election. It wasn't something that was far away, it was right on our doorstep. Perhaps I was just in a group that was politically conscious, but we were certainly very, very politically conscious, very very much so. So much so that we organised a sort of election campaign. A mini model election campaign, putting forward different ideas and programmes of the different parties to groups. We could get someone to advocate a Communist Party policy and a Labour Party policy and a Liberal Party policy, but not the Conservatives. We had to recruit someone to put forward what he thought was the Conservative Party policy who was actually a Liberal . . . The big thing which influenced the service personnel was the Beveridge Report.

Jim Tucker, Italy

For those not in the Forces, Labour's message was promoted through more traditional methods such as revues and public meetings. Hugh Dalton, the wartime Minister of Economic Warfare and Chancellor of the Exchequer in the postwar Labour government, wrote nearly two million words in his diaries. This is how he recorded victory in 1945: 'That first sensation, tingling and triumphant, was of a new society to be built, and we had the power to build it. There was exhilaration among us, joy and hope, determination and confidence. We felt exalted, walking on air, walking with destiny.'[7] His eloquence was recalled by Stanley Bell, while Josie Tipple recalled the one-time cotton weaver, county councillor and trade union official George Tomlinson who won a Parliamentary by-election in Lancashire Farnworth in 1938. He was appointed to be Parliamentary Secretary to the Minister of Labour in 1941 and held a number of other Ministerial posts. He was returned again in 1945:

I think I spoke on every platform, on every chair, on every street corner in the Northwich constituency, and I remember speaking in Sandbach waiting for George Tomlinson. He who became Minister of Education, of course, and he was late, and I'd nearly got to the point of telling funny stories when he arrived. I could tell the audience was getting restive and he had it under his thumb immediately. 'I'm sorry I'm late,' said George, 'my car is like the Tory Party, broken down.' He had them in his hands immediately.

Josie Tipple, Northwich

All this helped to build up a fighting force for 1945. First we had the General Election with George Elvin, who was the General Secretary of the cinematography workers [the Association of Cine-Technicians], as our Labour candidate. One of our rallies filled the Kingston Empire, that's about 2,000 people, with a big open-air overflow in the cattle market. Fortunately, George Elvin was a friend of J.B. Priestley, who came and spoke to a hushed audience. I had organised the collection, you know, donations from trade unions etc, and it all amounted to £478 which, by today's standard, equals about £5,000. Kingston had captured the headlines and amongst the many speakers who came were Manny Shinwell, Hugh Dalton and Dr Edith Summerskill.

Stanley Bell, Kingston-upon-Thames

So we set up this wonderful campaign, a committee really, of all the old boys who'd been in the party. They were getting on, but knew the area well and very slowly came together a whole lot of younger people, people who had nothing to do with politics, full of enthusiasm to come and help with not much idea of what to do, but once told they really got on with it and were splendid. Just outside the constituency was something called 16MU, which was a Maintenance Unit of the RAF with hundreds and hundreds, or even possibly a couple of thousand people working there, stuck with nothing much to do, the war was almost over, there was practically no work and they were bored. The main committee room was on the road leading out to this place and, after a very short time, we had committee room notices up outside, we had these RAF men coming secretly and saying would it be all right, if they came with a civvy suit, could they change in there because they wanted to help Stephen in the election. Dozens of them came, and they were marvellous canvassers. It was a wonderful experience. The main activities were public meetings in every single village, masses of villages, very rural area and in Stafford itself, which was the main town. There were three mining villages, quite small ones, to the south, there were the landed of Shrewsbury, Lord Stafford of Lichfield, about five or six large estates, and most of the people living in the villages worked on the estates and had tied houses, and for the very first time these villagers decided they were going to put up posters. I suspect they'd had letters from their sons who were serving miles away who said, whatever you do, don't vote for Churchill. I'm sure that it is how it happened, because these were people who'd never had any interest, but they would tell us, 'We've heard from our son that we've got to vote Labour this time', they would say when we went round canvassing. And these people would put up posters in the window. When the election was over and Stephen had become the Member of Parliament several, perhaps half a dozen of them, not only lost their jobs but lost their houses and we could do nothing to help. Without the postal votes of the soldiers I doubt if we would have won it. The most exciting thing I think that has ever happened, winning Stafford.

Anne Swingler, Stafford

On polling day I was working here, up and down on my bike. Our committee room was at 97 Fitzjohn's Avenue, which is now that private school, and that was the hub of that part of the election campaign. We had our headquarters in Broadhurst Gardens, 31 or 33. It was tremendously exciting. 'Make it a Field Day.' Bill Field was our candidate. He eventually became the member for North Paddington and became involved in some sex scandal.[8]

We had these revues with all the songs, you know. 'Build a better borough for your children to enjoy', and a wonderful one about 'When the railways are nationalised, we'll all have fun, fares will be cheaper and the trains will always run.' There was tremendous enthusiasm and great uplift and hope with the coming of the health service. The 1944 Education Act, of course, was already on the stocks.

Bea Serota, Hampstead

My husband and I went to a lot of Conservative meetings and we really heckled at the back and were very difficult. Because, you know, we were so fed up with these Tories, and we'd always had a Tory Member of Parliament.

Joan Baker, Gosport

I was living in Tavistock Square. I was interested in politics but at the time, as far as I can remember, it was a toss up between the Liberals and Labour. I had no strong socialist feeling whatsoever, I just wanted to be in something reforming after the war in the new world which was coming to pass, and I very nearly joined the Liberals. I can't remember what tipped me over in the end to join Labour instead, but I did . . . There was a very great feeling of building a new world somehow . . . I wasn't completely recovered from my illnesses, I still found difficulty getting around, but I was working full time in an office. I had also been doing a university degree and it was all quite a strain, but I was determined to be in on the election. I think I just found out where the local party rooms were and went along to them. It was South West St Pancras Labour Party. It was in a basement in Hampstead Road. It was terribly scruffy and most dangerous. It had electric fittings which were perfectly dangerous. I remember several of us got appalling electric shocks when we were trying to do something but, anyway, it was a place, it was a headquarters. Among the members was Michael Young, later Lord Young and the Denningtons, Evelyn and Cecil, and there were quite a lot of, I would say, intellectuals. There were also a lot of what were later called Militant but in those times were called 'Fellow Travellers'. In other words, near communists who were in the Labour Party to infiltrate. That was the in word. They were all in the same locality. The reason for this was that this did include Bloomsbury which is, of course, the university area, so you got mostly intellectual types. We went out canvassing on our own. I can't think how I had the courage to do it, knocking on doors. We had a large Greek Cypriot population, which increased even more later on. I'm going round the back streets behind Tottenham Court Road now, and some of it felt quite scary. I remember one canvasser saying she felt sure she'd found a corpse. One of the most eerie things that happened to me was putting a leaflet through a letter box and finding somebody took it from the other side. It doesn't sound much, but it was really a bit creepy. I can remember what irritated me most, and that was when it was the wife or woman in and she wouldn't answer her opinion, she just said: 'He settles all that.' A lot of us felt very irritated by that and I think it still happens.

Anna Clarke, St Pancras

Towards the end of the war, those of us still about started to build up the Labour Party and were amazed at the Sunday morning canvassing when literally hundreds of people joined. We could even set up sub-divisions of wards with street captains ready for the coming elections.

Stanley Bell, Kingston-upon-Thames

I was living in a village in Hampshire and several ladies with big houses in the district were, to my surprise, active Labour Party members. We did a lot of canvassing around the villages and public meetings for the 1945 election and of course that went extremely well for us . . . I even tried to get on the parish council.

John Horner, Hampshire

I had quite a lot of canvassing material and so on at home, and that was in a large house in Tavistock Square. And the person who I felt I had to hide it from was actually the woman who used to help my mother with the house, the cleaning lady. My mother and the rest of them were very worried that she shouldn't know that there was Labour activity in the house.

Anna Clarke, St Pancras

I went canvassing every day with the party, to try and win the election. I went canvassing from nine o'clock in the morning, to nine o'clock at night every single day for weeks, and weeks, and months.

Fred Neuner, Hornsey

The '45 elections, I worked both in Epsom, where I was studying during the week, and at home at the weekend. If I went home at the weekend I would help them there, canvassing and addressing labels, and knocking up, and the various things that one does in elections.

Maureen Dewar, Tottenham

We were absolutely over the moon. We didn't have to knock at doors. They were coming out: 'Yes, we're with you' . . . I kept writing to Sid: 'Don't know what you'd do if you was to see this.' And, as you know, everywhere else went overwhelming.

Vi Willis, Ilford

We had glorious posters the size of a wall on every possible corner and photos, enormous photos of me, the People's John.

John Platts-Mills, Finsbury

In Bloomsbury there was a lot of bombing because of the mainline railway stations, and there weren't any poster sites. Everybody was flyposting. Petrol was still rationed, we did have a car, we had a bit of petrol, and a bucket of paste, and a roll of posters, and off we went, slapping them up on bomb sites. Everybody was doing it.

Magda Clarke, London

Fly posting at that time wasnae illegal in '45. It only came in under the Representation of the Peoples Act, the fly posting stopped. But you didnae have much to fly post in 1945 because you didnae have any paper . . . Chalking on the streets and on the walls, but mostly on the streets. I can't remember very much about people sort of defacing walls. It was more that you did it on the street.

Alex Kitson, Edinburgh

There was a row of Cockney kids sitting on the wall. And we came along and they greeted us, said, 'Who's that for?' 'Labour.' 'Good.' The other side of the road there were a lot of Tory posters already up and one of the kids pointed to the Tory posters and said 'You mustn't put your posters over those. That would be un-English.'

Magda Clarke, London

Huge posters opposite the Tower, with Churchill on, and people tearing the posters down. Now this is something which I know from the Continent, that people do do that, but in England it's not done to do that, and so I was quite astonished how strong that was when I saw these torn posters of Churchill.

Irene Wagner, Holborn

Some of the enthusiasm for Labour was maintained for the local elections:

I had to get permission to stand [in the Metropolitan Borough elections], and [my employers] gave me permission because they never thought I'd win a seat. When they said, 'Where are you going to stand?' and I said 'Hampstead', they laughed. So I had no problems getting permission as a civil servant to stand. They thought it was hopeless but, in the event, we did very well in the late November elections. We won five out of six seats in the ward where I was standing, we won all six seats in Kilburn, and we won two if not three seats in Belsize, so we had quite a large group, and this really was a terrible shock to the Tories in Hampstead . . . It was a great shock to the officers of the council as well as the members.

Bea Serota, Hampstead

Labour's individual membership had fallen during the war from 409,000 to 218,000. However, it grew to 487,000 in 1945, and to 645,345 the following year. Maureen Dewar was one of the recruits, while Betty Crook realised that the heyday of the ILP was past. The party grew rapidly after the war to a peak of over one million individual members by 1952, or 6.2 per cent of those who voted Labour in 1951.

I joined the party in 1945, when I was eighteen, to win the elections. To get the Tories out.

Maureen Dewar, Tottenham

When it were the election in 1945, we all helped, the ILP, and we joined again, we all joined again. Because th'ILP had more or less died out. [It kept its three seats in Glasgow.] There were still branches in Nelson. Th'ILP was right, I think, their policies were right, but you couldn't make people believe in some way or other. You were losing all the time, you weren't getting new members.

Betty Crook, Chorley

Results

A number of interviewees recalled the day of the election and the day, three weeks later, when the results were announced:

On the Borough Council election in '45 some of the members actually hired a car, an old Rolls-Royce, or something, a rather spectacular-looking car, and parked it outside the LCC lodging house in Parker Street and ran to and fro taking men from the doss house to the vote.

Hugh Chaplin, Holborn

During the time leading up to the '45 election I had been transferred up to Epsom, and I was on night duty at Hammersmith Hospital, and I went down to Epsom to vote. My first vote I was able to have, and there were three of us who were going to vote Labour and three of us who were going to vote Conservative. We just didn't trust one another, so although we were all on duty that night, we all travelled down to Epsom to vote. Course, it was a lost cause for us, but at least we managed to record our votes, and we really felt that things were going to be absolutely marvellous. At that time I was secretary of the Socialist Medical Association in the hospital. One of the consultants was the chair. He was very left-wing. He was a Communist, and I was pressured a great deal at that time to join the Communist Party, but I decided that it wasn't for me, although I could see their points of view, but it wasn't quite what I wanted.

Doris Ashby, Perivale

In those days Stockport had two MPs. Labour got in nearly everywhere except Stockport, and one of the reasons for that was that they were Conscientious Objectors. Conscientious Objectors weren't appreciated just about that time. Since then I can quite appreciate it, but I'm sure other people were a bit iffy about it. The Tories got in on this.

Frank Booth, Stockport

The day the results were declared – we had various methods [if still serving in the army], you could either vote by proxy or you could vote yourself. I've got a feeling there was another method. It had to be done through the Army Post Office, so you got the ballot papers through applying and getting it back. It was great excitement. Great excitement and, on many occasions, fellows came along and said: 'Look, you know what to do with all of this.' So I'm afraid the Representation of the People Act was not strictly adhered to by myself. I can remember voting for Arthur Greenwood, Joe – I can't place all the names . . . to my vivid memory, to my great regret, one of them was Woodrow Wyatt. There was a fortnight's delay while they were taken in from the various war theatres and then they were declared a fortnight after. And I heard the results and read the results and heard it on the radio, coming back from Jerusalem across the Sinai Desert and reading in the *Palestine Post* that Tom Reed had been elected for Swindon with an 11,000 majority. And – yes, there was hope. Hope.

John Uzzell, Swindon

Although a civilian, I was made a member of the officers' mess. It was told to us that there were certain codes about the officers' mess. You didn't talk at meals

News of the Labour Party's resounding success was greeted joyfully by socialists worldwide

about ladies or politics or religion . . . When the 1945 election came we couldn't conceal the grins on our face.

John Horner, Hampshire

There was at the point when Labour won the election in 1945, just a tremendous feeling of exaltation that at last we were there and at last there might be an end to the horrors, at last people might begin to care for one another across the world. I used to go to the productions of Unity Theatre in Kings Cross in those days, and I can remember a revue which was put on within a fortnight of Labour's victory in '45. Labour won something like 392 seats in that election. I can remember the chant that came from the stage as we got there: 378, 379, 380 and so on – right up to whatever the total was.

Jack Lodge, Walthamstow

I was at Blackpool in 1945 and in a square there, they had the election results coming through in lights. What a thrill. I remember thinking, 'This is it. Now we shall get socialism.' Well we haven't got it yet, but some things are better than when I was young.

Betty Crook, Chorley

Coming on through the radio bits of [the results]. You didn't have no telly, did you? Couldn't go to bed, and couldn't sit, and walking in and out and – it was just out of this world. It was out of this world . . . Throughout our young life, all we had known were Tory governments, Tory rule and Tory-controlled councils, so when you started getting these things it fired you up.

Vi Willis, Ilford

The election night, everyone was jubilant because there'd been such a great victory. I was in the local Labour Club as the results came through. We had wireless in them days, we didn't have television, we just had to listen to the local radio.

Fred Brockbank, Pendlebury

Everybody went balmy. And when news came through that we were winning seats elsewhere as well, because they'd a radio there, and that kind of thing . . . and outside the baths [where the count was being held] it was pandemonium, the same as it was when we first got elected in 1934. The Tories had almost 100 per cent and we slung the lot out, the whole lot of councillors. There was just one or two aldermen left . . . And you should have seen the scenes outside the baths when the defeated Tory candidates came out, and they were booed and booed. It was really pandemonium.

Fred Combes, Southwark

The day that the results came through I walked from where I lived in Mount Florida to my sister's home in Moss Park. And her next door was a very delightful woman who was very active in the Labour Party after that. And we celebrated this glorious victory.

Helen Cameron, Glasgow

When they read out the results on the radio we were delighted. I don't think the majority of the airforce mess were quite so enthusiastic.

Alan Yates, Andover

The election took place, and they waited till the servicemen's votes came in. You'd to wait until the servicemen's votes were counted, and so on. And I was at my seat working, and the window was open. And I'm working, and my neighbour was out in the garden, and my next-door neighbour came down into her garden. Oh, she was so alarmed, so distressed. 'Labour have won the election. Labour have won the election.' And, of course, Peggy and I said, 'Oh, great, great, great.' And she was shocked to find that she'd Labour supporters living next door to her.

Isa Paton, Glasgow

Beer was still rationed in these days, pubs used to open only about twice a week or something like that, but we'd congregated somewhere and accumulated a few bottles of beer and what have you and we had our celebrations . . . Everyone was elated, like I suppose they'll be elated when the next election [in 1997] comes.

Alex Kitson, Edinburgh

I'd really overdone it completely, and I went and fell ill with pneumonia and got quite seriously ill, and I think it was almost on exactly the same day when I got the letter saying I'd got my Economics degree and also that Labour had won the election. I was beginning to improve then, my temperature had gone down, but I was very weak and not fit for anything much. I think it was too much for me. It sent it right up again. It was quite extraordinary . . . That was a tremendous government, the Attlee government. It was really amazing. Great, reforming government. One of the great wonders of English history, I would say. I wasn't disillusioned with them . . . It was tantamount to a revolution.

Anna Clarke, St Pancras

On 26 July the BBC gave the news hourly. When the first bulletin went out at 11 a.m., two Cabinet Ministers had lost their seats and Birmingham, a heartland of affluent working-class Conservatives, had swung to Labour. The Labour and Liberal Parties had decided not to stand against Churchill, but the independent farmer who did took over a quarter of the votes. At 7 p.m. Churchill resigned, and by the time the last results were announced at around 10 p.m., thirteen Conservative Ministers had lost their seats and it was clear that fifteen million votes had been cast against Churchill's government.

Nina Hibbin remembers the atmosphere at Hendon Aerodrome as the results were announced:

> There was a hut that was used for lectures and we had a huge map of the whole of the country there, with all the constituencies marked. As the results came through on the radio, we were sticking in red pins for the Labour victories, and blue ones for the Tory victories, and there was a huge crowd that gathered all day. There were great cheers every time there was another Labour victory.[9]

Frank Clayton remembers the results being announced in the factory where he worked:

> I was a toolmaker in an aircraft factory. In our workshop whenever anyone left or had something to celebrate, the whole shop would hammer on the benches – it made a tremendous sound. We were itching for a Labour victory. On this day every time the results came in, the whole shop would ring out. It was quite incredible.[10]

Michael Barrett Brown was in Yugoslavia:

> In Sarajevo we had a radio tuned into London and a copy of *The Times* – it was spread out in front of me, steadily filling in the results and adding them up. Our excitement grew as the possibility, and then the certainty, of a majority became clear, and finally as the size of the majority piled up. We celebrated with Yugoslav sparkling wine and plum brandy.[11]

> I was on a destroyer, going across to Halifax, Nova Scotia. We heard the results and there was great cheering all around – including the officers. I feel that four million servicemen were a solid vote for Labour.
>
> **Ernie Johnson, Salford**

Another serviceman who recalled hearing the results while at sea was on his way to India, where a red flag was hoisted outside the officers' mess:[12]

> I was on a boat going to India when the election results came over the tannoy. When we heard Labour had won – now this is a true story – all the soldiers on this troopship, thousands of them – got up and sang *The Red Flag*. The officers couldn't stop it. They didn't try.[13]

We had known, because of the results that had been declared and leaked, and that kind of thing, that the Labour Party were well in front. Well, it was great jubilation. I don't think there's a government has had a majority anything like they got . . . It was the start of a whole new life.

Alex Kitson, Edinburgh

I had to help for the '45 election, and we went on the knocker, and we leafleted and whatnot. We didn't expect to win. Everybody quoted the Wordsworth 'Joy was in that dawn to be alive'. It was like that. It really was. We really thought, 'Everything's going to be all right now.'

Donald Matheson, Liverpool

Needless to say I was out canvassing and, when the results came in, it was just amazing, it was a dream come true. *England Arise, The long, long night is over.* We were going to come out of our slums and we were going to have all the wonderful, decent things that everybody should have, education – and, of course, when the National Health Service started it just seemed as if the millennium had been reached.

Patricia Meitlis, London

The Conservatives did not have many ideas beyond the promotion of Churchill and the portrayal of their former coalition allies as extremists. Many people were voting against the Tories, who had been the dominant party of government since 1931. Officially Labour was committed to full employment, health, homes and low prices. Canvassers may have been even more fulsome in their promises and there were new opportunities within the armed services, which some left-wingers were able to exploit while others, such as Stanley Bell, were able to draw upon the work that they had put in on the home front. What distinguished the 1945 election was not the campaigning so much as the result and the implementation of the policies. As Tony Blair has pointed out, the election victory was an important landmark not only for that which it promised but also because of that which it delivered.

Labour in 1945 combined idealism and practicality in equal measure to lead a national crusade for a Britain based on social justice, equality of opportunity and social solidarity . . . To a remarkable extent, it succeeded.[14]

XI
Achievements

Many interviewees said that, in 1945, there was a national enthusiasm for co-operation, social reconciliation and substantial reforms, and that Labour won support because it appeared to be the party most likely to deliver them. Left-wingers John Platts-Mills and Alex Kitson extended the argument, and suggested that the electorate was ahead of the government in its enthusiasm for rapid change and that, in dampening down its demands, the Labour Party reduced the likelihood of social unrest. As Stafford Cripps claimed in the Commons: 'Socialist democracy is the true barrier against Communism'. Whether it was the views of the electorate or the party leadership which undermined the attempt to construct a Socialist Commonwealth, activists focused on the concrete. Labour may have wanted to build a new society with new attitudes, and there may have been a ground swell of support for this, but in interviews activists cited the achievements of the Ministry of Health, which was also responsible for housing, in building new units, not in shaping communities.

> Greatest thing ever was the 1945 election, and all the hard work that was put in. To me they were great achievements. Everybody feared, including the guys that had been conscripted, that it was going to be another 1918 fiasco, come back and no jobs and what have you. Well, if we hadnae had the Labour government we'd have had another war. I'm no talking about here, we'd have been involved in another war and it would have been against the Soviet Union . . . The 1945 period to me, that was a real revolution.
>
> **Alex Kitson, Edinburgh**

> There was a bit of unrest amongst different groups of workers but actually there was such a general feeling of triumph that that really covered the first few years of the Attlee government. Chaps put up with all kinds of impositions from employers that I think they wouldn't have put up with if Churchill had still been in power.
>
> **John Platts-Mills, Finsbury**

Health
Nye Bevan's father, a founder member of the Tredegar Working Men's Medical Aid Society, died in his son's arms of the pit disease, pneumoconiosis. Bevan was unemployed for years and had to rely on his sister's wages. Creating a universal, free

health system financed by the Exchequer, local rates and insurance was a personal goal. In 1945, at the age of forty-seven, Bevan became the youngest member of the Cabinet. As Minister of Health, he pushed through the National Health Service Act of 1946, which came into force two years later. He faced plenty of opposition, particularly from the main doctors' group, the British Medical Association. There were also attempts to stop the legislation inside Parliament.

The Bill was published on 26 March 1946, and there was a second reading on 30 April, after which it went to the committee stage. Within a week 132 columns of *Hansard* had been filled with debate on just three of the Bill's 74 clauses. Bevan had the committee meeting morning and afternoon in order to speed the bill's progress. Although during the war the Conservatives had claimed that the party favoured a national health service, the party's opposition in the Commons indicates otherwise. There was a third reading on 26 July and the bill received Royal Assent on 6 November.

There was public support both for the legislation and for Bevan, who was a popular speaker. His Labour College tutor, Mark Starr, recalled his style and persistence.

Many see 1945, when Labour and the country were victorious, as the party's finest hour

National Museum of Labour History

Aneurin Bevan was one of my students and Aneurin then had a first-class stutter, which he used as an attention-getter. He got it cured later on. But we used to keep our doors locked against Aneurin because he didn't get up early enough to get to lectures but he got up early enough to come and talk to you while you were trying to subscribe to the ordinary curriculum of the College.[1]

Mike Turner remembered the effect.

In the House of Commons, as a young man studying law and politics, I listened to Aneurin Bevan introduce the first National Health Bill. And I was amazed at the time with his eloquence, though he did stutter, I'm sure quite deliberately. But I was also amazed, and came away even more dumbfounded, that everybody on the opposition side voted against having a National Health Act, and I really couldn't understand that at the time, though I later did.

Mike Turner, Ruislip

I believe 86 Tories voted against the Second Reading, and a considerable number abstained, and they only had about 208 members at the time. And I absolutely bristle now when I hear them talking about how they were instrumental in supporting it from that day to this. I'm afraid I feel like throwing something at my television set.

John Uzzell, Swindon

The National Health Service. I can remember it being set up. I can remember my brother-in-law, my sister's husband, being very angry and saying 'My patients will be telling me what to do'. Doctors were against it, but the Labour Party very bravely pushed on and set it up. And now this lot are unpicking it . . . I was a nurse before it. It was awful. The way people were treated in hospital was awful. Bad food, it was awful. I remember they were given rice pudding every day. Every day. It was awful. And the discipline. I remember a man that I knew in my town, and I called him Bob, or something, and the sister saying to me 'You must not address patients by their Christian names, you address them by their surnames.'

Doris Partridge, Bromley

The thing that we achieved was the National Health Service. The introduction of the National Health Service and the '45–'50 Labour Government nationalisation of steel and the railways.

Jimmy Allison, Paisley

I thought: 'I've wasted six years in the army', and that struck me. I thought I'd wasted that six years in a way for one thing, that was free health for all people in England and Great Britain, that's the thing, and I became very strong Labour then.

Sam Waters, Stockport

The National Health Service was a necessity and has been marvellous. You see, in those days, operations that weren't necessary for medical reasons, cross eyes – lots and lots of little children had a cast in their eye – bent legs, rickets, things that weren't necessary weren't dealt with. People never went into hospital to have babies. They had them at home. And you couldn't. Sometimes people were too poor to afford a midwife, so a sister or somebody came. A midwife cost money, a doctor cost money, so you couldn't have either of them. If you became very ill, septicaemia, or something, you went into hospital, but generally you died.

Doris Partridge, Bromley

I think one of the achievements has got to be the National Health Service. I think that's taken a lot of fear from people that they might get ill and not be able to be looked after, and it's a great fear of mine that we're losing it . . . I think the Labour Party's always been there as a beacon.

Jean Goldie, Elderslie

Housing

Let Us Face the Future stated that there should be a Ministry combining Health's housing powers with the Ministry of Town and Country Planning's planning powers. This did not occur, and so the responsibility for housing fell between these ministries and the Ministry of Works. Bevan was so busy creating the NHS that he did not consider housing very fully. This was despite the fact that there were serious housing problems before the war and that during the war a third of Britain's houses had been damaged and many more had gone without repair. Overall there were 700,000 fewer homes than in 1939.

The most effective means by which Labour created and maintained a sense of community during the interwar period was through stressing how much better housing would be under a Labour administration. Where Labour councils built new homes and defended tenants and working-class owners, the party gained support. When the Lord Lieutenant of Surrey mentioned St Helier, a new London County Council estate in Surrey on which many artisans from Battersea were housed, it was with a degree of foreboding: 'I don't always welcome the LCC when they come into Surrey with their estates.'[2] There were three Labour councillors on the local council at that time. Three more swiftly joined them after the Labour Party supported a successful campaign for rent reduction on St Helier. In addition the county council seat of Merton South East, which included a large part of Morden, fell to Labour in 1934. Such victories were rare in Surrey.

In Stepney it was defiance which won Labour support. Activist Phil Piratin, reflecting on his activities there in the 1930s, concluded that 'many of the voters – stirred by the tenants' struggles, by the . . . fight against the building societies, and by the exposure of the National Government in its support of the building societies – turned with disgust away from Toryism to Labour.' In Feltham, he argued, it was on the basis of these activities that 'the Labour Party won the support of the majority of the people in the Council elections'.[3] Vi Willis recalled her father, who was in the Labour Party, taking action in the 1930s in an east London Labour stronghold:

> They had a rent strike. And Ulveston Road and Walton Road, and those women – it had to be women then because men couldn't stay at home from work if they were at work – and they all marched to Bow County Court. Dad was the leader. And the repairs had to be done.

Naomi Wolff, a Hammersmith councillor from 1934, looked back on the interwar years and commented that 'the domestic political thing – that was the basis of the Labour Party . . . Housing and health I think dominated the politics of the Labour Party at that time.'

Defence of working-class accommodation was also high on Labour's agenda after the Second World War. Mike Turner of Ruislip, who joined the Labour Party in 1945, recalled how he organised a squat of a former American camp of twelve large huts, which had been vacated by the American air force. In Putney Alf Barton cited a delegation to the town hall to get bomb-damaged houses repaired. 'That sort of thing gradually built up support for the party and that's what made the difference.'[4]

> In the north part of Ruislip there was an American camp of twelve large huts, which had been vacated by the American air force and were lying empty. Each hut had room for about twenty-four soldiers. So, in my efforts to improve the situation I organised a squat [with the Labour Party and Communist Party] of all these huts, and moved in twelve more or less homeless families, all of whom worked at the airport. The local council were responsible for these huts, and they had been instructed to knock them down. When they found that we had squatted in them, in those days squatting was unheard of, really. There was just a lovely opportunity, they were just right for the families who moved in. They decided that they would move families out one by one but house them in council accommodation, which was what we wanted anyway. But we decided that this was an opportunity to improve the housing problem which, after the war, was very acute in the Ruislip area. So, when the council workmen came to knock on the door of the empty hut they found, to their amazement, that there was another family in there, and they said, 'Well, who are you?' and they said 'We live here.' And this went on for a long time, and by that way we housed a lot of families . . . Because the borough was split between the rich and the poor, to some extent, we pressed for more rented housing in the north of the borough, to try and balance up the situation. And we used the powers of requisition so, as a large house became empty, say through the owner dying, the council were persuaded to requisition the property and convert it into flats for working-class people.
>
> **Mike Turner, Ruislip**

The housing shortage led many people to become squatters in otherwise unused accommodation

NMPFT/Science & Society Picture Library

I don't think [David Weitzman] was ever prominent as a national politician, though he was prominent in the House of Commons. He was an extremely able Member of Parliament, both in the House and as a constituency member. He worked very hard, he was very able, he was in the constituency every week and people who took their problems to him invariably thought that he'd done whatever he could for them.[5] Again I'm reverting to the theme, most of the problems were housing . . . The fact was, we had thousands of people who were seeking homes either because they didn't have homes as such or because their living accommodation was unsatisfactory and, as can well be imagined, we had a limited number of homes which we could provide. If we built a block of flats which could hold, say, 100 families, we would have something like 5,000 families who were looking for homes, the majority of whom needed new homes, although of course there were some who wanted to have something better. If we could build at the rate of providing 1,000 homes or 2,000 homes a year there would be a backlog of four or five years before people on the housing list would be re-housed.

The housing department and individual councillors and the mayor and the local MP were inundated with appeals from people, most of whom were genuine, for decent homes to live in. The housing department and the councillors and the mayor and the MP were simply unable to give a majority of these people the homes that they needed and probably deserved. There were occasionally cases which, while being further back on the list than they might have been because of certain circumstances or even perhaps because of additional circumstances, which from time to time we were able to help, but these were very few and far between because unless we adhered to a policy of housing those a) who were in the greatest need and b) then those who were longer on the list, we would have found ourselves in a chaotic situation, and so we had to be guided by those two conditions.

Joe Kahn, Hackney

Joe Kahn became chair of the Housing Committee.

The biggest problem of all was housing. We were very well served in Hackney by the chief officers. Hackney Council was run on the basis that policy was dictated by the councillors, that is by the Labour Party. Implementation was carried out by the chief officers. Chief officers had the right, and the duty, to advise, or oppose, decisions and to have those decisions discussed with them, and the views of chief officers were taken into consideration and from time to time were implemented in opposition to a policy that we had pursued, but once a decision was made the chief officers were then duty bound to carry them out. In this respect we were particularly fortunate in having a group of chief officers who, whilst they were probably all Tories, were even more local council officials and so they did their job exceptionally well. From 1950–57 we had an extremely efficient council and Hackney was a very nice locality for those years. Hackney had suffered as much as almost any part of London or the country other than the focal areas like the docks. This meant the number of homeless was very great, but it also meant there were large areas that could be used for building homes. Our main priority was building homes and we were very good at it. We had a chief officer in charge of housing, building, who had a labour force but who insisted on his labour force tendering for new developments so that we really got the best. He used his labour force either on a building programme where they succeeded or on the maintenance which was a very big issue anyway. It is interesting that the government who disliked Hackney and disliked Labour, when they had visitors, particularly from the eastern bloc, used to bring them to Hackney to show how well they were doing in the United Kingdom.

Joe Kahn, Hackney

Education
After health and housing people rated other aspects of the welfare state as being high on the list of Labour's achievements. Within the framework of the Education Act of

1944, which had been introduced by the Conservative R.A. Butler, Ellen Wilkinson raised the school-leaving age to fifteen, and increased government expenditure on education. Margaret Wright thought that Labour had achieved some changes which benefited working people:

> Looking back, it seems to me that the optimism was well founded. The Welfare State certainly made a big difference to all our lives. Thanks to a local authority scholarship I was able to go to university – the first in all our family to do so. We didn't have to worry any longer about the doctor's bills which had been a big strain on the family budget. And my parents could look forward to a state pension which took away the fear of poverty in old age.[6]

> People wanted a new kind of Britain. They wanted full employment, they wanted decent social services, they wanted housing and they thought the Labour Party was the vehicle through which these things could be obtained.
>
> **Jim Mortimer, Hounslow**

> We thought we were on the road to socialism, with the Beveridge Report and the Education Bill and the NHS, all that. We thought we were on the way to socialism and, of course all the building, council house building that went on, didn't it? We lived in a council flat until we moved here.
>
> **Dot Welsh, Paddington**

> We thought, what an exciting time it all is. Here, at long last, socialism is going to come into its own. Jobs for people, proper housing for people, proper education for people and, one thing that I do remember, one of the best things the Labour Party's ever done, was to open up the universities to all sections of societies, and I saw this happen in the ward that I represented, where there were operatic stars, there were doctors, architects, accountants, all come from a poor working-class district because the Labour government introduced this sort of education for all sections of society. That was one of Labour's greatest achievements.
>
> **Albert Huish, Cardiff**

> I was tremendously impressed with the Open University, and that's down to the Labour Party.
>
> **Jean Goldie, Elderslie**

Public ownership

In Cardiff Labour, having won all three Parliamentary seats in 1929, lost them all in 1931, when only one National Government candidate faced a Labour opponent. Labour was associated with Free Trade, and many East Moors steel workers deserted the party. The Conservatives maintained their grip on the city until 1945, when Labour won all three seats. Labour nationalised the steel industry and then, under a Conservative government, the steel works closed and the industrial base of Cardiff continued its decline. Before the closure of the East Moors works, 73 per cent of Cardiff's workers were in the service sector. This increased to 84 per cent after the closure. Bill Herbert recalled nationalisation:

Most of the management remained. And that was my one bitterness against it . . . The managing director down at East Moors was a real blue Tory and, as far as he was concerned – he did some damage there. If a bloke scorched a furnace prior to nationalisation he'd be sacked, he'd sack him like a dog. When we were nationalised, from having seven furnaces running, within eight weeks we only had two because they'd burn the roof and put the furnace off. Wouldn't sack them. He'd put the furnace off. It took a lot of work with the unions at that time, a lot of work to say – Hey, that's not on. Got to have some management. But really, if ever they nationalise anything like that, in my opinion, they need to put their own workforce. You've got to have people of your own. You've got to have people who are interested in running the steel industry for you. There were seven steel barons in those days. And those seven steel barons continued to run those steel works throughout its nationalisation. So it didn't get a fair crack of the whip.

Bill Herbert, Cardiff

A number of Ministers found that there was little by way of draft legislation. Manny Shinwell asked Transport House for its documents on coal nationalisation and discovered only two papers existed, and one of those was in Welsh. The government had little notion as to what to pay in compensation to owners. There were 800 coal companies, many of which also operated in other areas. Furthermore, many government advisors were from private firms and thus hostile to its plans. Ninety of the posts in the Ministry of Food were filled by staff from Unilever. There were complaints that public ownership was unnecessarily centralised, bureaucratic and managerial.

Nationalisation, if you've a Tory government, isn't a lot of good to you. It should have been socialisation. It should have been workers more on it. Nationalisation, we've had it under the Tories and they've just managed to do away with it all, haven't they?

Betty Crook, Chorley

The Attlee government achieved a lot. It may have achieved too much. It put its programme into action. Bevan and the National Health Service. Something which needs to be defended. I remember the problems Manny Shinwell had. He was Minister of Fuel. There were problems as far as the production of coal was concerned. The nationalisation of the coal industry, that was marvellous. That was one of the biggest things they did as some of us knew, some of my forebears knew. I used to see them coming home from the pits in their dirt. The thought of pit-head baths was out of this world. The trade unions had a very important role to play.

Jim Tucker, Redcar

One of the problems that arose from the Labour Party's mass transfer of organisations into the public sector, particularly in ones like civil aviation, was the fact that there were no managers who had socialist leanings, or were members of the Labour Party, to put in charge.

Mike Turner, Ruislip

I would still be a member of the Revolutionary Communist Party, of course, in 1945, and we were recoiling from, we were overthrown by these events. We were now in the postwar period, and not in the war situation as we knew it . . . We didn't get too euphoric about it because we knew that, basically, the Labour Party didn't know what to do either. It was only the programme of the first Labour Government was quite progressive, but it was not a programme that they had

In 1994 former miner Bill Herbert moved that Cardiff City Council give miners the freedom of the City

Bill Herbert's private collection

Despite lack of preparation, coal's long-promised
nationalisation in 1947 was popular
NMPFT/Science & Society Picture Library

thought out at all. The Nationalisation programme had been pushed on them . . .
Mikardo [later a member of the NEC, an MP and chair of the Labour Party]
points out that it was largely accidental that they had this postwar programme of
nationalising, of taking the railways and mines and so on, but it was trade union
pressures, particularly in relation to nationalisation of the railways and the mines
– though I don't think that Churchill opposed that – but these were more an
attitude of bewilderment than I think there was any thoroughly thought-out
system or programme of what a Labour government was likely to do. Attlee did
aid progression towards the ending of the colonial empire, and the development
of the Commonwealth of Nations freely joining together as exists today.

Syd Bidwell, Southall

After 1945

When considering that which the Labour Party had achieved, many people focused on
the Attlee government of 1945–50. However, approval waned for some when, in
September 1949, the Chancellor of the Exchequer, Stafford Cripps, devalued sterling
by 30 per cent, from $4.03 to $2.80 to the pound. This fuelled inflation and adversely
affected the government's popularity. Local councillors were also affected by the
swing against Labour. Labour only narrowly won the 1950 election with 315 seats, a
majority of six. In 1951 the Conservatives gained 321 seats and a majority of 16.
Some people began to be disillusioned, others looked forward to a new Labour

administration. Jean Goldie and Jimmy Allison referred to the importance of the government of Harold Wilson, which introduced the Open University, and Albert Huish was proud to have helped designate Wales nuclear-free.

When we started off, what you thought was: if you got socialism, that were Utopia, weren't it? That were th'end of everything. We never got it and we never will. I don't think we ever will.

Betty Crook, Chorley

In 1949 we had the Cripps budget and canvassing in the weeks after the Cripps budget leading up to the council elections was extremely difficult and in the council elections in 1949 we lost the seats in the West End ward and the Belsize ward. We were simply left with Kilburn.

Bea Serota, Hampstead

We were very much criticised as a council by the Tenants Federation because we weren't able to change things fast enough, improve things fast enough. This is the problem which is going to hit the next Labour government. As councillors you act as representative. You write letters. That was one of the boring things. Eventually we did get a system where we could phone in and dictate a letter, but that was much much later. We were having to handwrite letters on behalf of our constituents. I found that extremely wearisome – to the officers, to the MP, it depended. They would come to us with just a verbal account which was not very factual, and we would have to concoct a statement which would carry some weight. It was quite an arduous job.

Lyndal Evans, Hampstead

I think the Attlee government had some very good people in it, and we had everything going for us then because, like now, the Tories had done nothing for the working class and we needed changes so that more people could be helped and more people have opportunities, so I think it was very much on the right road, some of the people in it were very good. They were active for the people. The trouble is, we never stay in there long enough to make the impact we ought to make.

Joan Baker, Gosport

I also think that a lot of the acts that Harold Wilson did were very significant. People shouldn't forget that. The redundancy payment act, for a start, but also the legislation that we introduced about industrial relations and rights of trade unionists, equal opportunities, better deals for women, trying to move towards equal pay.

Jimmy Allison, Paisley

Local successes

A number of people mentioned the importance of the Labour Party within their own communities. Vi Willis and Naomi Wolff referred to events before the war, others to the post-war years. Several people reiterated the need to bolster that which had been created, as it was under threat from the Conservatives.

So many children were going to school in the middle of winter without anything on their feet. This is true. And if it wasn't for Councillor Taylor, as she was then – she organised what was called a Boot Fund . . . And then they brought in the free dinners. And there's a school down in Dursingham Avenue, and there's a brick building there and that was the dinner hall. And we really thought that was fantastic.

Vi Willis, Ilford

[On the council in 1934] we did a lot of simple things, like extending the library and that sort of thing. I know we had an arrangement. A lot of houses didn't have bathrooms in that year, and the Labour Party in Hammersmith agreed that families could collect tickets so that they or their children could use the public baths without paying. Little things like that.

Naomi Wolff, Hammersmith

I used the mayoral funds to host the biggest old people's party that had ever been held in Hackney. It was really very successful. We had engineers put in a special lift, we had cars going round and we had people, who, when my wife went round waiting at tables were holding her hand and crying that they hadn't been out of their bedroom for six years or whatever it was. Marks and Spencers gave us lots of sweets. I had a first-class West End variety show for which I had to pay full trade-union rates, but then they gave me the money back. I had an invitation to the Lord Mayor's Party and I wrote back and said I would come with pleasure if he came back and waited on my old people. He refused and so did I. It was exceptionally successful. They all went home with parcels.

Joe Kahn, Hackney

The Labour Party was extremely gentle, it was non-political almost, in Bedfordshire. There was no such thing as a Communist Party to stir things up anywhere in Bedford. The chairman of the Labour Party was the school mistress. It was all very gentle except that they had interests in the village. I remember vividly fighting battles for getting better sanitation in village schools.

Alan Yates, Cranfield

I was on Huntington Parish Council for twenty-five years. In that time, we were responsible for getting the school here. We had no education here. We had an all-age primary at Alford, which wasn't good enough for the children, and Cheshire County Council was a shocking education authority. [A school was built in 1957.] We both became governors of it.

Nancy Crawford, Chester

The Labour Party was instrumental in getting two schools, and we were also largely instrumental in getting a village hall in Huntington.

John Crawford, Chester

I was a member of the Schools Planning Sub-Committee [of the Inner London Education Authority] which went visiting schools to see how we could improve them and what the new developments would be. That was really fascinating, because one went into a school in any part of London, this wasn't confined to Camden, and could see, in some cases smell, the poverty, the damp coats in the cloak room. We had very good relationships with the staff and sometimes they would campaign to have new science blocks or a hall they could do drama in and all that sort of thing, and that came to the Schools Planning Sub-Committee.

Lyndal Evans, Hampstead

I arranged for the Hackney Empire to have symphony concerts which I thought would be welcomed, and was – by such a small handful of people – the mass of residents stayed firmly away and the concerts only lasted I think twice. One other incident that is quite interesting. There was in Stratford a theatre started by Joan Littlewood and Gerald Raffles and I thought this was an interesting thing. I went to see one or two productions but they were unable to get any funds from the government because their local authority wouldn't give them a grant. They approached me and asked me if I could get Hackney to give them a grant. I raised the matter in the council chamber and appealed and, although I was opposed by a number of Labour councillors, I did win the day and we decided to give a grant, not a very large one, to the Theatre Royal. As a result East Ham or West Ham, whatever it was, was shamed into giving a grant and they then got a government grant, and I'm rather pleased about this because, although I was attacked in council by members of the party who claimed that the mass of people did not want theatre like that, I think subsequent events show that this was a worthwhile effort because Theatre Royal Stratford became an extraordinarily well-known and much acclaimed theatre both in this country and abroad so, to that extent, perhaps I balanced the symphony concert on the one hand with the Theatre Royal on the other.

Joe Kahn, Hackney

We always sent a delegate to the women's conference. I remember seconding Dr Shirley Summerskill's resolution pressing for cervical cancer council clinics at one conference. Our section was instrumental in getting the health committee to set up cervical cancer clinics. We worked five years in introducing birth control clinics in the borough.

May Banks, Salford

Hornchurch Council. We brought in the free contraceptives for the young people and, of course, that was splashed all over the papers. I was associated with rabid sex.

Ron Whitworth, Hornchurch

When we took over from the Tories when they went out in '71, we found that they were only issuing meals on wheels twice a week, and we managed to get the meals on wheels up to seven days a week, because people needed them seven days a week.

Maureen Dewar, Tottenham

When I was chairman of county council, I arranged for all the peace movements in Wales to join us and to come to a meeting. It was held in the chapel in the centre of Cardiff, and I understood that that was the launch of the first European county to declare themselves nuclear free. That was 1984. That was Wales, the whole of Wales.

Albert Huish, Cardiff

You cannot ever, any more, think of the Labour Party as it was in the Thirties and Forties. Because you haven't got a nation like that any more. And you're never, never going to get young people to think and feel the same way as we did, because they've already got it.

Vi Willis, Ilford

In the Seventies, and certainly in the Sixties, political issues were there. People thought things very strongly. It was because of conviction and things like that, or oppression in some cases, but they fought their corner. And, beginning in the Eighties, things had got better and there weren't so many people that were so badly off that you had to go on your knees and pray to God. They were a bit more settled. That might be partly due to a certain political atmosphere before. A certain energy that was put into politics before helped to get to that position, but once you've got to that position, a certain lassitude takes over.

Ron Whitworth, Havering

Looking forward

Jennie Lee, the first Minister of the Arts in Harold Wilson's government, had been elected to Parliament aged twenty-four and then left the Labour Party in the 1930s. Her iconoclastic husband, Nye Bevan, was scornful of her because she would not compromise. 'Why don't you get into a nunnery and be done with it? Lock yourself up in a separate cell away from the world and its wickedness? . . . it is the Labour Party or nothing.'[7]

I am in my eightieth year, and for sixty-four of those years I have been a supporter of the Labour Party, and for many of those years an active member and a supporter. I haven't, however, been an uncritical supporter. I agree with Jennie Lee who said, 'One can do nothing with the Labour Party and one can do nothing without the Labour Party.'

Scott Garnet, Grantham

Unless we can set up – and it will be a long, long journey – unless we can set up what is called a classless society, Labour will always have a problem in bringing together what are called working-class people and middle-class people. Unless we can bridge in some way that divide. Apart from that, I think that Labour do very well, and they've tried hard, and that they've made enormous strides in my lifetime towards better standards of living for the poorest in the community.

Doris Partridge, Bromley

We had to fight to get our Welfare State. To get the National Health Service. And having established them, and got them working, and then got better working conditions. People got more money. They started buying cars, and they bought a house. They used to say, 'What do I want the Labour Party for? I've got a car. I've got a house. I'm happy. I don't want to have to vote Labour any more.' That's the way things went. I can't understand it. Absolutely crackers. If you've got a house and a car and everything through Labour Party activity, surely you want to keep voting for them?

Jack Coghill, Tottenham

The Labour movement has the seeds within it of its own destruction in that it agitates for full employment, it agitates for an advancement on merit in society, it agitates for available higher education. And the more its own people avail themselves of these facilities, the less time they have to give to the Labour movement itself. And that was certainly true of my Labour generation.

Tom Carbery, Glasgow

After a lifetime of commitment, people reflected on the way forward for Labour. Despite their attachment to how things have been done in the past, many of them stressed the importance of change in direction, to be prepared always to rethink strategy, that Labour should be a party of power not of protest. Roy Hattersley has stressed that

Socialism is far more than a theory of economic organisation . . . socialism is a philosophy, not a method of accounting . . . The glory of democratic socialism in Britain is the way in which its prophets have also been its practitioners, pursuing the ideal by perfecting the ways in which it can be achieved.[8]

Oral testimony indicates the extent to which, for activists, recruitment, social activities, political discussion and raising money, often through collecting subscriptions, were all related. Election agent Ron Whitworth made the point:

The social side is very important to consider in a political context, because if you can get your social activists and your political activists working together then you send out a bright message, don't you?

Josie Tipple and Jean Goldie emphasised that Labour was more than a political party, that it provided a social and ethical framework for socialists.

It is something like sacrilege to decide to abolish Clause Four yet it depends what's behind it, it depends what the motive is. If the motive is to change the party from being predominantly socialist to something which is just some sort of Liberal Party then I'd be completely against it but I think the present movement to modify Clause Four is historically sensible. I'm now satisfied. I've recently come to that conclusion because I was brought up on Clause Four. History tells us that the way it's been applied it doesn't mean complete blanket nationalisation. You can have socialism without that. I am just as encouraged today. The new leadership is in the interests of the party. It means winning elections. It is no good being a political party without winning elections. You've got to have control.

Jim Tucker, Stockport

What I'm afraid of. I'm not afraid of our lovely young Prime Minister that will be. I'm not afraid he will go away from socialism. But I do know it's going to be a different form of socialism . . . It's got to be different, but we're doing our utmost. And I'll support him all the way. When I listen to him, I support him all the way.

Vi Willis, Ilford

Before I die, I want to see another Labour government . . . You can't do a thing until you're in power, and there's a lot of people have got to be won back.

Magda Clarke, London

I feel I owe the Labour Party . . . I've had more out of being a member of the Labour Party than I've ever given to it in terms of friendship, in terms of hope for the future and some sort of route in your life. I owe it a lot.

Jean Goldie, Elderslie

The Labour Party has always been a crusade with me. It still is.

Josie Tipple, Winsford

Left-wing critic Raymond Williams argued that: 'Socialists in the Labour Party have been afraid, far too long, of describing it as it is. There has been a continual breeding of illusions and false hopes.'[9] The memories gathered here indicate otherwise. A number of interviewees said that they had little to gain from inhibition or deception and that they felt candour was beneficial.[10] Even if there are some 'false hopes', this testimony, the memories and perceptions of people who have a long-term commitment to socialism, offers far more than colourful illustrations of the nature of democracy, communities and the Labour Party in Britain. There are those on the left who have argued that Labour's position is influenced by media spin doctors, and those on the right who have said that it is dominated by doctrinaire socialists. Listening to those who are active within it indicates that the sentiments, the idealism and the selflessness, of the architects and builders of the party have also played a significant part in the creation of its ethos. It is not simply a machine for gathering votes in order to acquire power, it is a way of life which has sustained activists, just as they have sustained it. Many are still fully involved, knowing that while the battlefields may have changed, the struggle persists and will continue after their deaths. Perhaps with this in mind Vi Willis reminded her interviewer that every opportunity for recruitment should be seized to ensure that the torch of socialism is handed over to another generation of socialists:

Where do we go from here? Not us. Where do you go from here?

Vi Willis, Ilford

Biographies

Many of the people interviewed for this project have been lifelong activists, detailing up to eighty years of political experience. Left-wing commitment often extends for several generations, and many interviewees have mentioned grandparents or grandchildren in the Labour Party. It would be impossible to list all relevant details, the notes below are intended to form a context for the quotations given earlier. They are not complete biographies, just as the quotations do not form complete transcripts. The original recordings can all be consulted in the British Library's National Sound Archive. Telephone 0171 412 7405 for an appointment. All the accession numbers start with the code C609.

Jimmy Allison was born in Paisley in 1928 and applied to join the Labour Party in 1959, after years of involvement in the trade union movement. He took on many posts in his union and in the Party, rising steadily through the ranks, becoming a councillor in 1969, then Glasgow Organiser in 1971, Assistant Scottish Organiser in 1974, and Scottish Organiser from 1977. When interviewed in 1995 he was secretary of his constituency party. He is the author of *Guilty by suspicion. A life and Labour* (1995).

Doris Ashby was born in the 1920s to parents who were left-wing activists. She became a nurse and was active in the Socialist Medical Association and the Women's Co-operative Guild. A lifelong activist, she finally joined the Labour Party in 1980.

Joan Baker was born in Gosport in the 1920s, and she and her husband became active in the Gosport Labour Party in the 1940s. She had been active in the Women's Co-operative Guild from an early age, as her mother was chairman of the local branch. After she moved to Willesden in 1948, she became a Labour councillor, and she has also stood as a parliamentary candidate for Labour in Eastbourne and Barnet.

May Banks was born in Battersea in 1900 and remembers the funeral of suffragette martyr Emily Davison in 1913. She and her husband joined the very active West Salford ILP in 1922. Her daughter was named in the Socialist Sunday School. She became a Labour Party member in 1932, was active in the Women's Section, and later became ward secretary. When recorded in 1993 she was still a Labour Party activist.

Stanley Bell was born in Kingston-upon-Thames in 1915. A young activist, he attended Hyde Park demonstrations during the General Strike. He became secretary of the local League of Youth, where he met his future wife. They were temporarily suspended from the Labour Party, and their local party closed down for Popular Front activity. He later became Chief Whip of the Labour Group on the local council.

Syd Bidwell was born in Southall in 1917. His father was an active member of the ILP, and was on the General Strike committee. Syd joined the League of Youth in 1933 and then the Revolutionary Communist Party. He later joined the Labour Party and went on to become chair of the Southall Labour Club and a lecturer in the National Council of Labour Colleges. He became Labour MP for Southall in 1966.

Frank Booth was born in Stockport in 1920 to Conservative parents. He experienced poverty in the 1930s when his family were Means Tested. He went along to help the Labour Party in a 1945 by-election, and had been a member for forty-nine years when interviewed in 1994. In 1954 he became a Labour councillor, and went on to become a Labour alderman from 1960 to 1970 .

Edward Britton was born in 1909. He has had a lifetime involvement in education and the politics of education. He has also carried out trade union work at local, national and international levels, becoming

President and General Secretary of the National Union of Teachers, plus a member of the Warnock Committee and the International Labour Organisation.

Fred Brockbank was born in Pendlebury in 1923 and joined the Labour Party in 1945. He helped at his local MPs' surgeries for many years. In 1967 he was elected to his local council, becoming a city councillor in Salford after local government reorganisation. He became mayor in 1985.

John Broome was born in 1927. A trade unionist, he joined the Communist Party while working as a builder after the war, but found the party locally too academic, and left again. He and his wife Tessa (below) joined the Labour Party in 1952. He collected subscriptions for his local branch and went on to become secretary and chair of his constituency Labour Party.

Tessa Broome was born in 1927. As a student nurse she heard Nye Bevan speak on the eve of the creation of the National Health Service. After marrying John Broome (above) she joined the Labour Party with him in 1952.

Helen Cameron was born in Glasgow in 1919, the sister of Isa Paton (below). Her parents were in the ILP, and she was named in the Socialist Sunday School. She joined the Co-operative Party's Comrades Circle at the age of fifteen, and the Labour Party in 1942. She was election agent for many years, and one of two women from Scotland on the National Women's Advisory Committee, regularly travelling down to meetings at Transport House. She moved to Crieff in 1977. During the 1980s she and her husband became increasingly disillusioned with the Labour Party and left, later joining the SDP for a time.

Tom F. Carbery was born in 1925 in a Gorbals flat. When he was fourteen or fifteen a friend took him to the Co-operative Comrades Circle and he was very active in the British Federation of Young Co-operators, although his family was originally wary of his coming under 'communist' influence. After leaving the Forces in 1947, he joined both the Labour Party and the Co-operative Party, and found the Labour Party locally the livelier of the two. A lifelong political activist, he has never held office in the Labour Party but, when interviewed in 1995, had been on approximately twenty QUANGOs. His book, *Consumers in politics, a history and general review of the Co-operative Party* was published in 1969, and he is also the co-author of *Progress to Prosperity* (1968), published by the Scottish Council of Fabian Societies.

Hugh Chaplin was born in 1905, the son of a Wesleyan minister. He was a Conservative when he went to college, where he first came into contact with socialists. During the 1929 General Election he was in Belfast, where the choice was between a Unionist and an Independent Unionist candidate. He joined the Popular Front and then the Labour Party in 1935, when Mussolini invaded Abyssinia; and he and his wife campaigned hard for the Spanish Republicans and against fascism. In 1945 his wife was the local Labour candidate. Later she fought the Borough Council elections and won a Labour majority for the first time in Holborn. Hugh was active in the local branch as treasurer, secretary and chair.

Anna Clarke was born in 1919 in Cape Town, South Africa and later moved with her family to Canada and then to Oxford. She joined the Labour Party in 1945, and campaigned during the General Election that year. While living in London she was secretary and treasurer of her local party. She was asked to stand for the local council, but rejected the proposal. When she moved to Brighton in the 1960s she immediately became involved in the Labour Party there. She is the author of twenty-six novels.

John Morris Clarke was born in 1924 in Liverpool. His father was a Conservative, but his grandfather was an ardent socialist and one of his uncles a card-carrying Communist. John was involved in union activity, but did not join the Labour Party as an individual until 1955. His membership then lapsed, but he rejoined in the early 1960s. He became a borough councillor in 1979 and has been chair of Warrington North GMC and secretary of the European constituency of Cheshire East.

Magda Clarke was born in 1919 in Cape Town, South Africa, the sister of Anna Clarke (above). She joined the University Labour Club during the time of the Spanish Civil War, while she was at Oxford. In 1945 she was out campaigning in Bloomsbury every evening and took polling day off work. She campaigned again in

1950, but then dropped out of politics, only to rejoin under Neil Kinnock's leadership in the 1980s. When interviewed in 1995, she described herself as a staunch member of the British Labour Party.

Jack Coghill was born in Wood Green in 1916. Although he was brought up in a Tory household, Jack says he 'learned his socialism at grass-roots level' working in north London factories. He became a shop steward during the war, and during the 1940s he became a delegate to the Tottenham Labour Party. In 1979 he was Vice-Chairman of the Tottenham Labour Party and, when interviewed in 1995, was an active member of the Tottenham Pensioners Group.

Fred W. Combes was born in Islington in 1909, one of five children of a sheet metal worker. He joined the union at the age of sixteen and the Labour Party in 1929. He and his brother formed a local Labour League of Youth. He was deputy election agent for Southwark in the 1945 General Election and agent for subsequent London County Council elections. He worked for the Party as ward secretary for thirty-three years. In 1958 he became mayor, with his sister as mayoress, and was a local councillor for fourteen years.

John Crawford was born into a politically active family in Chester in 1915, and as a child helped Labour to win the 1924 General Election by running messages at the polling station. He joined the Labour Party League of Youth in 1931 and later the Left Book Club. In Egypt during the war his wife sent him political newspapers, and he took part in the Cairo Parliament. A parish councillor for forty years and a post-holder in his Constituency Labour Party for thirty-two years, John became a city councillor in 1979 and went on to become deputy mayor and mayor.

Nancy Crawford was born in 1915 and married John Crawford (above) in 1941. Her first job was in the local Co-op. After the war, local branch meetings were held at their house. She was a local parish councillor for twenty-five years and was still an active Labour Party member when interviewed in 1995.

Betty Crook was born near Bolton in 1908 and experienced poverty when her father died, leaving a young family. She joined the ILP Guild of Youth in 1924 and remembers continual activity, both political and social. She was a delegate from the ILP to the Labour Party, but found the ILP members far more active. She campaigned for Labour in the 1945 General Election and became secretary of her local Labour Party. She later resigned, although she continued to work for the party.

Miriam Crook was born in South Wales in 1910. A Labour voter all her life, Miriam joined the Labour Party in 1937, the year she married.

Maureen Dewar was born in 1925 in West Norwood. She was brought up in a socialist atmosphere, and her first political activity was delivering election leaflets at the age of ten. She joined the Labour Party in 1945 with the aim of getting the Tories out, and was voted in as secretary at her first meeting. Since then she has held almost every post there is, knocked on doors, canvassed, attended demos – 'you name it, and I've done it!'

Lex Diamond was born in 1921 in New York and came to Britain in 1939. During the war he became involved in the Communist Party, which was where he met his wife. As a member of the Amalgamated Engineers Union he was affiliated to the Labour Party, although he was unable to join any political party until he was naturalised. He was a delegate to and later secretary of the Ealing Trades Council. He left the Labour Party in 1992 because he considered it to have become anti-trade union.

Harold Edwards was born in Warrington in 1901 to Liberal parents. He started work for the Co-op at the age of fourteen and worked there for fifty-one years. In 1917 he joined the Co-operative Party and in 1922, as soon as he met the age requirements, he joined the Labour Party. He was a councillor from 1964 to 1967, served as mayor in 1979 and later received the MBE.

Marianne Elliott was born in Perivale in 1934. Her mother joined the Labour Party soon after her birth, and Marianne joined the Young Socialists in 1950. After being Assistant Secretary for a while she became Secretary of Ealing North Labour Party in 1960, held the post for thirteen years, and has also served as an alderman.

Lyndal Evans was born in East London in 1921. Her mother had strong political beliefs, had been imprisoned for her part in the suffragettes' campaign, and met Lyndal's father at a Fabian Society gathering. Lyndal was politically active from an early age. She has held many posts, including being on the local council for fourteen years and also on the Inner London Education Authority.

Martha Feeney was born in the East End of Glasgow in 1927. Her father was a member of the Communist Party, and a Stalinist till the day he died. He was blacklisted by employers for his beliefs, and so the family was not well off. She was always a political activist. Her union was affiliated to the Labour Party and she joined as an individual member in 1980, after the election of Margaret Thatcher. She was still very politically active when interviewed in 1995 and continues to attend meetings of the Women's Co-operative Guild.

Scott Garnet was born into a very Conservative family in 1915 and became a supporter of the Labour Party at the age of sixteen. In the 1930s he was literature officer and purchased many political pamphlets. He helped with the League of Nations Union Peace Ballot in 1934. He was elected on to Grantham Borough Council for nineteen years, then served on the District Council and became mayor in 1982.

Jack Gaster was born in 1907, the son of a Chief Rabbi of Sephardic Jews. During the General Strike one of his brothers volunteered as a blackleg. As a practising lawyer, he was heavily involved in legal protection of those who opposed the Blackshirts in the 1930s. He also defended the unemployed and tenants but placed these activities as secondary to his political life in the ILP (which he joined in 1926) and later the Communist Party. He stressed: 'I am not a drawing-room socialist'.

Jean Goldie was born in Sunderland in 1927. She was an active member of the League of Youth, taking part in social and political activities. At the end of the war she and her father went out and helped in the election campaign in Paisley, and she attended her first Labour Party meeting in 1946. After living in Portugal for thirteen years she rejoined the Party in 1964, which was 'like coming home'.

Douglas Hawkins was born in Barry in 1908. Encouraged by his mother, he joined the Labour League of Youth which, after differences of opinion with the Labour Party, later became the Barry Young Socialist League. He joined the Labour Party in 1923, collected subs for thirty years and was treasurer for fifteen years. An active trade unionist, in 1948 he tried to organise NCLC classes at his workplace, and was dismissed on a trumped-up charge. He was awarded the NEC's Certificate of Merit in 1984.

Owen Heather was born in Preston in 1918, the son and grandson of active suffragettes. His family moved to Withington, where he organised a Labour League of Youth and the Red Falcons – based on a German youth group of the same name. While a member of the Labour Party he joined the Young Communist League, and then the Communist Party in 1936. Expelled from the Communist Party, he joined the ILP and later rejoined the Communist Party, retaining Labour Party membership throughout. He was elected to Bedfordshire County Council in 1981 and served as a councillor for twelve years.

Bill Herbert was born in Blackwood, Monmouthshire, in 1921. He remembers attending union meetings with his father at the age of five, while scavenging for coal. His father had been a miner but left after being involved in an explosion. Bill went down the mines at the age of thirteen, but was buried underground for two days aged eighteen and never went down again. He joined the Labour Party in 1937, became a councillor in 1971 and was Lord Mayor of Cardiff in 1988. In the 1994 elections he stood against the Labour Party and was expelled.

Les Horne was born in Yorkshire in 1921 and brought up surrounded by politics and trades unions. His father was a miner, so the family had no income at all during the long strike of 1926. He first joined a trade union aged fourteen and was an active member, involved in many campaigns, until he retired at sixty-five, having been awarded the British Empire Medal. He joined the Labour Party before the war and became deeply involved when he moved to Swindon in 1946 but was very unhappy with the way it was run locally and recently stood as an Independent candidate.

John Horner was born in 1911 and brought up in Walthamstow. An active trade unionist, he was General

Secretary of the Fire Brigades Union for twenty-five years and was a Communist Party member for a decade. The Labour Party later approved his membership, and he became MP for the West Midlands seat of Oldbury and Halesowen in 1964, losing the seat to John Stokes in 1970.

Albert Huish was born in Cardiff in 1914 and grew up surrounded by poverty. He and his wife met through the Labour Party and have been members of the Co-operative movement since their marriage in 1938. He became a councillor in 1954 and a county councillor and Lord Mayor in 1974. Ten years later he was chairman of the county council, and was instrumental in having Wales declared a Nuclear Free Zone. His son, daughter and grandson are all Labour Party members.

Ernie Johnson was born in Salford in 1918. He joined the union when he started work and was very active in the Apprentices' Strike of 1937, which involved 15,000 apprentices in the Manchester area. He joined the Labour Party as soon as he left the Forces after the war. He became a councillor in 1951 and 'was on every committee that Eccles had, at various times'. In 1982 he took early retirement so he could fulfil his duties as chairman of the Greater Manchester Council.

Mervyn Jones was born in 1922. He joined the Young Communist League while at school, and later the Communist Party in Maida Vale. In 1951 he moved to Chichester and became a member of the Labour Party, where he was known as a Bevanite. He stood as Labour Party candidate in 1955 and later joined the editorial board of *Tribune* and was active in CND. He has written a biography of Labour party leader *Michael Foot* (1994).

Joe Kahn was born in London in 1916, the child of Russian Jewish immigrants who had arrived a few years earlier. He was active in opposing the fascists in the 1930s, and during the Spanish Civil War he led a convoy of five vans to Madrid, where he was eventually invalided out and arrested in France. He was a Communist Party member from 1936 to 1939, but joined the Labour Party during the war, and by 1945 he was a councillor in Hackney. He became chairman of libraries, baths, housing and finance committees and mayor of Hackney.

Alex Kitson was born in Kirknewton in 1921. His grandfather was politically active and Alex became

Jean Goldie, featured on a League of Youth leaflet in 1959
Jean Goldie's private collection

involved in the Labour Party at a young age. He joined the union as soon as he was old enough, was an official by the end of the war, and then took a full-time union position. He went on to become the General Secretary of his union and then Assistant General Secretary of the TGWU. From 1968–1988 he was on the National Executive Committee of the Labour Party and heavily involved in international politics.

Noreen Law was born in East Ham in 1918 and became politically aware at the time of the Spanish Civil War. She joined the Labour Party in 1949 and has since been involved in campaigning activities of all kinds. She was on the General Management Committee in Ealing and was elected as local councillor.

Margaret Lawson was born in Edinburgh in 1916. Her parents were both political activists, and she was a member of the Socialist Sunday School. She joined Central Edinburgh Labour Party in 1936. Her husband was MP for Motherwell from 1954 to 1974, and Margaret held office in her local party in Hamilton as secretary, treasurer and chair.

Margaret Lloyd was born in 1907 in St Helens. At the time her father was the full-time election agent for St Helens, being unable to find work as a miner because of his politics. At the age of sixteen she worked for her father, and did most of the work of agent when her father became mayor in 1926. She joined the Women's Section in the early 1930s and helped to organise election canvassing campaigns.

Jack Lodge was born in 1918. A trade union member, he was a pacifist during the Second World War. He has always voted Labour, but did not join the party until the year after his retirement in 1980.

Donald Matheson was born in 1928 in Liverpool. Influenced by the political ideas of his father and brother-in-law, he became a Labour Party member as a schoolboy. He later became disaffected with the Party and joined the Green Party for two years, although he has always voted Labour. He had recently rejoined the Labour Party when interviewed in 1994, and was an active member once again.

Maurita Matthewson was born in Bargoed in 1920. Her father worked at the mine, and the six children went to soup kitchens during the long miners' strike. Her family later moved to London, where she was involved in campaigning for the Spanish Republicans. She briefly joined the Communist Party. In the 1950s she moved back to Wales, where she became a Labour Party councillor in 1972. When interviewed she was hoping to become deputy mayor in 1996.

Helen McElhone was born in Glasgow in 1937. She met her husband in 1955. He was an avid member of the Labour Party and through him she became involved in organising, campaigning and raising money. Her husband became a popular local MP, and when he died in 1982, she stood for Labour in the by-election and was elected to parliament, but was replaced at the next general election.

Harry McNeill was born in Glasgow in 1924. He was delegated by his trade union to his local Labour Party constituency, and joined as an individual member in the early 1950s. He was councillor in Glasgow from 1972 to 1980 and, as vice chair of the planning committee for the district council and convenor of the Highways Committee for the corporation, helped to build the urban motorway through the city. When interviewed in 1995 his local constituency in Renfrewshire had been suspended by National Office for nearly a year.

Patricia Meitlis was born in Liverpool in 1925. After her mother died when she was six, she travelled widely with her father. In Southampton during the 1930s she met the daughter of Labour MP Horace King, who ran the Co-op choir, and through her she became involved in Labour Party activities. She joined the Communist Party in London during the war and trained to be a member of the Communist Resistance, should Britain be invaded. After the war she became a member of the Labour Party.

Jim Mortimer was born in Manningham in 1921. In 1934 he joined the Labour League of Youth in Portsmouth, then joined the Brixton branch on his first day in London. During the Second World War he joined the Young Communist League, but he was back in the Labour Party by the end of the war. He was a member of various groups within the Labour Party, including Victory for Socialism, and became General Secretary of the Party. He has written the history of the boilermakers' union in three volumes published between 1971 and 1994. He has also written, *A history of the Association of Engineering and Shipbuilding Draughtsmen* (1960), *Trade Unions and Technological Change* (1973) and, with Clive Jenkins, *British Trade Unions Today* (1965).

Fred Neuner was born an Austrian subject in Czechoslovakia in 1919. Like Irene Wagner in Dresden (below) and Owen Heather in Manchester (above) he joined the Red Falcons when young. As leader of the local Socialist Youth, he fled to Britain from the Nazis in 1938 and was interned on the Isle of Man. He was a councillor in Hornsey from 1954 until 1982, and became an alderman in 1979. He has been awarded the Labour Party Merit Award.

Ricky Ormonde was born in Carlow, Ireland, in 1924. He lived in America when young, before moving to Wales after the war. He joined the Labour Party in the 1950s after meeting Jim Callaghan, and was soon active locally, becoming secretary, chair, treasurer and election agent. He was himself elected to office, and became Lord Mayor of Cardiff.

Olive Parsons was born in 1892 and brought up in Bayswater. Her grandfather and uncle were both MPs and her family knew Ramsay MacDonald's family well. She worked for the Labour Research Department. She shared a cottage at Houghton, Arundel with fellow Labour Research Department worker Eva Reckitt, and in 1934 they established a socialist bookshop, Collets, together. She was on the original board and often helped out in the shop. Other branches were opened and Collets ran libraries, published booklets and arranged with publishers for the sale of cheap editions. A Collets' van accompanied the Scottish contingent of the 1936 Hunger March. Her husband Henry was secretary of the Labour Research Department 1945–65 and worked closely with Harry Pollitt, the Communist Party General Secretary. Olive Parsons died in March 1996.

Doris Partridge was born in Belfast in 1916, and moved to Barrow-in-Furness at the age of ten. She began work as a nurse aged sixteen and so is very aware of the benefits provided by the NHS. She became a Labour councillor in 1971 and is a Labour Merit Award holder. When interviewed in 1994 she was still an active party member, editing the local Labour newspaper *The Voice*.

Isa Paton was born in Glasgow in 1910, the daughter of a suffragette who took her to ILP propaganda meetings from the age of eight. She was a member of the Socialist Sunday School. Her father stood as a Labour Councillor in the 1930s and she helped him to campaign. She tried to join the Labour Party then but had no reply to her application and finally joined after the war. She and her family have always been activists and have helped to build the local Labour majority from 600 to 19,000.

Aileen Plant was born into a socialist household in Ashton-under-Lyne in 1913, and has lived in Stockport since 1924. She was a member of the Labour Church, the Labour League of Youth, and the Junior League of Nations, and ran the Anglo-Russia Friendship Council during the war. She trained as a teacher and has been active in the NUT and the National Association of Head Teachers.

John Platts-Mills was born in 1906 in Wellington, New Zealand. When he left Oxford University in 1931, he turned down the Duke of Devonshire's offer of a safe Tory seat in Eastbourne. He joined the Finsbury Labour Party in 1936. During the war, after being turned down for active service, he volunteered as a Bevin Boy, working as a miner. In 1945 he was elected as Labour MP for Finsbury, but was expelled from the party in 1948, and stood unsuccessfully against Labour in 1950. Twenty-one years later, there was no opposition to his rejoining the party. He has always been politically active and has represented hundreds of radicals during his career as a lawyer.

Olive Rainbird was born in Edmonton in 1915, and joined the Labour Party at the age of fifteen. She was very active in the Labour League of Youth, where she met her future husband. She worked at County Hall for the London Labour Party. She has held many posts in the party and, when interviewed in 1995, was on her local GMC and said: 'The Labour Party would probably be the last activity I would give up.'

Tom Riley was born in Battersea in 1917, the son of a staunch trade unionist father. He joined the Labour League of Youth aged fourteen, and remained in it until he was twenty-three. During elections he has always campaigned, delivered and written for the Labour Party. When interviewed in 1995, he felt that as a member of the Tottenham Pensioners Group he was more politically active than he had ever been.

Bea Serota was born in 1919 to a Russian father and an Austrian mother, and was brought up in Hackney. She joined Hampstead Labour Party in 1944 and was returned as a local councillor from 1945–49. She was co-opted on to the London County Council Education Committee in 1952 and returned as the LCC (or later GLC) Brixton councillor from 1954 to 1967. She became chief whip of the Labour Group on the Greater London Council and chair of the Inner London Education Authority, was created a life peer and later became a Minister.

Lew Smith was born to poor Jewish parents in Stepney in 1911. His father took him to political meetings when he was a child, and he joined the Young Communist League at the age of sixteen. He left the Communist Party over Hungary in 1957 and became 'a good Labour man'. He had always been a trade unionist, but for some years he belonged to no party, joining Labour in the 1960s. He now holds the Order of Merit for his long service in the party and, when interviewed in 1995, was vice chairman of the Labour Party in Hackney and active in the Tottenham Pensioners Movement.

Anne Swingler was born in Newcastle-upon-Tyne in 1915. At the age of seventeen she started work in the Labour Research Department, where she met and married a volunteer. He went on to become MP for Stafford and ultimately a Privy Councillor. She became a borough councillor in 1948 and continued her active involvement in Labour politics on moving to Hampstead.

Josie Mary Tipple was born in Acton Bridge in 1918. Her father was a radical Liberal. She joined the Labour Party in 1939 on her twenty-first birthday, and met both her husbands through the party. After the war she campaigned hard during the General Election, became branch secretary and later chair of the Women's Federation. In 1960 she moved to Winsford, where her second husband was mayor three times. In 1970 she joined him on the town council. She is a lifelong member of the NUT.

Harold Tomlins was born in Chester in 1923 and was brought up by his handicapped father. Encouraged by his father, he joined the Labour Party in 1947 and 'within three weeks I was the ward secretary'. He was also to become social secretary, chair of Chester Constituency Labour Party for eight years and parliamentary agent for twenty-one years. He was elected to the city council in 1954, became sheriff in 1972 and mayor in 1980. From 1984 to 1988 he was chair of social services and in 1992 became CLP chair once again.

Jim Tucker was born in Consett in 1916. His mother was in the Labour Party Women's Section and the Co-operative Women's Guild. He joined the Labour Party in 1935 and helped to form the Redcar branch of the Labour League of Youth. In 1959 he became chair of his constituency Labour Party and was later a local and a county councillor in Greater Manchester, and a treasurer, a councillor and an agent in Stockport.

John Tuffey was born in Kensington in 1911. He became political after the Second World War, and joined the Labour Party in 1957, when he helped a friend to canvas and became the local treasurer. He became assistant secretary of his union branch and held this post until he retired. He has been awarded the Labour Party Merit Award.

Mike Turner was born in Dorchester in 1926. His mother died when he was six and life was hard when his father was unemployed. He joined the Yeovil Labour Party and the union in 1945 and was elected to be shop steward the following year, then became chairman of his branch. After the war he organised a squat in an empty American base. On retirement he became an even more active party member, chair of the Eastcote Labour Party, served on many committees and campaigned against hospital closures. He is a Labour Party Merit Award holder and says, 'I've not finished campaigning yet.'

John Uzzell was born on the outskirts of Swindon in 1919. While in the army during the Second World War he attended the Cairo Parliament. He joined the Labour Party the day the NHS second reading was passed in the Commons, attended his first meeting in 1949 and went on to become chair of the Chippenham party. In 1960 he moved to Swindon, where he was treasurer, secretary and ward organiser before becoming a councillor in 1971. John Uzzell died in 1995.

Irene Wagner was born to Jewish parents in Dresden in 1916. She fled the country in 1938 after being locked up by the Gestapo for three days. She was naturalised in early 1945, and she and her husband immediately joined the Holborn Labour Party, and then the Co-operative Party. She ran the Labour Party library for many years, during which time she reclassified it entirely, provided the Parliamentary Labour Party with a press cuttings service every morning and founded an organisation for Labour librarians worldwide. When interviewed in 1995 she was an active party member, and membership secretary of her local branch. She is the Treasurer of Labour Heritage.

Sam Waters was born in Fleetwood in 1912. He joined the Labour Party at the age of sixty-five when he retired from his greengrocery business, having been unable to join earlier as he was not a union member. He joined in Stockport when he became eligible as he wanted to do something about unemployment and health issues.

Dot Welsh was born in Paddington in 1913. She was a member of the Kensington Young Communist League during the 1930s and was involved in joint activity with the Labour League of Youth. During the war, when the selling of the *Daily Worker* was prohibited, she was arrested for selling the Young Communist League newspaper, *Challenge*, despite the fact that this was not illegal. After the war she campaigned for the Labour Party.

Jean White was born in 1925 in Wallasey. Her mother was a member of the Co-op, and Jean went to the Children's Guild. Initially attracted to the Communist Party, she and her husband (below) were inspired to join the Labour Party in the 1950s by a friend. She started a Campaign for Nuclear Disarmament group in Ellesmere Port and rejoined the Labour Party in the 1980s in order to spread the message of CND.

Walter White was born in 1921 in Birkenhead. His father was a Conservative who would not let his wife join the Co-op. Walter began to find out about socialism when he went to work and he and his wife (above) attended Tribune Rallies on the Wirral in the 1950s. He joined the Labour Party in 1958 and left while Harold Wilson was in office, having previously campaigned hard for him. He feels the party is still on the wrong track, so he has not rejoined, although he attends meetings.

Ron Whitworth was born in Plaistow in 1921. He joined the Labour Party in 1947, and in 1953 started *Hornchurch Labour Journal*. He was a councillor in Hornchurch from 1957 to 1960, and in Havering from 1971 to 1986. He has been election agent for many people, including Carole Tonge and Ken Livingstone. A member of NATFHE for fifty-seven years when he was interviewed in 1994, his forty-seven years in the Labour Party had earned him a Merit Award.

Vi Willis was born in 1917 in Little Ilford. Her husband Sid was present when she was interviewed, and quotes are often from both of them. Her father was an 'absolute socialist'. When young, she used to deliver the left-wing *Citizen* newspaper in her doll's pram, while Sid carried his deliveries on a box tricycle. She joined the Labour Party aged sixteen and attended meetings with her father and Sid, who was converted to socialism by her father. The local party declined in the 1960s as people moved into high-rise flats and lost their feelings of neighbourliness. The local ward, of which Vi was chair, supported Reg Prentice, who defected to the Conservatives. They began to receive threatening phone calls and subsequently lapsed from the party.

Naomi Wolff was born in Walthamstow in 1910 and had to leave school early to run the household when her mother died. She was elected as the youngest councillor in Hammersmith in 1934. Her husband was Jewish and she was active in helping refugees from Nazi Germany. She later worked for the MP D.N. Pritt.

Alan Yates was born in 1913 in Halstead, the son of a Baptist minister and the great grandson of a Chartist. He voted Labour in Watford in 1935, and joined the Hampstead Labour Party in 1938 but it was disaffiliated from the Labour Party because members opposed the war. He was active in Unity Theatre 1939–40 and then he left the area and joined the party in Cove, near Farnborough. He was also active in the Anglo-Soviet Committee. In 1945 he campaigned for Labour in Andover. In 1949 he became a Bedfordshire county councillor and served for five years, and in 1950 and 1951 he was a Parliamentary agent. He retired to Hampstead, where he was made vice-chair of the branch and stood for the local council.

Notes

Unless otherwise stated all books referred to are published in London.

Chapter I

1. Prior to 1918 almost half the adult male population, and almost all women, were not allowed to vote.

2. Unless stated otherwise, all quotations are taken from the interviewees whose biographies are provided on pages 224–234.

3. In 1939 Walter Citrine enlarged and revised his *The Labour chairman and speaker's companion: guide to the conduct of trade union and Labour meetings* (1921) and published it as *ABC of Chairmanship*.

4. Sir Isidore Salmon was the Conservative MP for Middlesex, Harrow, between 1929 and his death in 1941. Helen Bentwich, who had previously stood as a parliamentary candidate in Camberwell, stood against him in 1935 and gained 37.3 per cent of the vote to his 62.7 per cent. The selection of women in seats which are considered unwinnable is an issue with which the Labour Party continues to grapple.

5. All four are quoted in H. Jenkins, *Rank and file*, Croom Helm, 1980, pp. 36, 58, 81, 150.

6. J. Wood, 'The Labour left and the CLPs 1931–51', 1982, Warwick, PhD, p. 343.

7. After that, in descending order of popularity, were responses about how people liked to engage socially with comrades, do a job for the party, see their candidate returned and feel influential. Four per cent felt that they were serving the country or the community. See John M. Bochel, 'Activists in the Conservative and Labour parties: a study of ward secretaries in Manchester', 1965, Manchester, MA, pp. 164, 190, 192–3.

8. R. McKibbin, *The ideologies of class: social relations in Britain 1880–1950*, Clarendon, Oxford, 1990, pp. 13–16.

9. D. Berry, 'Party membership and social participation', *Political Studies*, Vol. 17, 1969, pp. 205, 207.

10. P. Willmott and M. Young, *Family and class in a London suburb*, Routledge & Kegan Paul, 1960, p. 131. On the importance of urban communities to the Labour Party see F. Bealey and M. Dyer, 'Size of place and the Labour vote in Britain, 1918–66', *Western Political Quarterly*, No. 24, 1971, pp. 84–113; and W.P. Grant, 'Size of place and local Labour strength', *British Journal of Political Science*, No. 2, 1972, pp. 259–60.

11. This issue is examined in D. Weinbren, 'Labour's roots and branches', *Oral History*, Vol. 24 No. 1, 1996, pp. 29–38.

12. Response to Michael Mark Waite's questionnaire. See M. Waite, 'Young people and Communist politics in Britain 1920–91: aspects of the history of the YCL', 1992, Lancaster, MPhil, p. 245.

13. R. Samuel, 'The lost world of British communism', *New Left Review*, 154, November/December 1985, p. 53. The issue is also discussed in M. Waite, 'Manchester's Red Army', *Jewish Socialist*, No. 32, Autumn 1994, p. 30. P. Abrams and A. Little, 'The young activist in British politics', *British Journal of Sociology*, Vol. 16, 1965, p. 330 conclude from their survey that 'amongst the young activists of all parties there is a rather higher proportion of children of (white) immigrants than one would expect demographically'.

14. There is a discussion of how even those who call themselves 'born rebels' or 'lifelong socialists' cannot be politicised before birth in P. Thompson and R. Samuel (eds), *The myths*

we live by, Routledge, 1990, p. 9 and in R. Brunt, 'The politics of identity', in S. Hall and M. Jacques (eds), *New times: the changing face of politics in the 1990s*, Lawrence and Wishart, 1989, pp. 151–2.

15. On 4 June 1913, Emily Davison tried to disrupt the Derby horse race by running on to the course. Four days later she died of her injuries, and a funeral procession of 6,000 women took place in London on 10 June. Photographs and a description of the funeral appear in Liz Stanley with Ann Morley, *The life and death of Emily Wilding Davison*, Women's Press, 1988.

16. Four areas where there was high unemployment were officially designated as Depressed, later Special, Areas. One of the leaders of the unemployed movement, Wal Hannington, mocked these terms in the title of his book, *The Distressed Areas*, 1937.

17. Stephen Swingler won the seat at the next General Election, in 1945, with a majority of 1,423.

18. Quoted in P. Grafton, *You, you and you! The people out of step with World War II*, Pluto, 1981, pp. 142–3. Major Frederick Wise was a chartered surveyor, land agent, farmer as well as a rural district and county councillor. He stood for Labour before the war, and during the war he served as a RAF Land Officer and stood for Parliament as a candidate for Commonwealth. In 1945 he received over 3,000 more votes than the second-placed Conservative candidate.

19. Founded in 1936 the Left Book Club provided a sounding board for left-wing ideas. By 1937 it had a membership of 50,000.

20. Jenkins, *Rank and file*, p. 172.

Chapter II

1. Both the Conservatives and the Liberals also stressed the importance of the registration and canvassing of voters. P. Thompson, *Socialists, Liberals and Labour. The struggle for London 1885–1914*, Routledge & Kegan Paul, 1967, pp. 70–7.

2. P. Graves, *Labour women, women in British working-class politics 1918–39*, Cambridge University Press, Cambridge, 1994, pp. 47, 67. Between 1986 and 1990 she collected 24 interviews and, through sending out questionnaires, created a sample of 50 men and 50 women interwar activists; 68 of them were in the Labour Party, 23 of the women were in the Women's Co-operative Guild, 12 were in the ILP and 11 in the Communist Party. Some were in more than one organisation. See also M. Andrews, *Lifetimes of commitment: aging, politics and psychology*, Cambridge University Press, Cambridge, 1991.

3. Cited in John Ferris, 'The Labour Party League of Youth 1924–40', 1977, Warwick, MA, p. 161.

4. Abrams and Little, 'The young activist', pp. 330–1.

5. D. Butler and D. Stokes, *Political change in Britain: forces shaping electoral choice*, Macmillan, 1969, pp. 47–8, 250.

6. M. Childs, 'Labour grows up: the electoral system, political generations and British politics 1890–1929', *Twentieth Century British History*, Vol. 6 No. 2, 1995, pp. 134–5 employs evidence drawn from the 444 interviews which constitute the 'Family, life and work before 1918' study now stored as part of the Oral History Archive at the University of Essex.

7. Abrams and Little, 'The young activist', p. 331.

8. Butler and Stokes, *Political change in Britain*, p. 60.

9. See Weinbren, 'Labour roots and branches', p. 30. On the political influence of fathers see R. Dowse and J. Hughes, *Political Sociology*, John Wiley & Sons, Chichester, 1986, p. 6.

10. Helen Lilly in Hall Carpenter Archives Lesbian Oral History Group, *Inventing ourselves: lesbian life stories*, Routledge, London and New York, 1989, pp. 109–18.

11. Jimmy Allison with Harry Conroy, *Guilty by suspicion: a life and Labour*, Argyll Publishing, Argyll, 1995, pp. 59–60.

12. J. Seabrook, *What went wrong? Working people and the ideals of the labour movement*, Gollancz, 1978, pp. 48–9.

13. C. Wrigley, 'Labour's constituency activists', *Labour History Review*, Vol. 56 No. 1, Spring 1991, pp. 58–61.

14. R. Lane, *Political life: why and how people get involved in politics*, Free Press, New York,

1959, noted the relationship between strong community characteristics and participation in political activity. Geraint Parry and George Moser, 'Political participation in Britain: a research agenda for a new study', *Government and Opposition*, No. 19, 1984, p. 80, argue that 'the justification for taking part in politics is a concern for one's community . . . a strong sense of community enhances levels of political involvement'.

15. Bochel, 'Activists', pp. 54–5. The gender ratio is similar to that found in M. Benny, A.P. Gray and R.H. Pear, *How people vote*, Routledge & Kegan Paul, 1956, p. 50, which found that 68 per cent of Labour officers in Greenwich were men.

16. Bochel, 'Activists', pp. 64–5, 164. R. Rose, *Politics in England*, Faber, 1965, pp. 61–2, also makes this comparison.

17. Bochel, 'Activists', pp. 64–5.

Chapter III

1. Seabrook, *What went wrong?*, pp. 17–25.

2. Quoted in J.F. Reid, 'Socialist Sunday Schools in Britain 1892–1939', *International Review of Social History*, No. 11, 1966, pp. 46–7.

3. T. Anderson, *The red teacher*, quoted in R. Samuel, 'British Marxist historians part 1', *New Left Review*, No. 120, March/April 1980, p. 48.

4. Jimmy Maxton (1885–1946) was an ILP MP from 1922 to 1946, and an enthusiast for the Socialist Sunday Schools. The Reverend Campbell Stephen (1884–1947) was the ILP MP for Glasgow Camlachie from 1922 to 1929 and from 1935 to 1947.

5. Seabrook, *What went wrong?* pp. 88–93.

6. Seabrook, *What went wrong?* pp. 167–71. See also G. Hodgkinson, *Sent to Coventry,* Maxwell & Co, 1970.

7. N. Evans, 'Cardiff's Labour tradition', *Llafur*, Vol. 4 No. 2, 1985, pp. 80–1.

8. The agents' journal *Labour Organiser* also sought to gain young members. This section is based on Ferris, 'The Labour Party League of Youth'.

9. *Labour Woman*, 1 January 1925.

10. H. Jennings and C. Madge (eds), *May the twelfth, mass-observation day-surveys 1937 by over 200 observers*, 1st ed. 1937, Faber and Faber, 1987, p. 312.

11. In the 1930s the Labour Party League of Youth produced *New Nation*, and a faction within it published *Advance*.

12. Eric Voysey, interviewed by Maggie Voysey Paun for the Imperial War Museum.

13. Quoted in S. Gewirtz, 'Anti-fascist action in Manchester's Jewish community in the 1930s', *Manchester Region History Review*, vol 4, No. 1, 1990, p. 21.

14. Dalton, Attlee, Morrison, the *Daily Herald* and *Labour's Call to Labour's Voters* are quoted in S. Fielding, P. Thompson and N. Tiratsoo, *England Arise! The Labour Party and popular politics in the 1940s*, Manchester University Press, Manchester, 1995, pp. 79, 83, 91, 94, 95.

Chapter IV

1. K. Young, 'The LMS 1894–1963: a study in Conservatism and local government', 1973, London, PhD, p. 143.

2. Interview with E.G. Rawlinson in J.S. Rowett, 'The Labour Party and local government: theory and practice in the inter-war years', 1979, Oxford, DPhil, p. 37.

3. *Forward*, 18 March 1922.

4. D. Butler and J. Freeman, *British political facts 1900–1960*, Macmillan, 1964, p. 214.

5. Graves, *Labour women*, p. 76.

6. Between 1923 and 1927 *Workers Weekly* was the official newspaper of the Communist Party. The CP also ran the *Sunday Worker* from 1925 to 1930. After receiving almost £28,000 from the Soviet Union in 1928, the Communist Party launched the *Daily Worker* in 1930. Apart from when it was suppressed between 1941 and 1942, this ran until 1966, when it became the *Morning Star.*

7. Quoted in R.A. Leeson, *Strike. A live history 1887–1971*, George Allen and Unwin, 1973, p. 88.

8. Elijah Sandham (1875–1944) was elected to the Chorley Borough Council in 1906 and joined the ILP in the following year. He stood for Parliament in Chorley in 1918 and was a Labour MP 1929–31 for Liverpool, Kirkdale. He resigned from the ILP in 1934 and became

President of the Independent Socialist Party. Sandham's daughter, his son and his grandson all became local councillors.

9. R. Samuel, E. MacColl and S. Cosgrove, *Theatres of the left 1880–1935*, Routledge & Kegan Paul, 1985, pp. 23–45, 83–5.

10. S. Yeo, 'A new life: the religion of socialism in Britain 1883–1896', *History Workshop Journal*, No. 4, 1977, p. 35.

11. Cited in Francis Newton [E.J. Hobsbawm], *The Jazz Scene*, MacGibbon and Kee ed. 1959, Penguin ed. 1961, p. 254.

12. E. Greening, '1926 in Aberdare', *Llafur*, Vol. 2 No. 2, 1977, p. 35. Edwin Greening was born in 1910 near Aberdare, the son of a miner. He was in the ILP Guild of Youth from 1929 until he joined the Communist Party in 1933, he fought in Spain in the 1930s, and joined the Labour Party in 1948.

13. Quoted in Leeson, *Strike*, pp. 103–4.

14. John Stracey, a prominent left-winger, became an MP in 1929 but lost his seat and did not return to Parliament until 1945. Clifford Odets was a Communist active in a New York-based company Group Theatre. He wrote a one-act, agitational play, *Waiting for Lefty* in 1935, which was set against the background of the 1934 New York taxi-drivers' strike. It indicated the ways in which, in the face of hostility towards, and corruption within, trade unions people can still become committed to left-wing politics. It became very popular on both sides of the Atlantic.

15. Unity Theatre was established in March 1936 in London. Dr Edith Summerskill (Labour MP 1938–61) performed the opening ceremony.

16. J. Saville, 'Interviews in labour history', *Oral History*, No. 4, 1973, p. 95.

17. Quoted in Andrews, *Lifetimes of commitment*, p. 211.

18. Yeo, 'A new life', p. 42; and B. Barker, 'The politics of propaganda: a study in the theory of educational socialism and its role in the development of a national Labour Party in London and the West Riding of Yorkshire 1914–24', 1972, York, MPhil, p. iii.

19. 'O'Dee', *Failure and salvation of the Labour Party*, A. O'Donnell, Manchester, 1938, pp. 1, 4, 6–7.

20. Krishnan Menon (1896–1974), was the co-founder of Penguin and Pelican books and an advocate of independence for India. He served as a Labour Party councillor in St Pancras 1934–48 and was the first High Commissioner for independent India.

21. Manny Shinwell was born in 1884 and became President of Glasgow Trades Council and a Glasgow Town Councillor. He was first elected to the Commons in 1922 and served as an MP until 1966. He held Parliamentary posts in all the Labour governments from 1924 and became Minister of Fuel and Power in the 1945 Labour government.

22. Herbert Morrison was born in 1888. He was secretary to the London Labour Party from its inception in 1915 until 1940. He was a member of the London County Council from 1922, its leader from 1934, an MP from 1923 and a Minister in the second Labour government and in subsequent governments. Clement Attlee (1883–1967) was the Labour Party leader 1935–55 and Prime Minister 1945–51. Dr Edith Summerskill was born in 1901 and became a Middlesex County Councillor in 1933. She was elected to the Commons in 1938.

23. Bessie Braddock was born in 1899, became a shop assistant, and was elected as the Labour MP for Liverpool Exchange in 1945. Merlyn Rees was born in 1920, became a lecturer, and was elected to Parliament in 1963. He was a Minister between 1974 and 1979.

24. Quoted in Samuel, MacColl and Cosgrove, *Theatres of the left*, p. 19.

25. Hugh Gaitskell (1906–63), an economics lecturer, was elected to Parliament in 1945. He became Labour Party leader in 1955.

26. A gifted orator, Tony Benn was born in 1925 and became the Labour MP for Bristol South-East in 1950. He was a Minister between 1964 and 1979.

27. Martin Linton, 'Phones' vote of confidence', *Guardian*, 16 December 1995.

28. F.W. Bealey, J. Blondel and W.P. McCann, *Constituency politics*, Faber, 1965.

29. R. Hoggart, *The uses of literacy*, Chatto and Windus ed., 1957, Pelican ed., Harmondsworth, 1958, pp. 20, 264–5.

Chapter V

1. On the influence on policy making of activists see R. Rose, 'The political ideas of English party activists, *American Political Science Review*, Vol. 46 No. 2, 1963; R.T. McKenzie, *British Political Parties*, Heinemann, 1955, p. 581; and R. Milliband, 'Democracy and Parliamentary Government', *Political Studies*, Vol. 6, 1958, p. 170.

2. J. Jacobs, 'Personal reminiscences from Hackney', in Jeffrey Skelley (ed.), *The General Strike*, Lawrence and Wishart, 1976, p. 364.

3. Graves, *Labour women*, p. 163.

4. 'Reminiscences from the life story of Edward Cain', quoted in John Burnett, *Idle hands*, Routledge, 1994, p. 219.

5. P. Kerrigan, 'Personal reminiscences from Glasgow', in Skelley (ed.), *The General Strike*, pp. 315–17.

6. Bob Davies, 'Personal reminiscences from St Helens', in Skelley (ed.), *The General Strike*, p. 332.

7. Bill Carr, 'Personal reminiscences from the Yorkshire coalfield', in Skelley (ed.), *The General Strike*, pp. 340–50.

8. Quoted in Leeson, *Strike*, p. 77.

9. Quoted in Leeson, *Strike*, p. 101.

10. In 1859 Hospital Sunday Funds were created, and collections solicited from pulpits. These tended to be dominated by the middle class. In 1873 Saturday Funds were established, and thousands of pounds received, often in small donations, from the working class.

11. Quoted in A. Holdsworth, *Out of the Doll's House*, BBC, 1988, p. 191.

12. Cheshire Northwich constituency's Labour candidate, Barbara Gould, gained 15,473 votes and the Conservative Lord Colum Crichton-Stuart gained four votes more.

13. In 1929 J.W. Fawcett stood in Kingston-upon-Thames. He received 31 per cent fewer votes than the Conservative victor. He stood again in 1931 and received 65 per cent fewer. In 1935 he stood in Portsmouth South and received 50.4 per cent fewer votes than the Conservative. He did not stand for Parliament again.

14. In 1929 the Boards of Guardians were abolished, and in 1934 the Unemployment Assistance Boards took responsibility for relief payments to the jobless.

15. J. Gillespie, 'Industrial & political change in the East End of London during the 1920s', 1984, Cambridge, PhD, Chapter 2.

16. Entry of 25 August 1928, M. Cole (ed.), *Beatrice Webb's diaries 1924–1932*, Longmans, Green, 1956, p. 176.

17. J. Griffiths, *Pages from memory*, Dent, 1969, p. 174. Bochel, 'Activists', p. 164 and p. 174 notes that 42 per cent of those questioned in 1958 mentioned the pre-war Depression as an explanation for their support for Labour.

18. Quoted in J. Marriott, *The culture of labourism*, Edinburgh University Press, Edinburgh, p. 182.

19. Mary Agnes Hamilton, *The Labour Party today. What it is and how it works,* Labour Book Service, no date (1938?). On the life of a Labour councillor of the 1930s see J. MacFarlane, 'Interview with Robert Henry Shephard', *Bulletin of the Society for the Study of Labour History*, No. 25, Autumn 1972, pp. 82–100.

20. G.A. Phillips, 'The Labour Party and the General Strike', *Llafur*, Vol. 2 No. 2, 1977, p. 51.

21. J.A. Gillespie, 'Municipalism, monopoly and management: the demise of socialism in one county 1918-1933', in A. Saint (ed.), *Politics and the people of London: the London County Council 1889-1965*, Hambledon, 1989, p. 113.

22. Rowett, 'The Labour Party', p. 306. Labour's success at local level is outlined in John Gyford, *Local politics in Britain*, Croom Helm, 2nd ed. 1984, pp. 48–9.

23. There is a reproduction of the poster in J. Mack and S. Humphries, *The making of modern London 1939–45. London at war*, Sidgwick and Jackson, 1985, p. 185.

24. F.M.L. Thompson (ed.), *The Cambridge social history of Britain 1750-1950 Vol. 1: regions and communities*, Cambridge University Press, Cambridge, 1990, pp. 78–9; and Gyford, *Local politics*, p. 63.

25. As it soon dropped the word 'Committee' from its name it will be referred to as the NUWM.

26. Public Record Office MH 57/101 quoted in P. Kingsford, *The hunger marchers in Britain 1920–39*, Lawrence and Wishart, 1982, p. 146.

27. Kingsford, *The hunger marchers*, pp. 186, 200, 210, 215–16.

28. Ellen Wilkinson further publicised the cause in a book, *The town that was murdered: the life story of Jarrow*, Left Book Club, 1939. Although no concessions were granted at the time the Crusaders presented their petition in the Commons, a steel works was built in the town shortly afterwards.

29. Quoted in Judith Cook, *Apprentices of Freedom*, Quartet, 1979.

30. Ferris, 'The Labour Party League of Youth', p. 157.

31 *New Nation*, May 1933; Ferris, 'The Labour Party League of Youth', p. 162.

32. John Edmonds, *The lean years*, MS quoted in Burnett, *Idle hands*, p. 232.

Chapter VI

1. Quoted in Spanish Memories Group, *Changed destinies, memories of the Spanish community in London*, Kensington and Chelsea Community History Group, 1995, p. 53.

2. A description of the evacuation from Bilbao by one of the British doctors appeared in the *New Statesman* 29 May 1937. In September of that year the Left Book Club published Yvonne Cloud, *The Basque children in England. An account of their life at North Stoneham camp.*

3. Adrian Bell, *Only for three months. The Basque children in exile*, Mousehole Press, 1996, p. 147.

4. Bell, *Only for three months*, p. 69. Details about the Stoneham camp are to be found in this book.

5. S. Scaffardi, *Fire under the carpet: working for civil liberties*, Lawrence and Wishart, 1986, p. 65; and David S. Lewis, *Illusions of grandeur: Mosley, Fascism and British society, 1931–81*, Manchester University Press, Manchester, 1987, pp. 123–8.

6. *Daily Mail* 8 January 1934; *Sunday Dispatch* 7 May 1934.

7. Quoted in Andrews, *Lifetimes of commitment*, p. 123.

8. The two witnesses mentioned by Jack Gaster were both left-wing but not Labour Party members. Writer J.B. Priestley broadcast for the Labour Party in 1950 and was influential in the creation of the Common Wealth Party and the Campaign for Nuclear Disarmament. Vera Brittain was a writer who was active in the Peace Pledge Union from 1936. The condemnation of Mosley by such people aided the case for a coalition of interests against fascism.

9. Scaffardi, *Fire under the carpet*, pp. 123–32, 206.

10. M. Kundera, *The book of laughter and forgetting*, translated from the Czech by M.H. Heim, Penguin, Harmondsworth, 1981, p. 3.

11. On the value of oral testimony for what Geoffrey Alderman has called 'demythologising' political events such as the dramatic 'battle' of Cable Street see P. Catterall (ed.), 'Witness seminar: the battle of Cable Street', *Contemporary Record*, Vol. 8 No. 1, Summer 1994, pp. 105–32 for an account of a meeting of participants at this event.

12. J. Jacobs, *Out of the Ghetto: my youth in the East End. Communism and fascism 1919–39*, Phoenix, 1978.

13. Quoted in The Cable Street Group, *The battle of Cable Street 4th October, 1936*, The Cable Street Group, 178 Whitechapel Road, London E1, 1995.

14. N. Branson, *History of the Communist Party of Great Britain 1927–41*, Lawrence and Wishart, 1985, pp. 168–71.

15. M. Beckman, *The 43 Group: the untold story of their fight against fascism*, Centerprise, 1992, p. 32.

16. M. Daly, 'The social consequences of industrial transference: a reply', *Sociological Review*, No. 30, 1938, p. 259. See also D. Lyddon, '"Trade Union traditions", the Oxford Welsh and the 1934 pressed steel strike', *Llafur*, Vol. 6 No. 2, 1993, p. 108.

17. Quoted in H. Wainwright, *Labour: a tale of two parties*, Hogarth, 1987, p. 193.

Chapter VII

1. Bochel, 'Activists' p. 59.

2. Graves, *Labour women*, p. 4.

3. This argument may not hold true in regard to the memories of those who are politically influential. Philip Williams noted, after

interviewing over 300 people who had known Labour Party leader Hugh Gaitskell, that there was a 'strong propensity of politicians to interpret the past in the light of the present'. See Philip M. Williams, 'Interviewing politicians: the life of Hugh Gaitskell', *Political Quarterly*, No. 51, 1980, p. 311. A similar point is made in Willie Thompson and Sandy Hobbs, 'British communists on the war, 1939–41', *Oral History*, Vol. 16 No. 2, 1988, p. 32.

4. Journalist John Reed's account of the 1917 Russian Revolution, *Ten Days that Shook the World*, was published in Britain in 1926.

5. Labour Party, *Annual Report 1933*, p. 219.

6. B. Reed and G. Williams, *Denis Healey and the politics of power*, Sidgwick and Jackson, 1971, p. 25.

7. D. Hyde, *I believed, the autobiography of a former British communist,* Heinemann, 1950, pp. 65–6.

8. J.W. Kneeshaw letter of 4 December 1938 and the *London News*, March 1939 cited in Wood, 'The Labour left', pp. 151, 197–202.

9. Members included Sir Charles Trevelyan, who had entered Parliament as a Liberal in 1900 and been a Cabinet Minister in both Labour governments; Sir Stafford Cripps (1889–1952), a Labour MP since 1931 and a barrister whose father had served in two Labour governments; Aneurin Bevan (1897–1963) a Welsh coal miner who was an MP 1929–60, George Strauss, an MP since 1935 and the journalists Barbara Betts (later Castle) and Michael Foot, both of whom became MPs in 1945. Bevan, Strauss and Cripps were expelled from the Labour Party in 1939 but were later reconciled and became Ministers after the war.

10. Wood, 'The Labour left', pp. 147–57.

11. Autobiographical notes supplied by Owen Heather to the author.

12. *New Statesman and Nation*, 25 June 1938.

13. Fenner Brockway, *Inside the left*, Allen & Unwin, 1942, p. 268.

14. Ted Willis, *Whatever happened to Tom Mix?*, Eyre and Spottiswoode, 1970, p. 172.

15. Former Liberal MP Sir Richard Acland, a wealthy landowner who donated his hereditary estates to the National Trust, was a founder of Common Wealth.

16. Tom Wintringham, a former Communist and commander of the British battalion of the International Brigade, was a member of J.B. Priestley's 1941 Committee, a network of progressive intellectuals who wanted to give the war a left-wing emphasis. He stood for Common Wealth in the safe Conservative seat of Midlothian North in 1944 and lost only narrowly. Alex Kitson's treatment was not unique. Jennie Lee, a former Labour MP and wife of the expelled Aneurin Bevan, stood at Bristol Central as 'Independent Labour'. Those members of the local Labour Party who gave her their support were expelled.

17. P. Addison, *The road to 1945: British politics and the Second World War*, Jonathan Cape, 1975, pp. 134–40.

Chapter VIII

1. Quoted in Wainwright, *Labour*, pp. 191–2.

2. Newham Monitoring Project/Campaign Against Racism and Fascism, *Forging a black community, Asian and Afro-Caribbean struggles in Newham*, Newham Monitoring Project/Campaign Against Racism and Fascism, 1991, pp. 5–6, 31–2.

3. Peggy Duff, *Left, left, left,* Allison & Busby, 1971, p. 84.

4. D.C. Mathieson, 'Holborn and St Pancras South Labour Party 1947–1963', 1990, Huddersfield, PhD. One rebel later rejoined Labour and became a peer.

5. Fred Messer was an MP from 1929. Sidney Silverman an MP from 1935 and Richard Crossman and Barbara Castle were MPs from 1945 and later Ministers. Betty Boothroyd and Jo Richardson were MPs from 1973 and 1974. In 1952 six of the seven constituency seats on the NEC were won by Bevanites and the General Secretary of the TGWU, Arthur Deakin, demanded the dissolution of the Tribune Group. Victory for Socialism was a group associated with the left-wing MP Konni Zilliacus, who was expelled from the Labour Party in 1949. In 1952 the Parliamentary Labour Party imposed a ban on the Bevanites, who continued to organise in secret. The extra-parliamentary wing, which also included some MPs, was known as the Second Eleven. Those MPs who met with Crossman

once a week were the First Eleven. See Duff, *Left, left, left*, pp. 46–7 and the interview with Ted Castle in Mark Jenkins, *Bevanism, Labour's high tide: the cold war and the democratic mass movement,* Spokesman, Nottingham, 1979, p. 170.

6. John Freeman was born in 1915 and was the joint secretary of the liberal Union for Democratic Control prior to the Second World War. He was elected to the Commons in 1945. Harold Wilson was born in 1916 and became a University lecturer and then an MP in 1945. He was Prime Minister four times between 1964 and 1976. In April 1951 Hugh Gaitskell, the Chancellor of the Exchequer, faced with a £4,700 million defence programme due to British involvement in the Korean War, levied a charge on NHS patients acquiring teeth and spectacles. Bevan, Freeman and Wilson felt that this undermined the principle of free treatment and resigned. Labour lost the General Election that year.

7. D. Coates, *The Labour Party and the struggle for socialism*, Cambridge University Press, Cambridge, 1975, p. 194.

8. Mark Jenkins, *Bevanism*, p. 173.

9. The largest single voting unit at the Labour Party conference was controlled by the Transport and General Workers Union. Between the 1930s and the mid-1950s the union often supported the right of the Labour Party. In 1956 Frank Cousins became secretary of the union. He swung it against Labour Party defence policy and in favour of unilateral nuclear disarmament and, in 1960, the Labour Party conference supported him. In 1965 he was appointed Minister of Technology.

10. Labour Research Department, *Solidarity with the miners* cited in Wainwright, *Labour*, pp. 271.

11. S. Walmsley and B. Owen quoted in Wainwright, *Labour*, pp. 106, 272.

12. M. Crick, *The march of Militant*, Faber & Faber, 1986, pp. 177–8 and Zig Layton-Henry, 'Labour's lost youth', *Journal of Contemporary History*, No. 11, 1976, pp. 275–308.

13. Crick, *March of Militant*, p. 182.

14. See J.D. May 'Opinion structure of political parties: the special law of curvilinear disparity', *Political Studies*, Vol. 21, 1973, pp. 135–51; and H. Kitschelt, 'The internal politics of parties: the law of curvilinear disparity revisited', *Political Studies*, Vol. 37, 1989, pp. 400–21.

15. Quoted in Holdsworth, *Out of the doll's house*, p. 190.

16. Sally Alexander argues that London's interwar left 'was organised around notions of class . . . in which the individual subject was masculine'. See S. Alexander, 'Becoming a woman in London in the 1920s and 1930s', in G. Stedman Jones and D. Feldman (eds), *Metropolis London*, Routledge, 1989, pp. 246–7. Mike Savage argues that gender practices were fundamental to the specific politics of the labour movement. See M. Savage, *The dynamics of working class politics: the labour movement in Preston 1880–1940*, Cambridge University Press, Cambridge, 1987.

17. Quoted in Holdsworth, *Out of the doll's house*, p. 193.

18. A. Mitchell, *Election '45. Reflections on the revolution in Britain*, Bellew, 1995, p. 60.

19. Leslie Hilliard interviewed by Maggie Voysey Paun for the Imperial War Museum.

Chapter IX

1. D.W. Rawson, 'The lifespan of Labour Parties', *Political Studies*, Vol. 17, 1969, p. 316.

2. K.O. Morgan, 'The high and low politics of Labour: Keir Hardie to Michael Foot', in Michael Bentley and John Stevenson (eds) *High and low politics in modern Britain: ten studies*, Clarendon, Oxford, 1983, pp. 287, 311–12.

3. Percy Redfern quoted in Yeo 'A new life', p. 17.

4. Quoted in S. Fielding, 'Labourism in the 1940s', *Twentieth Century British History*, Vol. 3 No. 2, 1992, pp. 145–51.

5. Jack Dash, *Good morning brothers! A militant trade unionist's frank autobiography*, Lawrence and Wishart ed. 1969, Mayflower ed. 1970, p. 31.

6. Hamilton, *The Labour Party today*, pp. 62–4, 68–9.

7. N. Kirk, '"Traditional" working class culture

and the "rise of Labour": some preliminary questions and observations', *Social History*, Vol. 16 No. 2, 1991, pp. 212–15.

8. Autobiographical notes supplied by Owen Heather to the author.

9. N. Branson, *Poplarism, 1919–25*, Lawrence and Wishart, 1979, pp. 167, 179.

10. Marriott, *Culture of labourism*, pp. 179–82.

11. Quoted in Sarah Bussy, 'The Labour victory in Winchester in 1945', *Southern History*, No. 8, 1986, pp. 145–52.

12. Mitchell, *Election '45*, pp. 74, 78.

13. Linton, *Guardian*, 16 December 1995.

14. Quoted in Marriott, *Culture of labourism*, p. 182.

15. In 1945 in Kingston G.H. Elvin stood for Labour and gained 43.5 per cent of the vote. The Conservative, J.A. Boyd-Carpenter, gained 56.5 per cent of the vote. This was the narrowest victory (13 per cent difference) since the extension of the franchise to most men in 1918. Previous Labour Party candidates had trailed their rivals by between 23 per cent and 65 per cent.

16. Frank McElhone was born in 1929, became a Glasgow City councillor from 1963–74, and a magistrate. He was elected to Parliament in 1969 as MP for Glasgow Gorbals and became Parliamentary Private Secretary to Tony Benn, then at the Industry Ministry, between 1974 and 1975 and then Under Secretary of State for Scotland between 1975 and 1979. Following his death his widow was returned for the same seat until the following General Election.

17. Other interviews with Labour Party agents include D. Rubinstein, 'Interview with Tom Stephenson', *Bulletin of the Society for the Study of Labour History*, No. 22, Spring 1971, pp. 27–32 and C. Pearce, 'Interview with Wilfred Whiteley', *Bulletin of the Society for the Study of Labour History*, No. 18, Spring 1969, pp. 14–21.

18. Alan T. Lennox-Boyd was the Conservative MP for mid-Bedfordshire 1931–59. In 1950, although Labour's vote was down nationally, Lennox-Boyd won the seat with only 41.4 per cent of the vote against the Labour candidate's 36.3 per cent. Alan Yates was Labour's agent. In his unpublished autobiography Alan Yates recorded that 'Lennox-Boyd looked shaken and I felt very satisfied.'

19. T.E.M. McKitterick, 'The membership of the Party', *Political Quarterly*, No. 31, 1960, pp. 315–16.

20. Bruce Millan obtained a majority of 602; 50.8 per cent of the vote to his opponent's 49.2 per cent. In 1964 his lead was increased to 16.8 per cent and it was further strengthened in 1966 when he received 25.2 per cent more of the vote than his opponent.

21. P. Seyd and P. Whiteley, *Labour's grassroots: the politics of party membership*, Clarendon Press, Oxford, 1992, pp. 176–7.

22. Seyd and Whiteley, *Labour's grassroots*, pp. 196–9, 206.

Chapter X

1. The Liberals put forward only 306 candidates (compared to Labour's 603 and the National coalition's 618) and won 12 compared to the 21 the party had won in 1935. The Communist Party won two seats.

2. Angus Calder, *The People's War, Britain 1939–45*, first ed. 1969, Granada ed. 1971, pp. 666–8.

3. A. Brownjohn, 'Like 1945', in Nicki Jackowska (ed.), *Voices from Arts for Labour*, Pluto, 1985, p. 63.

4. Quoted in Mitchell, *Election '45*, pp. 24, 42.

5. Mass-Observation file report 2282 quoted Roger Eatwell, *The 1945–1951 Labour governments*, Batsford, 1979, p. 32.

6. Fielding, Thompson and Tiratsoo, *England Arise!*, pp. 28–30.

7. Quoted in A.J. Davies, *To build Jerusalem*, Michael Joseph, 1992, pp. 158–9.

8. W.J. Field gained 48.2 per cent of the vote in Hampstead in 1945, only 3.6 per cent or 1,358 votes, behind the Conservative C. Challen. In 1946 Field was elected MP for Paddington North.

9. Quoted in Mack and Humphries, *The making of modern London*, p. 170.

10. Quoted in P. Schweitzer (ed.), *When the lights go on again, memories of VE Day and after*, Age Exchange, Blackheath, 1995, p. 50.

11. Quoted in Schweitzer (ed.) *When the lights go on again*, p. 52.

12. Anthony Howard, '"We are the masters now".

The General Election of 5 July 1945', in Michael Sissons and Philip French (eds.), *Age of Austerity 1945–51*, first ed. 1963, Penguin ed. 1964, p. 19.

13. Grafton, *You, you and you*, p. 143.

14. Foreword by Tony Blair in Mitchell, *Election '45*.

Chapter XI

1. R. Hauben, 'A pioneer in workers' education: Mark Starr and workers' education in Great Britain', *Llafur*, Vol. 4 No. 2, 1985, p. 94.

2 *Surrey County Herald*, November 1937.

3. P. Piratin, *Our flag stays red*, first ed. 1948, Lawrence and Wishart (eds) 1978, pp. 46–7. Piratin was the Communist Party London Organiser, later West Middlesex Organiser and, from 1945, Communist MP for Mile End Stepney.

4. Jenkins, *Rank and file*, p. 39.

5. In the 1935 General Election David Weitzman stood as the Labour candidate in Stoke Newington, a seat which had been held by the Conservatives since 1924. He came second after Sir G.W.H. Jones. In 1945 Weitzman received 51.5 per cent of the vote and Jones only 28.4 per cent.

6. Quoted in Schweitzer (ed.), *When the lights go on again*, p. 52.

7. Quoted in Davies, *To build a new Jerusalem*, p. 184.

8. Preface to E. Durbin, *New Jerusalems*, Routledge Kegan Paul, 1985, p. xiii.

9. Raymond Williams *et al*, *May Day Manifesto, 1968*, Penguin, Harmondsworth, 1968.

10. On the possibility of left-wing activists pulling the legs of over-earnest interviewers see 'Editorial', *Bulletin of the Society for the Study of Labour History*, No. 27, 1973, pp. 2–3.

Bibliography

Tapes

Recordings of Eric Voysey and Leslie Hilliard are held at the Imperial War Museum. Other tapes are held at the National Sound Archive.

Diaries

Autobiographical writings were provided for the author by Alan Yates and Owen Heather.

Theses

B. Barker, 'The politics of propaganda: a study in the theory of educational socialism and its role in the development of a national Labour Party in London and the West Riding of Yorkshire 1914–24', 1972, York, M.Phil.

J.M. Bochel, 'Activists in the Conservative and Labour parties: a study of ward secretaries in Manchester', 1965, Manchester, M.A.

Ferris, 'The Labour Party League of Youth 1924–40', 1977, Warwick, M.A.

J.A. Gillespie, 'Industrial & political change in the East End of London during the 1920s', 1984, Cambridge, Ph.D.

D.C. Mathieson, 'Holborn and St Pancras South Labour Party 1947–1963', 1990, Huddersfield, Ph.D.

J.S. Rowett, 'The Labour Party and local government: theory and practice in the inter-war years', 1979, Oxford, D.Phil.

M.M. Waite, 'Young people and Communist politics in Britain 1920–91: aspects of the history of the YCL', 1992, Lancaster, M.Phil.

J. Wood, 'The Labour left and the CLPs 1931–51', 1982, Warwick, Ph.D.

K. Young, 'The LMS 1894–1963: a study in Conservatism and local government', 1973, London, Ph.D.

Newspapers and periodicals

Forward

Daily Mail

Guardian

Labour Woman

New Nation

New Statesman

Sunday Dispatch

Surrey County Herald

Annual report

Labour Party, *Annual Report 1933*

Journals

P. Abrams and A. Little, 'The young activist in British politics', *British Journal of Sociology*, 16, 1965.

F. Bealey and M. Dyer, 'Size of place and the Labour vote in Britain, 1918–66', *Western Political Quarterly*, 24, 1971.

D. Berry, 'Party membership and social participation', *Political Studies*, 17, 1969.

S. Bussy, 'The Labour victory in Winchester in 1945', *Southern History*, 8, 1986.

P. Catterall (ed.), 'Witness seminar: the battle of Cable Street', *Contemporary Record*, Vol. 8 No. 1, Summer 1994.

M. Childs, 'Labour grows up: the electoral system, political generations and British politics 1890–1929', *Twentieth Century British History*, Vol. 6 No. 2, 1995.

M. Daly, 'The social consequences of industrial transference: a reply', *Sociological Review*, 30, 1938.

'Editorial', *Bulletin of the Society for the Study of Labour History*, 27, 1973.

N. Evans, 'Cardiff's Labour tradition', *Llafur*, Vol. 4 No. 2, 1985.

S. Fielding, 'Labourism in the 1940s', *Twentieth Century British History*, Vol. 3 No. 2, 1992.

S. Gewirtz, 'Anti-fascist action in Manchester's Jewish community in the 1930s', *Manchester Region History Review*, Vol. 4 No. 1, 1990.

W.P. Grant, 'Size of place and local Labour strength', *British Journal of Political Science*, 2, 1972.

E. Greening, '1926 in Aberdare', *Llafur*, Vol. 2 No. 2, 1977.

R. Hauben, 'A pioneer in workers' education: Mark Starr and workers' education in Great Britain', *Llafur*, Vol. 4 No. 2, 1985.

N. Kirk, '"Traditional" working-class culture and the "rise of Labour": some preliminary questions and observations', *Social History*, Vol. 16 No. 2, 1991.

H. Kitschelt, 'The internal politics of parties: the law of curvilinear disparity revisited', *Political Studies*, 37, 1989.

Z. Layton-Henry, 'Labour's lost youth', *Journal of Contemporary History*, 11, 1976.

D. Lyddon, '"Trade Union traditions", the Oxford Welsh and the 1934 pressed steel strike', *Llafur*, Vol. 6 No. 2, 1993.

J. MacFarlane, 'Interview with Robert Henry Shephard', *Bulletin of the Society for the Study of Labour History*, 25, 1972.

J.D. May, 'Opinion structure of political parties: the law of curvilinear disparity', *Political Studies*, 1973.

T.E.M. McKitterick, 'The membership of the Party', *Political Quarterly*, 31, 1960.

R. Milliband, 'Democracy and Parliamentary Government', *Political Studies*, 6, 1958.

G. Parry and G. Moser, 'Political participation in Britain: a research agenda for a new study', *Government and Opposition*, 19, 1984.

C. Pearce, 'Interview with Wilfred Whiteley', *Bulletin of the Society for the Study of Labour History*, 18, 1969.

G.A. Phillips, 'The Labour Party and the General Strike', *Llafur*, Vol. 2, No. 2, 1977.

D.W. Rawson, 'The lifespan of Labour Parties', *Political Studies*, 17, 1969.

J.F. Reid, 'Socialist Sunday Schools in Britain 1892–1939', *International Review of Social History*, 11, 1966.

D. Rubenstein, 'Interview with Tom Stephenson', *Bulletin of the Society for the Study of Labour History*, 22, 1971.

R. Rose, 'The political ideas of English party activists, *American Political Science Review*, Vol. 46 No. 2, 1963.

R. Samuel, 'British Marxist historians part 1', *New Left Review*, No. 120, March/April 1980.

R. Samuel, 'The lost world of British communism', *New Left Review*, 154, November/December 1985.

J. Saville, 'Interviews in labour history', *Oral History*, 4, 1973.

W. Thompson and S. Hobbs, 'British communists on the war, 1939–41', *Oral History*, Vol. 16 No. 2, 1988.

M. Waite, 'Manchester's Red Army', *Jewish Socialist*, 32, Autumn 1994.

D. Weinbren, 'Labour's roots and branches', *Oral History*, Vol. 24 No. 1, 1996.

P. M. Williams, 'Interviewing politicians: the life of Hugh Gaitskell', *Political Quarterly*, 51, 1980.

C. Wrigley, 'Labour's constituency activists', *Labour History Review*, Vol. 56 No. 1, 1991.

S. Yeo, 'A new life: the religion of socialism in Britain 1883–1896', *History Workshop Journal*, 4, 1977.

Books

Unless otherwise stated, all books referred to are published in London.

P. Addison, *The road to 1945: British politics and the Second World War*, Jonathan Cape, 1975.

S. Alexander, 'Becoming a woman in London in the 1920s and 1930s', in G. Stedman Jones and D. Feldman (eds) *Metropolis London*, Routledge, 1989.

J. Allison with H. Conroy, *Guilty by suspicion: a life and Labour*, Argyll, 1995.

M. Andrews, *Lifetimes of commitment: aging, politics and psychology*, Cambridge University Press, Cambridge, 1991.

F.W. Bealey, J. Blondel and W. McCann, *Constituency politics*, Faber, 1965.

M. Beckman, *The 43 Group: the untold story of their fight against fascism*, Centerprise, 1992.

A. Bell, *Only for three months. The Basque children in exile*, Mousehole Press, 1996.

M. Benny, A.P. Gray and R.H. Pear, *How people vote*, Routledge & Kegan Paul, 1956.

N. Branson, *History of the Communist Party of Great Britain 1927–41*, Lawrence and Wishart, 1985.

N. Branson, *Poplarism, 1919–25*, Lawrence and Wishart, 1979.

F. Brockway, *Inside the left*, Allen & Unwin, 1942.

A. Brownjohn, 'Like 1945', in Nicki Jackowska (ed.), *Voices from Arts for Labour*, Pluto, 1985.

R. Brunt, 'The politics of identity', in S. Hall and M. Jacques (eds), *New times: the changing face of politics in the 1990s*, Lawrence and Wishart, 1989.

J. Burnett, *Idle Hands*, Routledge, 1994.

D. Butler and J. Freeman, *British political facts 1900–1960*, Macmillan, 1964.

D. Butler and D. Stokes, *Political change in Britain: forces shaping electoral choice*, Macmillan, 1969.

The Cable Street Group, *The battle of Cable Street 4th October, 1936*, The Cable Street Group, 178 Whitechapel Road, London, 1995.

A. Calder, *The People's War, Britain 1939–45*, first ed. 1969, Granada edition 1971.

Bill Carr, 'Personal reminiscences from the Yorkshire coalfield', in J. Skelley (ed.), *The General Strike*, Lawrence and Wishart, 1976.

Y. Cloud, *The Basque children in England. An account of their life at North Stoneham camp*, Left Book Club, 1937.

D. Coates, *The Labour Party and the struggle for socialism*, Cambridge University Press, Cambridge, 1975.

M. Cole (ed.), *Beatrice Webb's diaries, 1924–1932*, Longmans' Green, 1956.

J. Cook, *Apprentices of Freedom*, Quartet, 1979.

M. Crick, *The march of Militant*, Faber & Faber, 1986.

Jack Dash, *Good morning brothers! A militant trade unionist's frank autobiography*, Lawrence and Wishart 1969, Mayflower ed. 1970.

A.J. Davies, *To build Jerusalem*, Michael Joseph, 1992.

B. Davies, 'Personal reminiscences from St Helens', in J. Skelley (ed.), *The General Strike*, Lawrence and Wishart, 1976.

R. Dowse and J. Hughes, *Political Sociology*, John Wiley & Sons, Chichester, 1986.

P. Duff, *Left, left, left*, Allison & Busby, 1971.

E. Durbin, *New Jerusalems*, Routledge Kegan Paul, 1985.

R. Eatwell, *The 1945–1951 Labour governments*, Batsford, 1979.

S. Fielding, P. Thompson and N. Tiratsoo, *England Arise! The Labour Party and popular politics in the 1940s*, Manchester University Press, Manchester, 1995.

J.A. Gillespie, 'Municipalism, monopoly and management: the demise of socialism in one county 1918–1933', in A. Saint (ed.), *Politics and the people of London: the London County Council 1889–1965*, Hambledon, 1989.

P. Grafton, *You, you and you! The people out of step with World War II*, Pluto, 1981.

P. Graves, *Labour women, women in British working-class politics 1918–39*, Cambridge University Press, Cambridge, 1994.

J. Griffiths, *Pages from memory*, Dent, 1969.

J. Gyford, *Local politics in Britain*, Croom Helm, 2nd ed. 1984.

M.A. Hamilton, *The Labour Party today. What it is and how it works*, Labour Book Service, *c.* 1938.

G. Hodgkinson, *Sent to Coventry*, Maxwell & Co, 1970.

R. Hoggart, *The uses of literacy*, Chatto and Windus, 1957, Pelican edition, Harmondsworth, 1958.

A. Holdsworth, *Out of the Doll's House*, BBC, 1988.

A. Howard, '"We are the masters now". The General Election of 5 July 1945', in Michael Sissons and Philip French (eds), *Age of Austerity 1945–51*, first ed. 1963, Penguin ed. 1964.

D. Hyde, *I believed, the autobiography of a former British communist*, Heinemann, 1950.

J. Jacobs, *Out of the Ghetto: my youth in the East End. Communism and fascism 1919–39*, Phoenix, 1978.

J. Jacobs, 'Personal reminiscences from Hackney', in J. Skelley (ed.), *The General Strike*, Lawrence and Wishart, 1976.

H. Jenkins, *Rank and file*, Croom Helm, 1980.

M. Jenkins, *Bevanism, Labour's high tide. The cold war and the democratic mass movement*, Spokesman, Nottingham, 1979.

H. Jennings and C. Madge (eds), *May the twelfth, mass-observation day-surveys 1937 by over 200 observers*, 1st ed. 1937, this ed. 1987.

P. Kerrigan, 'Personal reminiscences from Glasgow', in J. Skelley (ed.), *The General Strike*, Lawrence and Wishart, 1976.

P. Kingsford, *The hunger marchers in Britain 1920–39*, Lawrence and Wishart, 1982.

M. Kundera, *The book of laughter and forgetting*, translated from the Czech by M.H. Heim, Penguin, Harmondsworth, 1981.

R. Lane, *Political life: why and how people get involved in politics*, Free Press, New York, 1959.

R.A. Leeson, *Strike. A live history 1887–1971*, George Allen and Unwin, 1973.

D.S. Lewis, *Illusions of grandeur: Mosley, Fascism and British society, 1931–81*, Manchester University Press, Manchester, 1987.

Helen Lilly in Hall Carpenter Archives Lesbian Oral History Group, *Inventing ourselves: lesbian life stories*, Routledge, 1989.

J. Mack and S. Humphries, *The making of modern London 1939–45. London at war*, Sidgwick and Jackson, 1985.

J. Marriott, *The culture of labourism*, Edinburgh University Press, Edinburgh, 1991.

R.T. McKenzie, *British Political Parties*, Heinemann, 1955.

R. McKibbin, *The ideologies of class: social relations in Britain 1880–1950*, Clarendon, Oxford, 1990.

A. Mitchell, *Election '45. Reflections on the revolution in Britain*, Bellew, 1995.

K.O. Morgan, 'The high and low politics of Labour: Keir Hardie to Michael Foot', in Michael Bentley and

John Stevenson (eds) *High and low politics in modern Britain: ten studies*, Clarendon, Oxford, 1983.

Newham Monitoring Project/Campaign Against Racism and Fascism, *Forging a black community, Asian and Afro-Caribbean struggles in Newham*, Newham Monitoring Project/Campaign Against Racism and Fascism, 1991.

Francis Newton [E.J. Hobsbawm], *The Jazz Scene*, MacGibbon and Kee 1959, Penguin ed. 1961.

'O'Dee', *Failure and salvation of the Labour Party*, A. O'Donnell, Manchester, 1938.

P. Piratin, *Our flag stays red*, first ed. 1948, Lawrence and Wishart ed. 1978.

B. Reed and G. Williams, *Denis Healey and the politics of power*, Sidgwick and Jackson, 1971.

R. Rose, *Politics in England*, Faber, 1965.

R. Samuel, E. MacColl and S. Cosgrove, *Theatres of the left 1880–1935*, Routledge & Kegan Paul, 1985.

M. Savage, *The dynamics of working class politics: the labour movement in Preston 1880–1940*, Cambridge University Press, Cambridge, 1987.

S. Scaffardi, *Fire under the carpet: working for civil liberties*, Lawrence and Wishart, 1986.

P. Schweitzer (ed.), *When the lights go on again, memories of VE Day and after*, Age Exchange, Blackheath, 1995.

J. Seabrook, *What went wrong? Working people and the ideals of the labour movement*, Gollancz, 1978.

P. Seyd and P. Whiteley, *Labour's grassroots: the politics of party membership*, Clarendon Press, Oxford, 1992.

Spanish Memories Group, *Changed destinies, memories of the Spanish community in London*, Kensington and Chelsea Community History Group, 1995.

L. Stanley with A. Morley, *The life and death of Emily Wilding Davison*, Women's Press, 1988.

F.M.L. Thompson (ed.), *The Cambridge social history of Britain 1750–1950 Vol. 1: regions and communities*, Cambridge University Press, Cambridge, 1990.

P. Thompson, *Socialists, Liberals and Labour. The struggle for London 1885–1914*, Routledge Kegan Paul, 1967.

P. Thompson and R. Samuel (eds), *The myths we live by*, Routledge, 1990.

H. Wainwright, *Labour: a tale of two parties*, Hogarth, 1987.

R. Williams *et al*, *May Day Manifesto, 1968*, Penguin, Harmondsworth, 1968.

T. Willis, *Whatever happened to Tom Mix?*, Eyre and Spottiswoode, 1970.

P. Willmott and M. Young, *Family and class in a London suburb*, Routledge & Kegan Paul, 1960.

Index

(Page numbers in *italic* refer to illustrations.)

248